S0-BDM-462

Integrated Business Leadership Through
Cross-Marketing

To Mother, With Love

Integrated Business Leadership Through
Cross-Marketing

THE CRITICAL LINK
TO A CUSTOMER-DRIVEN BUSINESS

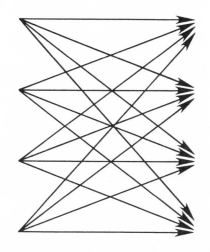

by

Michael F. Baber

WARREN H.GREEN, INC.
St. Louis, Missouri, U.S.A.

INTEGRATED BUSINESS LEADERSHIP THROUGH
CROSS-MARKETING

Copyright © 1986, by Michael F. Baber

Printed in the United States of America

All rights in this book are reserved.
No part of the book may be used or reproduced in any manner whatsoever without
written permission of the author, except in the case of brief quotations embodied in
critical articles and reviews. For information address Warren H. Green, Publisher, 8356
Olive Boulevard, St. Louis, MO 63132.

ISBN 0-87527-400-5

CONTENTS

LIST OF FIGURES

Preface

HOW TO USE THIS BOOK, AND WHY!

This book was written for 6 reasons or purposes:

(i) To present in a comprehensive and integrated form the practices of business and personal leadership and effectiveness; as I have seen them practiced over the past twenty years,

(ii) To define and expand on the concept of Cross-Marketing™, and its importance to business leadership; and to present some new and related marketing concepts,

(iii) To emphasize and explain the importance to business success of every word in the phrase, "every employee working effectively and together with every other employee with a focus on serving the commercial customer,"

(iv) To present in a comprehensive and clear way what is required from management and from each employee to cause the "statement" in (iii) to happen,

(v) To present specifically what each person needs to do to make it happen, and how to do it, and finally,

(vi) To serve as a detailed, back-up reference and guidebook for my clients and those who attend our company's seminar programs.

This book can be helpful to any corporation or organization of any kind, and its people, in a number of ways:

(1) For upper management, it summarizes today's wisdom on how to operate a successful organization, and explains the importance of a new concept, Cross-Marketing™. This is based on personal study and observation, literature analysis, and personal experience over a twenty five year career.

(2) It explains to management and supervision at all levels how to be truly effective, results-generating, people-motivating leaders. For the less experienced manager it can be a comprehensive short-course in corporate

business management and leadership. It contains not only what to do, but why and how to do it learned from years of study, observation and practical experience. Through illustration and example it gives insight into the responsibilities and challenges of various positions in a company and various types of businesses (banking, health care, hotels, industrial corporations, etc.). Higher management people forget, and most in lower management never had the experience.

(3) It explains to front line employees, and to all employees, the importance of customer and team orientation; and specifically what they need to do to produce desired results, and how to do it. It contains a short-course on customer relations and inside sales, which benefits the customer and generates sales at the same time. Chapter 11 is addressed specifically to front line employees.

(4) It explains clearly what customers, superiors, subordinates, and peers want and need from each of us, and how to provide those wants and needs in a professional and effective way.

(5) It explains how to serve the customer better, how to get more business and more recognition for us and our organization, and how to be positive, effective, productive persons.

The book is written in an unusual style. Each chapter stands alone and can be read as a short book on that subject. Consequently, some very important principles and practices are presented in a number of chapters. The chapters all tie together to present the bigger picture.

The material is presented in a very organized fashion with many headings and sub headings. This makes it easily useable as a reference work. The table of contents, the index, and the first pages of each chapter are arranged to give a clear understanding of the book's contents, and where to find information on any specific topic.

The material is presented with sufficient explanations and illustrations to clearly cover each point, but with as much fluff and excess baggage removed as possible. As a result, the book contains many times the quantity of valuable, pithy information as does the average business book. It can be somewhat tiring (although interesting) reading, since every paragraph and every sentence is meant to convey valuable information.

From a brief scan of the table of contents you will get an accurate impression that this book deals with all of the following topics: business leadership, personal leadership, market development, customer service, customer relations, human relations, Cross-Marketing, personal performance, personal image, group performance and teamwork, motivation, management and supervision, finding and solving customer problems, selling yourself, professional sales, effective communications, persuasive communications, why and how to be an effective front line worker, and how to successfully implement programs and systems within your organization. All of these are needed in a truly effective organization and by a truly effective management leader, and they are integrated into a system of business and personal leadership.

The introduction contains additional information on why the book was written and how it can help you.

If I as the author have accomplished my purpose, you will want every person in your organization to read part of this book, and many all of it; and your copy will be one of the five most valuable books in your library. You will read it from cover to cover, and you will do something different and better as a result. You, your customers and your subordinates will benefit substantially therefrom. You will continue to keep it readily available as a problem-solving reference.

I would enjoy receiving questions or comments on anything presented in this book. These can be addressed to the publisher, or in care of Michael Baber & Associates, P.O. Box 2707, La Jolla, California 92038; or phone 619-454-2099.

Michael Baber
July, 1986

DEDICATION

This book is dedicated to three important people who have shared themselves with me in different ways.

TO PETER DRUCKER
For providing me over the years with truth and wisdom.

TO PETER JOHNSON
For naming Cross-Marketing, and for his many ideas.

TO CAROLE BABER
For inspiring me, for allowing me the time to write,
and for helping me with this work.

INTRODUCTION

WHY CROSS-MARKETING*, AND HOW IT WILL
HELP YOU AND YOUR ORGANIZATION

Why is it that a few organizations both large and small, and a few people in most organizations, are so effective and so successful, while the rest are not? There are no easy answers. But there **are** some clearly-identified principles and practices employed by the winners - the IBMs, the Procter & Gambles, the Citicorps, the British Airways, the Lee Iacoccas, the Andy Groves, and probably the top institutions in your city or town - that explain why they **WIN**. Many are presented in this book; and one of the most important is explained in detail. That one is **CROSS-MARKETING.***

This book explains what Cross-Marketing is, and more importantly, how it can be used to make a winner out of your organization and you. This is a *how-to* book.

Mr. or Ms. President, as a result of implementing the principles and practices explained herein your corporation or institution can take even larger strides toward out-performing your competition. IBM did from the beginning, and Scandinavian Airline System recently used them to make a remarkable turnaround. Department managers, professionals, front line workers, and their departments, can reach levels of effectiveness and recognition only dreamed about. I have seen it happen and have enjoyed being involved in making it happen.

How can these statements be true? Over 20 years of study and experience have demonstrated that they are true, simply because so few

---

*Cross-Marketing™ as a concept is defined in chapter 3 as: "Activities by which solutions and benefits are effectively communicated from numerous parts of a supplier to numerous receivers, and ultimately to the commercial customer." A simpler way to say this is, "Everyone in the organization works effectively, and with everybody to effectively serve the customer." To accomplish this a number of personal and business effectiveness practices must be integrated and employed by the people in the organization at all levels. The Cross-Marketing™ system consists of the concept plus the integrated practices required to make it work.

organizations and individuals understand and apply the basic principles of customer-oriented effectiveness and high performance. And that is what this book is about.

Cross-Marketing is a concept or philosophy*, integrated with a number of how-to personal business practices to form a system. These practices include being customer driven, teamwork driven, personal performance, group performance, finding solutions to customer problems, communicating those solutions effectively and persuasively, and effective implementation. Individual employees at all levels employ these practices in the positive and supportive business environment described in chapter 1.

A personal note. Some years ago I read a book on how to play golf by Ben Hogan entitled **Power Golf**. Within only a few weeks my average golf score dropped by ten points from the mid 80s to the mid 70s. This improvement in performance resulted simply from my practicing and applying easy-to-learn principles and practices of an effective golf game. Correspondingly, it has been my experience that any organization or person which will practice and apply the easy-to-learn principles and practices of Cross-Marketing, will achieve an equivalent improvement in business performance.

This book originally was conceived for companies which directly serve the public: banks, savings associations, credit unions, hospitals, hotels, restaurant chains, transportation companies, and the like. However, major industrial and commercial corporations in numerous industries have risen to the top using the Cross-Marketing principles: among them; IBM, 3-M Company, Johnson & Johnson, and the non-high tech Deluxe Check Printers. My consulting with and studies of companies with sales from over $10 billion to below $1 million indicate that the level of a business's effectiveness and commercial standing is heavily influenced by its emphasis on, or lack of emphasis on, the key principles and practices in the Cross-Marketing system.

This book was written for three separate categories of readers, although one reader can fit into two or three categories:

(1) *Policy makers* - on how to establish a customer-oriented and people-oriented environment, and what policy makers need to commit to, as compared to just providing lip-service. For example, I refer to the statement by Francis G. "Buck" Rogers, Vice President of Marketing for IBM from 1974 to 1984; "A customer-driven atmosphere is essential to long term growth. All members of an organization - not just the sales representatives - should be sensitive and responsive to customers and in tune with the market place." Buck has made similar observations about people-orientation and commitment.

(2) *Managers at all levels* - on how to effectively *lead* their people to

implement a productive, team-oriented, customer-oriented organization and Cross-Marketing system. And,

(3) *Professionals and workers at all levels* - on how to improve their personal performance, how to make their customers feel well served, how to find and solve the problems of customers and associates, how to effectively and persuasively communicate those solutions, and how to work with them effectively.

There are concepts presented which may be new to some of our readers. Included among these are: "Anyone who uses what you do is and should be treated as a customer," "The commercial customer should be the focus of everything you do," "You are the company to your customers," "The customer's problem is your opportunity," "If you don't ask the customer you may be providing the wrong services and satisfying the wrong needs," "The department manager is the "chief executive" of his or her department and must address *chief executive* concerns," and "Treat your subordinates as your partners, and as if you owned a company and had to get results." Every person at every level is shown how to be more effective by believing in what they do, being more innovative, concentrating their efforts, touching others in a human relations way, communicating and listening, being more persuasive and offering more effective service to both commercial and personal customers. The concept of the *personal customer* is explained.

Chapter 1 explains the seven keys and the twelve steps to business effectiveness, with Cross-Marketing being the twelfth step. Chapter 2 contains a business and personal assessment on customer oriented business leadership. It then presents some important definitions and assumptions upon which the book is based. Chapter 3 then introduces the Cross-Marketing system. It defines Cross-Marketing, the Cross-Marketing System and the Process of Cross-Marketing, and explains their benefits. It explains the keys to effective customer support, and the steps to customer service management. The remaining chapters put meat on the Cross-Marketing skeleton; presenting segments of the system and the practices which make them work.

In chapters 4 and 5 methods for increasing personal performance and image are explained. Chapters 6 and 7 show how to be an effective leader and manager of people, with emphasis on motivation and how to *cause* effective performance. Chapter 8 addresses who your customers are, how to determine their needs, and how to find and solve their problems. Chapter 9 presents the keys to communicating more effectively with everyone, and especially your customers and those who use what you do. Chapter 10 gives the principles and the process of persuasive communications and to being a more persuasive person. Chapter 11 presents Cross-Marketing from the viewpoint of the front line worker.

Chapter 12 discusses the principles of effective implementation, especially as they relate to a program or system of "Integrated Business Leadership Through Cross-Marketing™."

Although chapter 1 reviews in detail the principles and practices of the nation's most successful companies, this book is not meant to be a textbook on total business success. For instance, it is not comprehensive about what it has to say on corporate finance, research or manufacturing. It doesn't cover the implications of the recent advances in manufacturing technology, or the effect of world money values. However, for most companies and organizations, in our present deregulated and competitive environment, the principles and practices of Cross-Marketing appear to be more critical and more timely than those. This book describes practices which generate both organizational and personal effectiveness, with an emphasis on what each individual, at every level, can do to help the organization be more effective and successful.

The book contains numerous illustrations and examples. Most are real incidents which come from my experience and research. Others are analogies, but represent what really can and does happen. A number of corporations and organizations are referred to, with probably more references to IBM than to any of the others. IBM is perhaps the most successful company in the history of the world, and it has consistently followed the customer driven philosophy supported by Cross-Marketing. It should be understood that the Cross Marketing system was developed based on working with and/or researching the experiences of these successful companies. Most did not employ the total Cross-Marketing system, specifically, to achieve their success, although some used parts of it.

As a final note, the Cross-Marketing™ system is not offered as a short term *miracle* program or drive. It consists of fundamental practices of good business and personal operations. When they are implemented, they should be part of a continuing system or program, which has the full commitment of whoever is in charge. When applied consciously and consistently the practices of Cross-Marketing will, without a doubt, raise the levels of performance of your people individually and of your organization as a whole. Increased performance and how to achieve it should be the prime objective of workers, managers and stockholders. If this is your objective, this may be the book you have been waiting for.

Integrated Business Leadership Through
Cross-Marketing

1

"The one who is tenacious of purpose in a rightful
cause is not shaken from his firm resolve."
Horace (23 B.C.)

BUSINESS LEADERSHIP

THE PURPOSE OF A BUSINESS
KEYS TO BUSINESS LEADERSHIP
TWELVE STEPS TO BUSINESS EFFECTIVENESS
PERSONAL BUSINESS LEADERSHIP
FROM BUSINESS PURPOSE TO CROSS-MARKETING

What separates the successful and leading businesses and organizations of all sizes from the less successful? What separates the more effective and more successful people in those organizations from the less effective and less productive? That is the subject of this chapter. How to make that success happen in *your* organization and for *you* is the subject of the remainder of the book.

The world is changing and yet everything stays the same. Allied Chemical Corporation (now Allied-Signal) was the odds-on favorite to become the leading company in the chemical industry back in the 1920s, and yet by the late 1940s DuPont was well ahead to stay. Ford was dominant in the automotive industry, and then just about went bankrupt, being replaced by mighty General Motors, which in turn now is scrambling to stay up with the Japanese. In the late 1940s IBM knew very little about computers and yet by the late 1950s had firm control of the market. In the early 1950s a number of successful restaurant chains were in operation and no one had heard of McDonalds. They have now! British Airways and Scandinavian Airline System were in trouble in 1981 and have since made dramatic turnarounds. A number of new high growth companies have caught the public eye in information systems and other high technology areas. A few of these will grow to become successful giants; most will falter and not reach their potentials. Why the difference?

Numerous studies have been made of companies, large and small, to determine what differentiates the winning companies from the losers. The winners are those that reach or are reaching their potentials, and often have more than double the productivity, market growth, and profitability as compared to the average. One of these studies was by Peters and Waterman of McKinsey and Company and was reported in the 1982 bestseller, **In Search of Excellence.** Another was performed by Clifford and Cavanagh for The American Business Conference, and resulted in the 1985 book, **The Winning Performance - How America's High-Growth Midsize Companies Succeed.**

Each of these studies reveal important characteristics and practices of the successful companies; and each misses the mark in its own way. For instance, neither of these two explain the serious impact of the recent advances in Japanese manufacturing technology. My studies confirm and add to what has been said before, but they too are incomplete. However, by understanding and making use of the following observations the business executive will walk a path of proven success, and will avoid most of the obstacles known to the author.

THE PURPOSE OF A BUSINESS

It is the responsibility of every manager and every person in an organization, business or otherwise, to work toward the purpose of that organization. As indicated above, there are principles and practices which contribute to the effective performance of every organization. A number of these have been combined in a new way into a system named *Cross-Marketing*. To understand how and where to incorporate the Cross-Marketing system into your operations, let us first look at your organization's purpose.

The PURPOSE of a business, **or of any organization, is to** *effectively provide* **a** *needed product or service to a customer* **or a group of customers, and to provide it in such a way that it**

is *most useful to the customer*(s) and that the business can continue to provide it for a *sufficient length of time* to satisfy the customer(s), the people who make up the business, and the investors in the business.

This statement of purpose is true for a Fortune 500 corporation, for a small business, or for a non-profit institution. It also is true for a department within an organization or any single job in the organization. More on this later; let's examine the statement for an effective business or organization - corporation, bank, hospital, university, etc.

Effectively provide - The organization and the people who make up that organization (officers, managers, professional workers, non-professional workers) need to do what they do well, if they are going to be effective. Products need to be of sufficiently high quality to satisfy customer needs, and produced at low enough costs to compete in the marketplace. Leadership must be provided so everyone at every level knows what is to be done, by whom, when, and how to do it most effectively. The leadership must inspire and motivate the people (everyone in the organization), help them when needed, and measure and reward their performance.

Needed product or service - The product(s) and/or service(s) provided by the organization must be designed to fill the needs of the marketplace. This means we must understand quite well the workings of both the markets we serve and the industries and customers within those markets. We must understand how each market fits into the overall national and international environment and what trends, changes and events may change the needs for our products and/or services. We need to understand, sometimes better than the customer, how our products are used by the customer, and how well our products fulfill customer needs as compared to those of our competitors.

To a customer - Customers are the focus of our entire business effort. Without customers we have no business. Having examined ourselves to determine what capabilities and resources we possess, we determine which markets and which (type of) customers can benefit most from what we have to offer. We then identify major customer needs, and develop products, services and systems to serve those needs over a substantial time period. We develop close business relationships with as many (major) customers as possible.

Most useful to the customer - We attempt to modify and add to what we have (our products, services, systems) to fulfill the needs of the customer, and help the customer more effectively serve "his" customer. Thereby, the customer will grow, and his needs for our products and services will grow. We do not, except in exceptional circumstances, try to get the customer to adjust his systems and needs to fit in with what we have to offer. We train and lead everyone in our organization to be sensitive to customer needs and to work together cooperatively to effectively serve the customer and keep him happy with our organization, and with each of us as individuals.

Continue for a sufficient length of time - The customer wants to deal with someone who is committed to him and his business, will be around for a long time, and continues to develop new ways to help him (the customer) to grow and be more effective. A "good" business is made up of "good" people. If a business wants to keep good people it must establish an environment in which they can produce results and grow as individuals. Top management must manage in such a way as to make the majority of the people believe that "this organization is going somewhere," and "there is a place for me." Finally, the stockholders in a profit-making organization, and the trustees in a non-profit organization, must be convinced that both the business concept and the people involved are of sufficient quality to continue to generate both satisfied customers and needed financial results.

During the past twenty five years I have operated businesses and have consulted with and studied hundreds of businesses and non-business organizations. Some were rapidly-growing, well managed and profitable; most were not. I also have reviewed in depth the results of studies by others on the most successful American and foreign corporations. As a result, there have emerged *seven key principles* to business leadership and *twelve performance practices* employed by the leading, most effective organizations. These will be discussed in the following two sections of this chapter.

KEYS TO BUSINESS LEADERSHIP

Summarized below are the seven basic principles to effective business leadership.

BUSINESS LEADERSHIP KEYS
(The leading, successful businesses are:)

a. **Market and Customer Driven**
b. **Clear in their Business Base**
c. **Encouraging toward Innovation and Entrepreneurship**
d. **Mission Oriented**
e. **Results Oriented**
f. **Communications Oriented**
g. **Employee Oriented**

Each of these will be discussed in turn.

A. Market and customer driven. The top companies study intently, and stay in *close contact with*, their *markets and their customers*, especially their top customers. They remain aware of trends and events worldwide which could influence their businesses. They define their markets broadly and realize that major changes frequently come from organizations and technologies foreign to present market leadership.

They, in effect, treat their major *customers as partners*, and learn their customers' businesses so well that they become consultants to them. They stay in touch with technical and market trends and events. They work jointly with customers on new and innovative ideas to develop new products, and to help them compete more effectively. They realize that the customer looks at the business entirely differently from the way the suppliers normally look at the business. They learn to look at values and needs through the eyes of the customer.

They identify what it is that the customer most wants from them from the standpoint of problem solving and customer service. They then methodically set out to meet the *customer's needs* and desires. They develop a customer service mentality within the entire organization, and design systems and procedures for providing effective customer service.

They concentrate more on quality, and *value* to the customer, than on low price.

They frequently find *niches*, or market segments, where their capabilities fit. They then develop leadership positions in those niches. The 3-M Company is particularly expert at working within niches, and then dropping product lines if they become low profit commodities. An example would be their specialty product line of floor maintenance pads, carpet cleaners, etc., for the sanitary maintenance industry, where they are still strong. These companies avoid concentrating in business areas which are likely to develop such large volumes they draw in large, low cost producers, unless they have the manufacturing technology and economics to compete effectively. In some industries, such as automobiles, machine tools, and now semiconductors, it has been difficult for even the most advanced American companies to compete with the advanced Japanese manufacturing technologies.

They have a tendency to *decentralize*, thereby organizing into business groups with a *mini-president* in charge of each group. This decreases direct upper management control, and allows lower management people the opportunity both to grow managerially, and to demonstrate their abilities to run an entire small business or profit center. It also generates the development of more expertise in the specific areas (niches), because they are managed by area or niche specialists.

Their upper managers get into the field and directly observe what is happening with employees and with customers on a *first hand basis*.

B. Clear in their business base. The top companies clearly understand what businesses they are in and where their strengths and limitations lie. They work at developing *expertise* in certain *clearly-defined areas*, and build their business growth in those areas and around that expertise. This expertise can be technical, market, or customer-industry based. They remain at the cutting edge of knowledge and technology in their core businesses.

Dunkin Donuts branched out into a number of franchise businesses and concluded its business base was a knowledge of franchising. After many problems and failures it sold off most of the businesses and decided its business base revolved around making and serving the best donuts and coffee in the world. Now that it is clear in its business base it is performing very well.

The top companies *understand their businesses* and have a feeling for what is happening nationwide and worldwide, which may affect their ability to compete.

They are organized with as *few levels* as possible. Some huge companies have only five levels from president to the first level worker.

C. Encouraging toward innovation and entrepreneurship. These companies do an effective job of managing and marketing today's business and today's products. However, they commit substantial energy, resources and encouragement toward *improving* today's products, processes and marketing, and toward *developing* and marketing new products and new, related businesses. They *encourage innovation and entrepreneurship* in numerous ways. They seek to develop a culture which supports creative thinking, new and odd-ball ideas, trying and failing and trying again, and allocating financial resources on a limited basis to numerous innovative people and ideas. They hold opportunity meetings, and encourage the identifying of opportunities in situations, not just problems.

They continually *challenge* their own assumptions and ways of doing business, and they encourage others to do the same. They agree with Harry Olson, CEO of Deluxe Check Printers, a rapidly-growing, market-driven Fortune 500 company, that the number one threat to effective business growth is complacency.

While they encourage informal and numerous approaches to innovation, they also establish *structured approaches* to innovation and to the development of new business opportunities. They seek to *allocate high quality resources*, especially manpower, to tomorrow's winning products and opportunities as compared to protecting and supporting yesterday's fading winners. They also seek to increase resource allocation to the 10-20% of the business which generates over 50% of the company's income; as compared to the remaining 80-90%, which normally consumes 80-90%

of the resources. They remove resources from fading products and secondary opportunities; frequently discontinuing low-result efforts entirely, thereby freeing up resources for more important efforts.

Thomas Edison tried over 100 different ways to make a light bulb before he was successful. Successful companies realize they must make *multiple attempts* to solve problems and to start successful new ventures. For this reason they generally start small.

They definitely want to grow, and generally do outgrow their competition, but they *plan for growth*, and prevent run-away growth which can get out of hand and lead into trouble.

They keep lots of new products and product-related ventures *coming along*. They realize that the existing is soon outdated.

They remain alert and *flexible*, to be able to take advantage of surprises or quickly-occurring opportunities.

They *diversify* their products and businesses carefully into areas with which they are *familiar*, or those that are closely associated. Rather than jumping into new and unknown waters, they edge into associated markets with versions of present products. They then develop new products for these new markets after gaining a foothold, and learning something about them. They stay alert to major changes in the environment, world economy, society, and technology, and their effects on the business.

Experimentation and testing are encouraged. Instead of studying projects to death they encourage trying them out on a small scale. They are tolerant of leaky systems and failure. They realize that many programs must be tried to find one large winner, and if kept small, failures do not cause excessive damage. They also realize that motivated "fanatics" often generate successes in spite of the better judgement of established, more conservative managers.

D. Mission oriented. The top companies identify the specific strengths of their businesses - technology, market and industry expertise - and specialize in and build additional knowledge and expertise in those strength areas. They *focus* their present and future business efforts into those areas, so they excel there. They know they cannot do everything well, so they *concentrate* their resources into a few business areas. They continually introduce new products into these areas and feed resources into those which are accepted by the market and which build their business positions. When they diversify they edge over into related markets or technologies, rather than jumping into something new and foreign.

They *plan strategically*, positioning themselves favorably in relationship to their and their competition's strengths, and market trends and needs. They plan effectively so as to have the correct type and amount of financial and managerial resources when needed.

They develop a well recognized *organization culture*, with customer-oriented and effectiveness-oriented *values*. Everyone in the company knows what are the values of their organization. "IBM means service," is an example. McDonalds stands for, "quality, cleanliness, value and service." These shared values and beliefs are deeply ingrained and serve as the basis for decision making.

E. Results oriented. All of these companies operate with some form of *management by objectives*, although frequently it is informal and operated by line management. They measure results and feed them back to the personnel involved for self control. They maintain tight control over important cost areas. The controls are tight, but few and simple. They apply pressure selectively to accomplish important results in a few areas.

They realize that numerous wasteful systems and unnecessary departments will grow up if they are allowed to. They are *anti-bureaucracy*, and work very hard at keeping the organization simple and as lean as possible.

They pay relentless attention to *business fundamentals*. They realize that Peter Drucker was right when he reported in his book, **Management in Turbulent Times**, "The fundamentals deteriorate unless they are being managed carefully, consistently, consciously, and all the time. Indeed the greatest danger to most enterprises today - business, non-business, and public service institutions alike - may not be public hostility to business. It may be a hidden deterioration in the fundamentals."

They continually *push for increased performance* and productivity. Instead of the former credo, "If it ain't broke, don't fix it;" they have a new credo, "If it ain't broke, fix it or it soon will be broke." They realize that productivity can be increased substantially in most areas. They concentrate productivity-improving efforts in areas of greatest opportunity, rather that just across-the-board.

They perform the *basic management functions* effectively. They manage and train their people so that they plan, organize, direct, and control for effective results.

They *avoid unsound business practices* such as reducing quality in bad times, dropping promising long term development programs to save money over the short term, or knee-jerk reacting to business pressures. They don't swing back and forth from a customer service emphasis after receiving a number of customer complaints to exclusively a results-oriented emphasis when bottom line performance drops. They continue to emphasize both. This is in spite of the fact that the stock market tends to value stocks based on projected short term performance. They do not let their concern for short term performance overshadow attention to and the devotion of resources to *long term performance*. This is one of the reasons for the success of many Japanese corporations as compared to similar American corporations.

They *avoid crash programs* and drives. They encourage steady, continuous programs with a sound base.

They are *action oriented*. As Lee Iacocca of Chrysler said, "Do something, don't just stand there."

They identify and encourage *high leverage activities*; those activities which affect others and have a high payout in sales, income, cost reduction, and productivity improvement.

F. Communications oriented. The effective organizations encourage intense communications. They go to great means to encourage their people to talk to each other. They establish plenty of conference rooms and marking boards, and even structure the organization to encourage communications.

During one of my open seminars a number of years ago a hundred supervisors and managers were asked what was their biggest problem. For over half their biggest problem was communicating with their direct superiors. However, none believed he had a problem communicating with his subordinates. Likewise, in over twenty surveys we performed of first line corporate employees, every one has indicated that the employees feel they are not being kept adequately informed by their superiors.

The effective organizations encourage *small work groups* and use short term task forces. Experience has shown that in many cases small groups have out-performed much larger and better financed groups working on the same or similar projects. Larger and medium sized companies have had a great amount of success with short term or ad hoc task forces to solve major problems. These groups include both knowledgeable specialists and decision makers. A not-so-small task force was used by IBM during the mid 1960s to develop the 360 line of third generation computers, which changed the face of the industry.

They encourage *informality*, generating an atmosphere of congeniality and information-sharing between unconnected groups.

G. Employee oriented. They treat their *employees as if they were partners* in the business. They treat them with respect. This is discussed later in this chapter and later in the book. They also attempt to design the organization and manage it in such a way as to make as many middle level managers as possible feel and act like owners. Many of the more successful mid-size and smaller companies have stock sharing plans.

They continually *develop their people* for increasing responsibilities and more effective performance. Again, IBM is an example. IBM spends tremendously on personnel development at all levels. The top Japanese companies have a similar commitment to people development and training, and this has contributed substantially to their recent successes.

They make *decisions* at the *lowest possible level*, realizing that the working specialist and the low level manager frequently know more about the problem and how to solve it than those up the line. If they have received developmental training, then they should have the capability to make high quality decisions.

TWELVE STEPS TO BUSINESS EFFECTIVENESS

There are twelve distinct steps which a business or organization takes to effectively satisfy *"the purpose of a business"* defined in the first section of this chapter. In the top organizations, these steps are taken in conjunction with the recommended business principles just discussed.

BUSINESS EFFECTIVENESS STEPS

Step 1 - Know the Environment and the
Marketplace
Step 2 - Know your Resources, Strengths and
Values
Step 3 - Develop Meaningful Strategies and Plans
Step 4 - Commit to Markets, Strategies and Plans
Step 5 - Acquire the Proper Resources
Step 6 - Develop the Correct Product Line
Step 7 - Market Expertly
Step 8 - Sell Professionally
Step 9 - Develop Individual Effectiveness
Step 10 - Lead People to Results
Step 11 - Manage the Business Productively
Step 12 - Cross-Market Enthusiastically

Business situations vary. A potential entrepreneur can have an invention or a new business idea. A corporation may be having problems, or alternately, it may be looking to expand into related markets or product technologies. A business or institution may be either improving its present operations, or continuing its effective present operations. In any of these cases the same principles and steps apply, but the emphases and the methods of application will vary.

The following are the twelve steps to business effectiveness; the practices which are followed by the winning organizations as they study and understand what to do, gear up to do it, and then implement effective performance.

Step 1 - Know the environment and the marketplace. A common failing of businesses, and institutions as well, is to concentrate internally on providing good products and on operating effectively, without paying enough attention to the business environment and the marketplace. While we are busy developing new and wonderful products, and improving our operating systems for producing and delivering those products, the entire market can be changing or even disappearing. The railroads suffered drastically because they did not see, understand or effectively react to the changes in transportation technologies and customer preferences. The same has been true in the steel industry, the automobile industry, the electronics industry, and more recently for many companies in computers and the entire financial industry.

We need to understand demographics, political trends and life-style trends - internationally, nationally and as they directly affect the markets and industries in which we are involved. We need to know and react to certain economic, market and technical factors and trends.

For instance, a business, a bank or otherwise, serving a farming community is affected by foreign and U.S. production and consumption of crops; political and economic trends and events which will affect these; pending federal legislation; new industries entering the area, and factors affecting the futures of those industries. If the business serves a grain farming area one thing it needs to know is about the future of gasahol. This in turn is dependent on petroleum supplies, impending gasahol production technology, future consumption of gasoline products in all transportation industries, and government policy. The business in question needs to know which businesses in town are and will be prospering, why, and if it can help in any way. It needs to know what types of products and services would be most acceptable to all local customers, both business and personal.

If it is a bank, it needs to know what new products and services it might develop and market effectively, both banking oriented and non-banking oriented. It needs to know what products that banks in other parts of the country are offering, that are being well-received; as well as the advantages and disadvantages of the bank's present offerings as compared to local competition. It needs to know what other businesses (savings associations, credit unions, insurance companies, department store chains, consultants, out-of-state banks, etc.) are potential competitors; and what are potential new areas in which to offer its own products and services. It needs to know what areas of specialization would be most fruitful. It needs to know, in each market it serves, which are the trend-setting companies; those which influence the business decisions of other companies in the area.

The business in question needs to know everything it can about its markets, the major customers in those markets, and what will influence their future growth, business health, and purchasing decisions.

Some of this information can be obtained from market research, customer surveys, and purchased market studies. Some is available from published sources such as newspapers, periodicles and government and trade association studies. These sources generate valuable information, but that information tends to be *quantitative* - how much? when? where?

It also is valuable, and frequently imperative, to obtain substantial *qualitative* information about the market - a "gut feel" for what will happen and why, plus a basic understanding of the market, how it operates, why it operates that way, and how the various factors and influences interrelate. A skilled market analyst, from inside or outside the company, can rather quickly obtain a certain "feel" for the market by studying the literature and through individual and group interviews with customers and other knowledgeable personal sources. However, the best way to obtain this qualitative "feel" for the business and the market, which frequently leads to better decisions than a quantitative analysis, is to personally become submerged in the business over a period of time. Many high level executives of successful companies spend a large amount of time "in the field" personally talking with salespeople, customers, industry experts, and the like. Usually the best way to find out what a customer wants and needs, as well as what he likes and dislikes about our company and its products, as compared to competition, is to ask him.

As a result of studying and knowing the environment and the marketplace we have both hard data and perspective for judging market trends and needs. We have a basis for determining what our position should be; and what products, services and business approaches would be most successful.

Step 2 - Know your resources, strengths and values. We need continually to be appraising our strengths as compared to market needs. On a regular basis, more frequently than most usually do, we need to methodically and systematically take a *business xray*. Peter Drucker in his book, **Managing For Results,** outlines one method for doing this.

We need to answer questions such as: What are our present and potential financial resources? What are our capital and equipment resources, and what changes and additions are needed? Do we have the right people in the right positions; should we transfer people, remove people, or add new technologies and capabilities? Do our people have the attitudes and abilities to accomplish present and anticipated objectives? What strengths do we have in the areas of market and technical expertise, locations and facilities, and present and potential products, which could be utilized to grow, or expand into new areas? Which products should be discontinued; which barely supported; and which are the winners and future winners which should be heavily supported with money and manpower?

We also need to know what dangers, trends or opportunities we learned about from our market analyses that we could exploit effectively to expand or protect our present business, or build a new business? Do we have an effective management and leadership system in place? Where are we suffering in effectiveness, efficiency and resulting productivity; and what corrective systems, equipment and training would pay for itself? Which of our products are superior to competition; which are inferior; and what can be done about it? How do customers rate our products, our service and our company; and what can we do to improve our ratings? What are obvious business needs and voids which we already have the capabilities to satisfy? These are some of the questions that need to be answered before we move ahead with step 3.

We need to ask what we are in business about, what we stand for, and what are those basic values upon which the business is based? As will be discussed in later chapters, the "values" of a business permeate the organization and influence its decisions and how it operates. This can be seen by observing the very successful McDonalds hamburger chain, which professes to have the values of, "quality, service, cleanliness and value."

Step 3 - Develop meaningful strategies and plans. We now have the bases for developing effective strategies and operational plans, first for the business as a whole, and then for each sub-business and/or functional area (eg. marketing). A number of the considerations which should be taken into account while developing business and marketing strategies were discussed in the section above on business principles. Some of the considerations include:

- concentrating on market segments and niches
- developing leadership positions in those segments
- being customer and market driven
- having systematic approaches to innovation and entrepreneurship
- diversifying into related rather than completely unknown areas
- responsibly reacting to change
- systematically creating and fulfilling new market trends and needs
- developing strategies for productivity improvement
- being long term oriented, and
- addressing the market through decentralized business units.

Among the books on business strategy two of the most useful were written by Peter Drucker, **Managing For Results** (1964), and **Innovation And Entrepreneurship** (1985). Michael Porter's **Competitive Strategies** (1980) also is helpful.

Chapters 4, 7 and 12 of this book contain some general guidelines for developing action plans. The compilation of strategies and plans into thick, well-written tomes can be an exercise in systematic thinking, forcing one to clearly think out all factors and considerations. However, more often than not they are a waste of time and effort, and sit on shelves, never to be read again. Many companies spend hundreds of man days doing what a few knowledgeable people could accomplish together in a properly designed planning session of a couple of days, a week apart, with perhaps a man week of staff work in-between.

Step 4 - Commit to markets, strategies and plans. "What you do speaks so loud I cannot hear what you say." This anonymous quotation explains why this step is included and why it is so important.

Some experts believe that the United States lost the Vietnam War because of a lack of commitment to win. The country kept sending more and more men and supplies, but just enough to keep from losing; never enough to get the job done. And no serious effort seems to have been made to determine what was really wrong and what was required to "win." There seems to be a penchant for management at all levels to follow the Vietnam example, and the higher the level the stronger the tendency.

When top management makes a true commitment to a market, a strategy and a plan of action everyone knows it: middle management; the troops on the front line in sales, production, accounting, research and staff; the customers in that market; industry professionals; the media; everyone. When top management says it has made a commitment, and really has not, which occurs too frequently, everyone knows that too. When a commitment is made management at all levels is involved; asking questions, looking at results, making suggestions, demanding action, recognizing and rewarding results, solving major problems, providing ample resources, visiting major customers, redrafting failing plans.

A frequent indication of a lack of serious top management commitment is when top management sincerely believes that middle management and the troops "have gotten the word" and are are really moving out on a supposedly agreed-upon plan of action, **and they are not.** Top management wonders why the results are not forthcoming as projected, while key employees down-the-line are taking delaying, modifying and blocking actions. Instead of wondering, top management should be down in the ranks looking!

Why does this happen? Sometimes the new strategy and plans are a threat to the positions and the job knowledge of key employees. Sometimes there is a fear of change, and that the job cannot be accomplished properly. Sometimes there is resistance to the extra work involved. Sometimes there is inadequate communication on what is needed, why it is important, and how it will benefit those involved. Sometimes inadequate resources are provided, and this is interpreted as an indication of a lack of importance. Always there is a lack of upper management involvement: checking on results, requiring results, and rewarding results.

Step 5 - Acquire the proper resources. Important business, product and marketing efforts require high quality resources and enough of them to properly get the job done. Providing the proper finances, buildings and equipment, and top management involvement are important. But the most important resource of all is manpower.

Generally the quality of the people assigned is even more important than the quantity. The most capable people should be assigned to the most important tasks. Too often the most important tasks involve the future - developing products and developing new businesses. They are smaller and are incorrectly treated as less important. They often are considered to be of lower status by everyone in the company. Consequently, higher management must be very convincing and provide extra incentives, to motivate established executives to leave secure positions with large budgets and take charge of smaller, less secure business development projects.

Step 6 - Develop the correct product line. If we are committed to selected markets, then over time our organization and certain people in our organization will become extremely knowledgeable about those markets. This will include knowledge of the major customers in the markets, what they produce, how they produce it, who they produce it for, what opportunities they have, what problems they face, what they need from us, why they need it, and how valuable it would be to them.

If we are customer oriented and customer-service oriented, then we will be developing close relationships with a number of customers, especially major ones. We continually will be upgrading our product line and developing new products to serve customer needs. As a result, our line of products will closely match the needs of the marketplace and will be continually improved and upgraded as market needs change. Also, as a result, we will be an influential and often preferred supplier to the market.

The sales force finds it both easier to get motivated and easier to get results when it is proud of its product line, and can clearly explain the advantages and resulting benefits to present and new customers. Also, when the company and its people are recognized for providing quality products that solve problems, prices and profit margins can be a bit higher. This in turn furnishes the resources to provide high quality products, problem solving expertise and outstanding service. This improves our market standing, and the cycle continues in a positive direction.

Step 7 - Market expertly. Customers define what is value to them, what are the problems they need solved, and what satisfactions they are willing to pay for. Their purchasing behavior is influenced by many factors in addition to product quality, as important as that is. Consequently, an effective marketing program is a must.

Market development should be continuous. It includes four stages: (a) market analysis - similar to that described in step 1 above, (b) market position - the prognosis of where we stand, (c) market objectives, and (d) a market plan including strategic positioning in the market, product mix, market organization and staffing, pricing, sales promotion, etc. A plan should be developed for each separate market and should be tailored to the needs and opportunities in that market.

The market plan should take into account marketing principles such as developing continuing business relationships, product life cycles, proper timing for new product and new business introductions, and creative destruction - replacing our own products with those which serve customer needs even better, before competition does so.

Every effort should be made to differentiate our products and services from those of the competition. We can be different and better in a number of ways. These include our advanced technology, our commitment to the market, our specialized knowledge of the market and its problems, our knowledge of our customers and their technologies, our knowledge of the needs and problems of our customer's customers, our abilities to solve customer problems, our innovative approach to helping customers, the willingness of our technical people to work on customer problems, the advantages and benefits of our products, and the supporting evidence for those advantages and benefits. It includes our company's reputation for quality, advanced technology and good service, our quick reaction to customer requests, the friendliness and cooperativeness of our people, the effectiveness of our customer communications, the ease of doing business with us, and the specialized and efficient service of our sales and customer service people. Our differences and advantages should be clearly spelled out in our market strategies, in our advertising and sales promotions, and in our sales programs.

To support many of the differentiations and advantages listed above we should encourage a corporate policy or "value" of, *in our organization marketing and customer service is everyone's business.*

Step 8 - Sell professionally. During recent years customers have become much more sophisticated in their buying attitudes and behaviors. Consequently, it has become increasingly necessary to approach the marketplace in a more professional manner.

There should be a written sales plan for each sales representative and for each major customer. These should be kept simple and clearly stated, frequently consisting of a single page. Sales managers at all levels should be true managers and leaders of people, not just good sales people who were promoted.

The sales staff should be trained to be competent "sales consultants" whenever applicable. Every sales representative needs adequate product knowledge, and most sales consultants need considerable knowledge about the technology used by the markets and the customers. Sales skill training should be "professionalized" by being concentrated in *eight major high productivity areas:*

1. SALES STRATEGY. Determining what industries, markets and customers on which to concentrate, and when and how to work with them most effectively.
2. SALES TOOLS. Developing demonstration kits, testimonials, references, creative evidence, and other *tools* which help the salesperson to make convincing sales presentations.
3. POSITIVE, CONFIDENT ATTITUDE. Developing in our sales people attitudes which inspire both the customer and the salesperson to *get on* with the process of making the presentations, solving the problems, and writing the orders.
4. PROSPECTING AND MAKING QUALIFIED APPOINTMENTS. Identifying those prospects with the biggest problems which will yield the highest results; and then using proven techniques to cause the *decision maker* to be eager to meet with you.
5. MAKING AND KEEPING FRIENDS. Realizing that people buy from their *friends* in whom they have both trust and confidence; and developing proven skills for making good business friends.
6. DETERMINING PROSPECT PROBLEMS, WANTS AND NEEDS. Leading prospects to tell you how to develop effective business relationships with them and their companies, what are their problems and needs, and how to match your products and services to their wants and needs - utilizing effective question organization, question asking, active listening, and analytical skills.
7. GENERATING ACTION AND CLOSING SALES PROFESSIONALLY. Effective and proven methods for solidifying relationships, generating action and positive decisions, and obtaining signed contracts.
8. PERSONAL PLANNING, ORGANIZATION AND TIME MANAGEMENT. Skills which increase results and sales productivity.

A ninth fertile area for sales training is *effective and persuasive communications;* especially the six keys presented in chapter 9: believe, innovate, concentrate, touch, communicate and serve.

Step 9 - Develop individual effectiveness. Managers and professionals at all levels should identify for themselves and their people specific areas and skills on which to concentrate to improve personal effectiveness. In addition, there are some important skills and activities for which organization-wide training and management systems might be advisable. These could include holding effective meetings, goal setting and planning, time management, and any company-wide management systems such as "management by objectives."

Peter Drucker, as presented in his book, **Managing in Turbulent Times**, is just one authority to identify that in any industry the leading organization operates at 1.5 - 3 times the productivity of the average organization in that industry. Likewise, within an organization one individual can operate at many times the effectiveness, generating many times the meaningful results, of others in the organization. This shows the importance of each of us working to improve our personal effectiveness. Chapters 4 and 5 discuss how to accomplish this in further detail.

Step 10 - Lead people to results. The two primary factors affecting the success of most organizations are the quality of its people and the leadership provided those people at all levels. The quality of people is heavily influenced by hiring, placement, and in-company education and training. More emphasis and expertise should be placed on all three of these than presently exists in most organizations, especially the first two.

Dwight D. Eisenhower defined leadership as, "getting people to do what you want them to do because they want to do it." How do we accomplish this? We might consider three recommendations.

People make the effort to be effective when they believe in what they are doing. They need to believe in the organization and its leadership, the worthwhileness of the endeavor, that they can be effective if they try, and that it will benefit them sufficiently to do so. The effective leader makes sure that the above it true; and then communicates with his people and *sells* these truths to them.

The second recommendation is to operate in such a way as to *cause* our people to be successful - to generate effective results. To accomplish this we should utilize, and help our people utilize, the principles discussed in chapters 6,7 and 12; principles such as setting objectives, making action plans, being supportive and encouraging, measuring results, giving support and help when needed, removing unnecessary obstacles, and adequately recognizing and rewarding results.

Even though most employees are not legal partners in the business, the third recommendation is to, *treat your people as partners.* This could be clarified to say, *treat your people with respect, and give them sufficient support to get their jobs done and at the same time enjoy doing them, just as you would partners.* To accomplish this, we should be genuinely interested in them and helpful in a friendly way, effectively communicate and listen to them, be positive and supportive, inform them how their jobs fit into the overall mission and objectives, help them to be effective now but show them how they can advance and reach their personal objectives later, make clear what is expected of them, allocate adequate resources to their tasks, listen to and act on their ideas, design their jobs to be interesting, delegate responsibility to them when they can handle it, keep their paperwork to a minimum, make them feel as secure in their jobs as possible, and work with them to improve both their performance and their advancement potential.

Step 11 - Manage the business productively. There should be a business focus with all employees feeling a "sense of mission." If the business is too large for a single focus then it should be separated into business groups or marketing efforts. Unnecessary activities should be totally abandoned, thereby loosening resources for the more important. There should be a continuing search for where resources are being misallocated.

The most successful companies follow the seven *keys to business leadership* presented in the section above. They encourage innovation, change, experimentation and low-level risk taking. They realize that markets and technologies are constantly changing, and if the company does not continually change it will fall behind or lose out altogether. They continue to bring new products to the market. They encourage that the related decisions be made at low levels, since lower level "specialists" frequently have a better feel for market and customer needs. They operate with as few organizational levels as they can. They encourage small units where as many people as possible can see the "big picture," and thereby have the perspective to make meaningful contributions. They discourage bureaucracy, unnecessary paperwork, and large staffs and central offices. They encourage informality and intense communications throughout the organization.

On the other hand they pay close attention to the fundamentals. Lack of attention to fundamentals is a major problem for the less successful organizations - businesses and sports teams as well. They are performance oriented and have effective control systems which feed back results to those who are performing the work. They concentrate on even further improving the performance of the already high-performers. They also concentrate performance improvement in high-leverage activities, those where improvements will generate cumulative increased productivity. They avoid replacing sound, long term business programs with short term "drives," or pushes for improved results. They avoid unsound business practices such as cutting back on important new product developments or supplying cheapened products during hard times. They anticipate what is likely to happen regarding customers, competition and employees, and prepare contingency plans.

Step 12 - Cross-Market enthusiastically. When everyone in the organization is working effectively with everyone else, with a focus on serving the customer, the organization almost has to prosper.

There are a number of keys to successful business performance which most managers agree with, but which few think of employing *together*, as part of one system. It is bringing these practices together and causing them to happen simultaneously which helps to make the few truly top-performing companies into industry leaders; into champions. We have identified a number of winning business practices, and have developed a system for simultaneously implementing them within an organization. We named the comprehensive system, Cross-Marketing.

The following are eight of the *effective business practices which are* incorporated into the Cross-Marketing system:

- The organization and every person employed by it is market oriented and customer-service oriented.
- Every person identifies who uses what he or she does, and then plans to provide effective service to them, whether they be commercial customers, internal departments, or individuals in the organization.
- Every person learns and utilizes specific skills for developing and offering even more effective service to commercial customers and to others who make use of their output.
- Every person takes specific actions to improve his or her own personal skills and performance.
- Every person works as a cooperative and communicative team member, and even provides unofficial leadership when applicable.
- Every manager utilizes effective leadership and motivational management principles and practices.
- Every manager and professional person, and many non-professionals, learn how to identify and solve the problems of those whom they serve, especially commercial customers, and they apply that problem-solving knowledge when possible.
- Every manager, professional and customer-contact person learns and uses the skills of persuasive communications to communicate effectively what they have to offer, both to commercial customers and to others within the organization.

As a result, everybody is in the marketing department; everybody is in the sales department; everybody is in the productivity improvement department; and everybody is working together with everyone else to effectively serve the customer.

PERSONAL BUSINESS LEADERSHIP

A business or organization is effective only if it is led by effective, results-oriented people. If those people happen to be in top leadership positions, and have vision and/or charisma, they can establish a focus for the organization and inspire the entire organization to address that focus with dedication and excitement. Such was the case with both Tom Watsons of IBM, Jan Carlzon of Scandinavian Airlines, Colin Marshall of British Airways, and John Hanley of Monsanto Company.   Lee Iacocca's performance at Chrysler is legend, as are the leaders of many of the fastest growing mid-size companies to their own people.

The above two sections have discussed the keys and steps to effective leadership for businesses and organizations. A close examination shows that the same principles apply to effective personal business leadership. To test this for yourself, think of the names of some national and local effective leaders with whom you are familiar. Whether by purpose or by design, they will have applied these principles and employed these steps in their personal business lives. If we personally do the same, we and our organizations will enjoy the resulting effective performance.

We personally should be (a) *market and customer driven.* We should be asking, "Who do I serve, and who uses what I do in my job?" and, "What can I do to serve them more effectively?" We should stay in close contact with our personal markets and customers and other who use what we do. We should work with each of these as partners. We should find our own personal niche, where our specialized knowledge offers special value. We should concentrate on the quality and value we offer our personal customers.

Likewise, we should be (b) clear in our personal business base, what we know and can do to make the most effective contribution. We should be (c) innovative, (d) mission oriented, (e) results oriented, (f) communications oriented, and (g) people (employee) oriented.

We should take the *twelve steps to our personal business effectiveness.* We should know (1) our personal business environment, and (2) our resources, strengths and values. We should (3) develop meaningful strategies and plans, (4) commit ourselves to personal markets, strategies and plans, (5) acquire the proper personal resources and skills, (6) develop the proper business knowledge and experience, (7) market ourselves and our people expertly, (8) sell and communicate our ideas and job output effectively, (9) improve our individual effectiveness, (10) lead our people and associates to results, and (11) manage our own personal business and job effectively.

Finally, we should (12) cooperatively work with everyone appropriate in our organization with an eye to effectively serving the commercial customer; we should use Cross-Marketing principles and practices. Having already embarked on steps (9) and (10) above, and having identified who are our personal and commercial customers, we should continually be finding and solving their problems. We then should be using effective communications and persuasion skills (in other words, selling skills), to communicate our solutions to our personal and commercial customers, so they will accept and use them. Only if our customers accept and use our solutions and our job output will we be making an effective contribution to our organizations, and thereby demonstrating *personal business leadership.*

As we continue throughout this book, we will see how the *Cross-Marketing* system assists us in carrying out the keys (principles) and the steps (practices) of personal business leadership. If we personally carry out these keys and steps, then we will personally become effective, recognized and successful. If our entire organization carries our the keys and steps, then our organization, like IBM and the others cited, will be effective, recognized and successful - it will be demonstrating BUSINESS LEADERSHIP.

FROM BUSINESS PURPOSE TO CROSS-MARKETING

"The purpose of a business, or of any organization, is to effectively provide a needed product or service to a customer or a group of customers, and to provide it in such a way that it is most useful to the customer(s) and that the business can continue to provide it for a sufficient length of time to satisfy the customer(s), the people who make up the business, and the investors in the business."

As indicated above, this *purpose* will be served by any business or organization which effectively carries out the seven **Keys to Business Leadership** and the **Twelve Steps To Business Effectiveness**. Cross-Marketing, the twelfth step and the subject of this book, is consistent with the seven keys, cuts across a number of the twelve steps, and helps to tie them all together. It provides a framework for building business leadership on personal and team effectiveness and a customer orientation. Consequently, understanding the Cross-Marketing concept should make it clearer to businesses and organizations how to become effective industry leaders. The remainder of this book further defines Cross-Marketing, and outlines the tools whereby organizations and individuals can use its practices to perform more productively, and to serve their customers in a more effective and business-generating way.

CROSS-MARKETING PARTS AND CHAPTERS

2

"Anyone who makes use of the output
of your job is your customer."
Baber

GROUNDWORK FOR CROSS-MARKETING

BUSINESS ASSESSMENT
PERSONAL ASSESSMENT
CUSTOMER DRIVEN
COMMERCIAL AND PERSONAL CUSTOMERS
BUSINESS ASSUMPTIONS

Before specifically defining and explaining Cross-Marketing (chapter 3) and examining the practices of the system, let's first take a look at our present status, and the definitions and assumptions upon which the Cross-Marketing system is designed.

In the first section below we examine how our organization or corporation stacks up from the standpoint of customer oriented business leadership. In the second section we ask ourselves some questions about our personal work situations, to determine our level of awareness on how to be effective, customer oriented performers. Then we discuss some definitions and business assumptions upon which the Cross-Marketing system is based.

BUSINESS ASSESSMENT

Listed below are 25 characteristics or criteria of an organization which is a customer oriented business leader; resulting from implementing the Cross-Marketing system or its equivalent. The criteria are listed in three categories depending on the level to which they pertain:

(a) top management and policy makers,
(b) managers and supervisors, and
(c) professionals, non-professionals, and managers in their own work.

> Category (c) refers to the work attitude and performance of everyone in the organization, at all levels, as regarding their personal positions and responsibilities.

To rate your company or organization, read each statement (1-25) as it pertains to your organization and your people as a whole. Assign a point score rating to each criteria of from 0 to 4 points, based on your judgement as to how well and how often the criteria is met, according to the point score below. Attempt to be objective and score as if you were a hard-nosed outside consultant.

4 points	-	Yes, all the time
3 points	-	Frequently
2 points	-	Sometimes
1 point	-	Seldom
0 points	-	Never.

After rating all 25 criteria, then refer to the end of this section to compile and analyze the ratings.

CHARACTERISTICS OF A CUSTOMER ORIENTED BUSINESS LEADING ORGANIZATION
(Rate your organization from 0-4)

Score

A. Top Management and Policy Makers

_____ 1. Top management and policy makers are committed to customer support and customer service, and provide the resources, direction and inspiration to all the company's people to insure that the commitment is effectively carried out as company policy.

____ 2. They have developed a meaningful customer service theme which clearly conveys to our people and the customers what our service objectives are and how they will benefit our customers. They have effectively communicated this theme from top to bottom within our organization.

____ 3. They believe that all the company's people are important, that they should be treated with respect, that they should be given whatever information and resources are required for them to perform effectively, and that they should be rewarded more than adequately in proportion to their performance and results.

____ 4. They provide leadership from the top by making policies clear, by being visible, and by doing whatever is required to demonstrate full support for the major systems and programs implemented by the company.

B. Managers and Supervisors

____ 5. Managers and supervisors have a clear understanding of the principles and practices of the most successful companies in our industry, and how our company differs from the top companies, if it does.

____ 6. They have researched their customers and/or the users of the services of their departments, to determine what are the wants and needs of the users as compared to what their department does or provides. They have a clear understanding of their users' and customers' wants and needs.

____ 7. They have analyzed the customer service aspects of their departments to determine which factors most influence the relationships between the department and its customers and users; and they have systematically addressed the objective of improving customer service.

____ 8. They have a clear understanding of the present attitudes and beliefs of their people at all levels toward (a) our company's industry and the industry's health and worthwhileness, (b) our company and its policies and top management, (c) their immediate superior as a manager and leader, (d) the importance of their own jobs, and (e) the company's products and services.

____ 9. They are thought of by their people as inspirational leaders, rather than just operational managers.

____ 10. They believe that everyone in the organization is important and treat them that way.

___ 11. They are thoroughly grounded in the knowledge and skills of working with people to achieve a high level of performance.

___ 12. They know how to inspire and motivate superior performance from their people, regardless of skill level, and use that knowledge so their people are indeed inspired and motivated.

C. Professionals, Non-Professionals, and Managers in Their Own Work

___ 13. Everyone in the organization is continually aware of all customers they come in contact with, and are sensitive to serving all customers and knowing and responding to their needs;

> and as a result, our customers receive rapid response and high quality service from all our people most of the time, and prefer to do business with us.

___ 14. Our people consider all superiors and associates who they work with to be the equivalent of customers, and are sensitive to being cooperative with them and serving their business needs;

> and as a result, our people work together cooperatively and as a team and effectively supply each other's needs, which will result in a higher lever of performance from everyone.

___ 15. They understand and use the principles of good human relations, and develop close business relationships with important customers and business associates;

> and as a result, our customers like them and feel comfortable with them; and their business associates like them, feel comfortable with them, and readily communicate with them.

___ 16. They have a problem-finding mentality and the trained ability to seek out and solve customer problems;

> and as a result, our company and its people are effective in problem seeking and problem solving. This results in more problems solved, more and better products and services provided, and customers which are more satisfied, more successful and provide us with more business.

___ 17. They are confident in themselves and their abilities to accomplish their jobs. They become authorities in their specialized areas of interest;

> and as a result, they step out and try new ideas and better approaches because they have less fear of failure. As a further result, the people in our organization provide better products

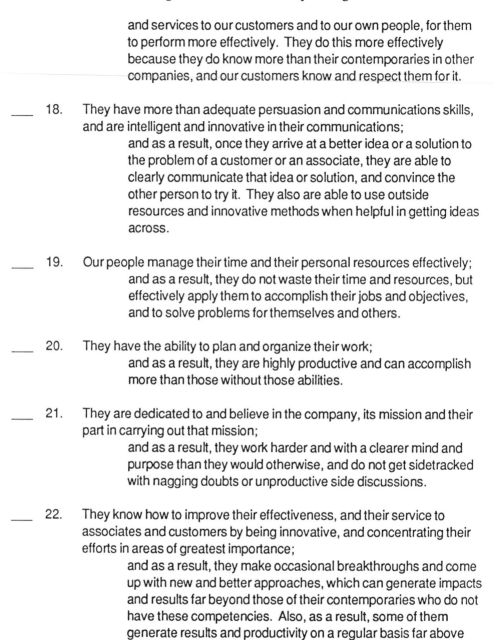

and services to our customers and to our own people, for them to perform more effectively. They do this more effectively because they do know more than their contemporaries in other companies, and our customers know and respect them for it.

____ 18. They have more than adequate persuasion and communications skills, and are intelligent and innovative in their communications;

and as a result, once they arrive at a better idea or a solution to the problem of a customer or an associate, they are able to clearly communicate that idea or solution, and convince the other person to try it. They also are able to use outside resources and innovative methods when helpful in getting ideas across.

____ 19. Our people manage their time and their personal resources effectively;

and as a result, they do not waste their time and resources, but effectively apply them to accomplish their jobs and objectives, and to solve problems for themselves and others.

____ 20. They have the ability to plan and organize their work;

and as a result, they are highly productive and can accomplish more than those without those abilities.

____ 21. They are dedicated to and believe in the company, its mission and their part in carrying out that mission;

and as a result, they work harder and with a clearer mind and purpose than they would otherwise, and do not get sidetracked with nagging doubts or unproductive side discussions.

____ 22. They know how to improve their effectiveness, and their service to associates and customers by being innovative, and concentrating their efforts in areas of greatest importance;

and as a result, they make occasional breakthroughs and come up with new and better approaches, which can generate impacts and results far beyond those of their contemporaries who do not have these competencies. Also, as a result, some of them generate results and productivity on a regular basis far above that of other people in similar positions.

____ 23. They are not afraid to be held accountable for accomplishing their jobs and their agreed-upon objectives;

and as a result, they are very cooperative in working with their superiors to establish what needs to be done, and by when, to support the corporate and department mission; and they commit themselves to those objectives.

____ 24.   They understand and are satisfied with how they are rewarded for their performance and what they must do to move ahead in the company; and as a result, they obtain fair rewards for their performance; and believe the company is fair, and over time will act to improve their positions and levels of contribution according to their motivation, abilities and performance.

____ 25.   They are inspired and turned on by their company top management, their superiors, their jobs and the idea of giving excellent customer service; and as a result, they enjoy their jobs and look forward to working with and helping their customers and associates. As a further result, they perform effectively, are motivated, have good attitudes and are a positive influence and an inspiration to their fellow workers.

Organization Rating

To arrive at a rating for your organization, add all the point totals for criteria 1-25, and arrive at a sub total. Then adjust the sub total as follows.

An adjustment is made for criteria 1,3 and 4 because of the extreme importance of the attitudes and actions of top management and the policy makers. (This is not to mean that criteria 2 is not also important.) Consequently, for criteria 1,3 and 4:

- For every rating of 4, add 5 points
- For every rating of 3, add 0 points
- For every rating of 2, subtract 5 points
- For every rating of 1, subtract 10 points
- For every rating of 0, subtract 15 points.

SCORING BOX

Sub Total (criteria 1-25)   [_____]
Adjustment, criteria 1   _____
Adjustment, criteria 3   _____
Adjustment, criteria 4   _____

TOTAL BUSINESS LEADERSHIP SCORE   [_____]

Based on the scoring of other companies, a score of 75 would indicate barely satisfactory performance as far as an organization being a customer oriented business leader. IBM, as a corporation, scores an even 100.

PERSONAL ASSESSMENT

The previous section was designed to rate or assess your organization as a customer oriented business leader.   However, it contains some questions which relate to your personal effectiveness and customer oriented performance.   This section contains fifteen additional sets of questions related to you personally.

The purpose of the following questions is for each of us to use to measure our personal effectiveness and customer service performance - and to determine the extent to which we are operating with Cross-Marketing practices.   If we are managers we can ask our people to complete the assessment and discuss it with us.

The questions can be answered from the following different perspectives. We should use ones which are appropriate to our situations:

(a)   our personal performance, or that of our people or department,

(b)   serving commercial customers, or serving internal people and
       departments who use what we do or produce, and

(c)   as our organization directly serves the public (eg., as we are
       a bank, hospital,etc.); or as we serve specific, non-public customers (eg.,
       those customers being corporations, institutions or internal departments of
       organizations).

After answering these questions we will better understand which parts of the remainder of the book will first be most helpful to us.

PERSONAL ASSESSMENT QUESTIONS

1.   What is the most important task for me or my people to complete in the next
      30 days? Why is that task the most important? How do I plan to accomplish
      it? How does it tie into the corporate mission or objectives? What will
      happen as a result of it being completed?

2.   Who are the three (or more) customer departments or companies (or
      classes of them) which benefit the most from what I or my people do, in my
      position or department? How do they benefit? How could I increase the
      benefit to them?

3. What are the biggest problems or challenges presently facing the three customers listed above?

4. When did we last ask them, by personal interview or survey, what they most want from us?

5. What job behavior or results that I or my people should generate is most important to the commercial customers, and to the internal departments we serve or provide input to?

6. How do they rate us as to how well we are projecting that behavior and providing those results?

7. As I or my people encounter our customers and associates on a daily basis what are the most important recurring events which give them reason to judge our service highly or poorly?

8. As compared to competitors, or other associates, where do our customers judge us to be the strongest, and where the weakest?

9. What strengths or resources do we have or do we have available to us, which we could employ even more effectively to accomplish even more, and give more benefit to those we serve (our customers and associates)?

10. What single objective could I accomplish, which would benefit my company and/or my commercial customers the most, and which would bring positive recognition to me and to my department or organization?

11. What could I do to help my people to be even more effective, and to receive even more recognition?

12. What are three instances in the past week when I could have given (or did give) appreciation to or noted (recognized) the positive performance of one of my people, or a fellow employee?

13. How do I now communicate with commercial customers? What events occur which cause me to communicate with them? What channels (phone, mail, via a salesperson, etc.) do I use, and which are most effective? How do I define effective?

14. What could I or my people do to improve our relationship with customers, and to make them even happier with us and our company?

15. What is the single most important action I can take to encourage my people and others to be more concerned with effective customer service?

CUSTOMER DRIVEN

There is much discussion in the early part of this book about an organization being customer driven. Exactly what does this mean? As an answer, the following are twenty characteristics of a customer driven or customer service oriented organization.

Organizations which are Customer Driven -

1. Stay close to market trends,
2. Communicate effectively with customers,
3. Listen to customers, especially industry leaders,
4. Get feedback from customers,
5. Tailor products and services to market segments,
6. Know the benefits of their products and services,
7. Are sensitive to customer needs,
8. Innovate based on customer and industry needs,
9. Respond rapidly to customer needs,
10. Solve customer problems,
11. Are highly committed to quality, reliability and service,
12. Learn how customers think,
13. Perform as if they are on the verge of losing every customer,
14. Have senior management involved with customers,
15. Motivate workers down-the-line through customer involvement,
16. Realize that service objectives inspire ordinary people,
17. Change service incentives often,
18. Make all employees in some way accountable for customer service and results,
19. Stress customer service to their people, and
20. Become partners with their customers.

COMMERCIAL AND PERSONAL CUSTOMERS

One concept which is important for understanding Cross-Marketing is that of the *commercial* vs the *personal* customer.

An insurance sales person knows who his commercial customer is. It is his next door neighbor, or anyone who purchases an insurance policy from him. The *customer* of a bank new accounts representative is the person who opens a new account, or takes out an IRA, or in any way purchases from her. A customer of the hospital, and of the nurse on the floor, is the patient. The airline customer flies from one place to another.

When IBM sells a large computer to Monsanto Company, then Monsanto Company is the customer. There also are important buying influences within a corporate customer such as a division manager who signs a $3 million purchase order, a purchasing agent who processes the purchase order, and a systems engineer who evaluates and recommends the IBM computer. All of these buying influences should be considered to be "commercial" customers.

But who is the customer of the research scientist? If he visits the commercial customer with a sales person to solve a customer problem, then, yes, he knows who his commercial customer is. It is both the company being visited and the individual who represents the company. But suppose he spends all his time in the research laboratory and never works on a commercial project for a commercial customer? Does he then have no customer?

Who is the customer of the personnel manager or the personnel specialist? Who is the customer of the production foreman, the department secretary, the file clerk, the group vice president, or the computer systems analyst? Who is the customer of the credit union controller, the hotel or motel housekeeping supervisor, the airline baggage handler? They all *do* have customers to serve. Everyone has one or more customers for the products or services that they provide in their job, whether or not they ever contact a *commercial* customer. Then who are they?

Anyone who makes use of the output of your job is your customer. If that organization or person purchases your products or services they are a *commercial customer.* If they work within your organization and make use of your products or services (your research, your management, your help, your typing, etc.) then they are your *"personal customer."* (Note: Some personal customers do not work in your organization, as for instance, your national and your state senators, if you are a high level corporate official.)

For example, the bank new accounts representative starts a new account for, or sells an IRA or travelers checks to, the bank's, and consequently her, commercial customer. But, in addition, she reports to and provides information to her boss, who is one of her personal customers. She provides completed customer information forms to the accounting department; so the accounting department is one of her personal customers.

The head floor nurse in a hospital serves her commercial customer, the patient. She also provides supervision and management services to the other nurses on her floor, so they would be her personal customers; as would be the physicians to whom she provides information on the patients. (This is a special case. In a hospital the physicians frequently are considered to be commercial customers, along with the patients.) The director of nursing, her superior, would be her personal customer. The supervisor of housekeeping would be her personal customer because she provides information to the supervisor of housekeeping on what needs to be cleaned and where. In reverse, the head nurse is a personal customer of the housekeeping supervisor.

What this all boils down to is that each of us needs to determine who it is we serve, who it is to which we provide services, and treat each one of them as if they were an important customer of ours and we wanted to effectively serve them to maintain an effective business relationship. When we do this, we are taking the first step toward applying the practices of Cross-Marketing and becoming a winning organization.

BUSINESS ASSUMPTIONS

The Cross-Marketing system, and the remainder of this book, is based on the following assumptions about business reality. These are assumptions which I have developed during the past 25 years as a businessperson and consultant; and my studies show they are the assumptions upon which the leading and most successful businesses in this nation are based. Before you reject any of them, please first read and think on assumption no. 9.

A. About Being Customer Driven

1. For most businesses and organizations of all types, a customer driven or customer oriented orientation with emphasis on effective customer service, will not only pay for itself, it will generate the highest long term results in business health, sales and business volume, employee satisfaction, and financial results.

2. It is not natural for the majority of people and organizations to evolve customer oriented values and systems. It takes purposeful and continuing leadership from the top to accomplish this. Note: it is more natural to be concerned with internal operating efficiency and the employees' own convenience.

3. Most organizations are not nearly as customer driven, or effective at customer service, support and satisfaction as they think they are.

4. It is best and easiest to be customer driven from the outset of an organization's existence. However, there is ample evidence of organizations turning their fortunes around totally, from unprofitability to profitability and industry leadership, by effectively implementing a customer driven system such as Cross-Marketing.

5. Organizations with strong customer service orientations generally are well managed overall. They are high performing organizations, not just high performing service-oriented organizations. One reason for this is that it takes a high level of leadership and general management ability to implement and institutionalize a customer oriented system.

6. To implement an effective customer driven system within an organization there are policies and systems which must be instituted by the organization, at the top management level, and there are principles and practices which must be implemented by managers and front line people on a daily basis. Both are required.

7. If your organization indeed has a customer driven or customer service oriented culture, then it will have developed "war stories" about effective customer service; no war stories - no culture!

8. It should be the objective of the organization that every employee in every department be customer service oriented. Anyone who is not customer support oriented becomes introverted in view and thinks and acts as a bureaucrat.

B. About Change and Selling the System

9. People at all levels of an organization are naturally resistant to change; they are amazingly attached to their habits and procedures. However, they will change once convinced that upper management means what it says and knows what it is doing. Convincing them of these two facts is more difficult than most people realize.

10. Complex concepts seldom trickle very far down the organization. They need to be presented directly to front line personnel, especially when significant changes in attitude and performance are desired.

C. About Customer Satisfaction

11. Effective customer service can be an active marketing tool, and has been so used by a number of leading business organizations. Customer service can become a critical differentiator between your organization and your competitors.

12. Customer loyalty is circumstantial, fragile and fleeting. Especially with the existence of an effective competitor, the customer is continually asking, "What have you done for me lately?"

13. We get no special credit from the customer for delivering a high quality of service if it is the standard for the industry. We get credit for extra service, when it is above that of our better competitors. We get demerits and lose business from a level of service that is less than the standard for the industry, or less than our better competitors if we are one of the industry leaders.

14. The level of service required to generate customer satisfaction changes over time. It generally becomes more demanding as the performance of competition improves, and as the customer becomes used to a level of customer support and service, and considers that to be normal.

15. Each one of your people is the company to the customer when they are in direct contact with the customer. Each has the opportunity to significantly affect the customer's opinion of your organization.

D. About Leadership

16. People can and will improve their attitudes and their performance if they are led and managed effectively.

17. It is not natural for most people and organizations to have respect for the individual and to develop policies and systems which effectively utilize the brainpower and knowledge of front line personnel. This has to be cultivated by a knowledgeable and far-sighted management.

18. In dealing with customers, especially in organizations which deal directly with the public such as banks and hospitals, there are so many customer interactions and opportunities to make mistakes (both in performing tasks and in interacting with customers) that it is necessary to motivate and educate front line people sufficiently that they will perform effectively with or without supervision. Most customer encounters occur out of the observation of management. Responsible surveys have shown that less than ten percent of unhappy customers complain, but most tell a large number of other potential customers.

19. Effective feedback to employees positively affects their performance.

20. People tend to do that which is recognized and rewarded.

21. Dissatisfied employees tend to give unsatisfactory performance, regardless of the rules and restrictions applied.

E. About Front Line Employees

22. Employee attitudes and performance can be changed somewhat simply by collecting information from customers and showing it to the employees in a meaningful form. Employees want to satisfy their customers.

23. An effective way to gain employee commitment to customer service from front line employees is to ask them to define good service and to develop methods for improving and measuring customer service. This relieves managers of the task of specifying good behavior, and releases a tremendous amount of creativity at the gross roots or front line.

24. Front line employees are a good source of information and ideas on how to improve customer service, and how to measure that improvement.

F. About Personal Performance

25. By identifying a few specific skills or practices which will significantly improve personal performance, and by concentrating on developing those skills or making a habit of those practices, one's personal performance can be increased substantially.

G. About Customer Problems

26. If we do not effectively learn the customers' wants and needs we may be trying to appeal to them with things they don't really care about.

27. By proper investigation and analysis we can identify and understand specific wants and needs of customers, and those problems relating to our capabilities which need to be solved.

28. Once we understand which unfulfilled needs and which problems our customers have, we can fill many of the needs and solve many of the problems by matching them to our resources and strengths, using non-sophisticated problem solving methods.

29. It is not enough to give our customers good service and effectively solve their problems; it is important for us to effectively communicate to them that we are doing so. Sometimes customers are getting good or exceptional service, don't realize it, and don't give us any special credit for it. Also, if we do not effectively and persuasively communicate to the customer that we have a solution to his problem, he may never make use of it.

3

"In Cross-Marketing everyone works effectively
and with everybody to serve the customer."
Baber

THE CROSS-MARKETING SYSTEM

What is Cross-Marketing? What sets it apart from strategic marketing, or customer-oriented marketing, or customer relations or cross-selling? Does it include these, or is it something entirely different? What makes up the *system?* Does it include a specific set of principles and practices? What are the benefits of Cross-Marketing to our customers, to my company and to me? This chapter is designed to answer these questions.

BENEFITS AND CHARACTERISTICS OF CROSS-MARKETING

Chapters 1 and 2 refer repeatedly to the policies and practices of the most successful organizations. These can be grouped by categories. Three of the most important are (1) a consistent orientation toward customers, (2) actions which generate effective team performance in the organization, and (3) a high level of personal performance and individual productivity.

The Cross-Marketing system, which is described in this chapter, emphasizes these three areas; and the remainder of this book presents specific principles and practices for accomplishing them. The Cross-Marketing system encourages the following practices and generates the following benefits.

CUSTOMER ORIENTATION.

Companies which Cross-Market -
- Have concern for customer welfare
- Provide effective customer service
- Know their customers, and determine customer wants and needs
- Know how their products and services benefit their customers
- Continually evaluate performance against customer expectations
- Meet customer wants and needs
- Have internal customer service themes
- Apply innovative thinking to customer problems
- Actively solve customer problems and provide consulting
- Earn customer and employee loyalty
- Have fewer customer problems than their competitors
- Serve as being on the customer's team
- Help their customers to be more competitive and successful
- Receive referrals from satisfied customers
- Earn a high level of customer satisfaction
- Earn a favorable business reputation.

TEAM OR GROUP PERFORMANCE.

Companies which Cross-Market -
- Achieve effective teamwork and a winning team spirit
- Provide a positive, supportive work environment
- Generate an enthusiastic work force
- Achieve employee belief in the company and its products
- Earn employee confidence in management
- Provide management support of worker needs
- Provide leadership throughout the company
- Achieve effective communications with their people
- Keep everyone informed
- Provide sensible delegation
- Train and motivate their employees effectively

- Provide effective coaching and counseling
- Have consideration for the feelings of their members
- Have an understanding of employee needs
- Generate high morale
- Generate company and personal pride
- Develop a motivated work force.

PERSONAL PERFORMANCE

Companies which Cross-Market -

Train and manage their employees to generate -

- increased personal effectiveness
- effective time management
- increased personal strengths
- confidence, assertiveness and skill
- increased productivity
- higher quality products and services.

THE DEFINITION OF CROSS-MARKETING™

The *purpose of a business* defined in chapter 1 is supported by Peter Drucker, in his 1954 classic entitled, **The Practice of Management,** with his statement, "There is only one valid business purpose: to create a customer." Creating customers requires effective marketing.

Webster's dictionary defines *marketing* as, "activities by which transfer of title or possession of goods and services from seller to buyer is effected including advertising, shipping, storing and selling." This definition of *marketing* is modified by Baber to be, "activities by which solutions and benefits are effectively communicated from a supplier to a receiver; i.e., the customer." (Remember the concept of commercial customer and personal customer explained in chapter 2.) Webster's dictionary defines *cross* as, "to move from one side to another; to intersect."

Baber combines the definitions of cross and marketing to generate the following definition of Cross-Marketing (or Cross-Marketing™, because the expression is a trademark of Baber Marketing):

Cross-Marketing: "Activities by which solutions and benefits are effectively communicated from numerous parts of a supplier to numerous receivers, and ultimately to the commercial customer."

This is illustrated In Figure 3-1, entitled **The Cross Marketing Flow of Solutions and Benefits.** The figure shows four types of

Figure 3-1

THE CROSS-MARKETING
FLOW OF SOLUTIONS
AND BENEFITS

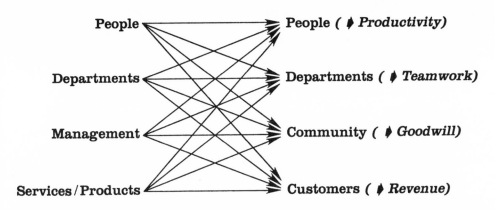

Suppliers	Receivers

People   People (⬧ *Productivity*)

Departments   Departments (⬧ *Teamwork*)

Management   Community (⬧ *Goodwill*)

Services / Products   Customers (⬧ *Revenue*)

suppliers and four types of receivers. The diagram is illustrative, and the *four* could have been any number. Referring to the discussion in chapter 2 on commercial and personal customers, the first three items listed on the right side are personal customers: people, departments, and community. The final item, *customers,* is meant to represent all commercial customers. There can be many other suppliers within a particular organization and many other receivers, both commercial and personal customers.

The message of Cross-Marking is that to be a winning company like IBM, Procter & Gamble, Deluxe Check Printers, or the top company in your city, you need to manage your company in such a way that *every employee, every department and every function works effectively to serve every other employee, every other department and every other function, all with a focus on serving the commercial customer.* This should be done with the dedication of serving a valuable commercial customer. This bears out what Ted Levitt said in the introduction to his 1983 book, **The Marketing Imagination,** "Marketing is, indeed, everybody's business, and everybody had better know it, no matter how deeply buried one may be in far away R&D or out at the telephone switch board."

THE CROSS-MARKETING SYSTEM

The title of this book is **Integrated Business Leadership through Cross-Marketing.**   Chapter 1 discusses business leadership from a corporate standpoint, and presents the seven keys to business leadership and the twelve steps to business effectiveness, with Cross-Marketing being the twelfth step.

In balance to chapter 1, which addresses the practices of corporate policy makers, the Cross-Marketing system addresses the practices of all the <u>individuals</u> in the corporation (or organization of any type).

The Cross-Marketing <u>system</u> consists of integrating with Cross-Marketing eight "performance increasing," "how-to" business concepts into one integrated system, so that everyone in the organization is working effectively and with everyone else to serve the customer.   These eight concepts are as follows.

1. Business leadership; understanding the principals and practices of business leadership and how to apply them at your level in the organization.

2. Customer driven; why and how to effectively work with customers and seek out and serve customer needs.

3. Teamwork driven; why and how to effectively support customers by cooperatively working with associates, subordinates, and superiors.

4. Personal performance; how to work more effectively and more productively, and be recognized for it.

5. Group performance; how to lead individuals and groups to effective results through inspiring, motivating and causing performance.

6. Finding solutions; how to seek out, find and solve the problems and opportunities of both customers and associates.

7. Communicating solutions; how to plan, organize and implement both effective and persuasive communications.

8. Implementation; how to effectively implement the Cross-Marketing™ system, and any program or system.

Chapter 2 presents a business and a personal assessment to determine if your organization and your people are operating consistently with the Cross-Marketing concept. Chapter 2 defines "customer driven," "commercial and personal customers," and the 29 business assumptions upon which the Cross-Marketing system is based. The remainder of this chapter, chapter 3, discusses seventeen ways to provide customer support, which are required to be *customer driven* (concept 2 above). It also presents "customer service management," a new concept which can help many companies to be more customer driven.

Finally, the immediate next section in this chapter presents *"The Process of Cross-Marketing."* This four step process supports most of the eight concepts listed above, and specifically 4-7. It is the subject of most of the remainder of this book. The eighth concept, implementation, is discussed separately in chapter 12.

THE PROCESS OF CROSS-MARKETING

To accomplish Cross-Marketing, and to support the Cross-Marketing system, everyone at every level in the organization should be effective in four stages or four sets of practices. These four stages are outlined in Figure 3-2, entitled *The Process of Cross-Marketing.* They are:

1. **Effective Personal Performance**
2. **Effective Group Performance**
3. **Finding Solutions to Customer Problems, both commercial and personal**
4. **Communicating Those Solutions Effectively to Customers.**

1. Personal Performance. Regardless of level or position, there are certain personal management practices we need to perform effectively in our own jobs so we will be generating effective results. We must manage our time and our performance so as to be performing the correct tasks, and performing those tasks efficiently. We need to project a positive image and attitude so as to effectively represent ourselves and our departments. How to do these is discussed in chapters 4 and 5.

2. Group Performance. Most organizations are a team affair. As a team member each of us needs to be cooperative and supportive of our leadership and our fellow employees. As a corporate manager, or as a team leader, we need to handle ourselves in such a way as to provide a motivational and results-oriented influence on the other members of the team. The principles and practices of leadership and team performance are presented in chapters 6 and 7.

3. Finding Solutions. We need to understand and seek out the wants, needs and problems of our customers, both commercial and personal. We need to use our abilities and resources to be service oriented and to devise solutions to the problems we find.

Looking at this from the corporate or overall standpoint, our organization needs to determine what customers want and need from our

Figure 3-2

THE PROCESS OF
CROSS-MARKETING

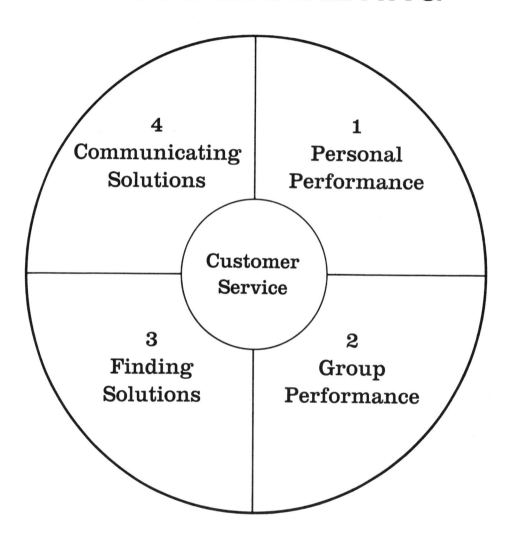

organization and from our people; as well as what are the critical incidents, those continuing customer interactions which most influence our relationship with customers. Part of this information might be supplied by a marketing research department and part by the individual people and departments.

From a personal standpoint we as individuals need to identify, both generally and specifically, what the customers we encounter want from us, what is most important to them, and what needs and problems they have which we might solve. The following are three examples related to finding and solving solutions to customer problems and needs.

If we are department managers our people (who are some of our personal customers) probably have the following needs or problems which we should supply or solve. They need from us information as to what are the current department objectives, how their personal objectives support department objectives, and which of their projects and assignments are most important to the company at this time, and why. They need sufficient resources and support to accomplish their assignments, assistance in solving certain critical problems, timely review meetings to insure they are on track, and appropriate appreciation and recognition.

At the airline ticket counter our customers may have problems which require us to supply the following: the technical knowledge to rearrange flights in difficult circumstances; the patience and human relations skills to remain calm and friendly in difficult circumstances; care and concern for the customer dilemmas we encounter; the ability and willingness to bend the rules as needed to help out the customer; and the willingness to make amends and apologize when and if the customer is inconvenienced (by canceled flights, etc.).

Looking at a specific problem solving situation, a nurse might want to encourage one of her personal customers, a physician, to admit even more patients to her hospital rather than to another hospital. From the nurses' standpoint this would generate support, income and jobs for her hospital, and better patient care. To accomplish this she would look at what that physician needs to perform more effectively in her hospital. The physician may need a time-saving mechanism to alert her as to when she is needed at the hospital and when she is not. The nurse might solve the problem by establishing a system of observing the patients' charts more systematically and more often, and making phone calls to the physician's office at regular intervals, updating the physician on patient conditions. This would be a solution to the problem.

The finding of solutions to customer problems is further discussed in chapter 8.

4. Communicating Solutions. Having arrived at a solution to our customer's problem, we need to effectively communicate that solution to the customer. It does little good to solve a customer's problem if we cannot communicate properly. The customer must be clearly informed that the solution exists, and be convinced to use it. This requires both effort and skill, especially when the customer is acting dense and uncooperative.

As an example of solution communication, let's refer to the above hospital problem. The nurse, after analyzing the hospital problem or challenge, develops the solution indicated in 3 above. The communication might include, after clearing it with proper hospital authorities, writing a comprehensive report to explain clearly to the physician how the problem can be solved and what are the benefits to the physician. Then a meeting might be arranged, and the report explained clearly to the physician and to others on the hospital staff. Once the first physician is convinced that the solution will help her, and it is successfully implemented, then this same solution might be implemented with other personal customers, in this case the other physicians on the staff. These and other practices of effective and persuasive communications are dealt with in chapters 9 and 10.

CUSTOMER SUPPORT

In a customer driven, Cross-Marketing organization both the organization and its people direct their attentions to learning and supporting customer needs. Chapter 2 lists twenty characteristics of a customer driven organization which offers strong customer support. This section expands on that listing.

The *Marketing Department* develops strategies and plans for making customers and potential customers aware of our company, and how good are our products and our people. The *Sales Department*, often under the direction of the Marketing Department, personally contacts customers and prospective customers, determines their problems and needs, and sells them both (a) problem-solving products and services and (b) the concept of maintaining a continuing buying relationship with our outstanding, customer-oriented company. *The rest of us* have the mission of proving to the customer that our company indeed is outstanding and customer-oriented. We do this by providing outstanding customer support so the customer will desire, and even prefer, to continue to do business with us, and over a long period of time.

Listed below are seventeen ways, or practices, for providing outstanding customer support. Depending upon the type of business our organization is in, and upon our personal positions, some of these, as for example market research, may be performed for us. But if they are not, we should assume responsibility for them, whether we are serving commercial customers or personal customers.

For those in organizations which directly serve the public (financial institutions, hotels, airlines, etc.), plus direct customer contact people at the front line in all organizations, the following discussion may have to be modified slightly to be applicable. However, for this group the next section on *Customer Service Management* presents a specific approach to applying these practices.

CUSTOMER SUPPORT PRACTICES

1. Perform market and customer research. By researching our customers and their markets we will better understand them and their problems and needs, both individually and as a class. As a result, we will be better able to serve and satisfy their problems and needs. We can do this through background reading, telephone and written surveys, personal interviews and/or listening and taking notes during daily contacts. We should listen carefully to any communications concerning customer problems and needs, whether they come from the customer, from the community, or from within our own organization. We then should analyze and categorize them to see what patterns emerge which we can take action on. If we are representing a corporation, as an executive, this research may require the resources of many people. Alternately, if we are dealing with a limited number of customers personally, we may perform the research ourselves through general reading plus on-the-spot discussions with a few of our more important customers.

2. Locate and communicate with all customer buying influences. For a corporate commercial customer these buying influences could include a number or people; for example, a high level manager, a technical expert, an operations department manager, a purchasing department representative, and even a first level user of the product or service. Generally, in a corporation, only one or two people can authorize a purchase but a number of people can veto a purchase or a business relationship. For an individual commercial customer, such as a patient in a hospital, these could include people who influence the customer such as the physician and the visiting relatives. For a personal customer within our organization these could include the individual with whom we are in direct contact, that person's immediate superior, that person's secretary or assistant, and an advisor in a different department.

It may be worthwhile to pause here and address a question which could be in your mind, that question being - if I'm trying to effectively serve another member of my organization, a personal customer, why should I go to the trouble of identifying all of these other associated personal customers and attempt to communicate to them as well? The answer is - we are attempting to do whatever we can to make our organization, our department and ourselves as effective as we possibly can, and to provide as much service to as many people as possible. One of our important personal customers, maybe our most important, may not be informed enough to totally realize the value of our services to them, especially in a single important area. For this reason, we may need to persuasively communicate how we can help them, both to them personally and to their associates. Even a secretary or an assistant can have some negative words about our input or solution, thereby persuading their boss to take action which would be detrimental both to our purposes and to the effectiveness of the overall organization.

3. Assume Personal Responsibility.   Assume personal responsibility and accountability for providing outstanding service, for identifying and solving as many customer problems as possible, and for effectively and persuasively communicating those solutions to the customer. Emphasize both quality and reliability of service.   There are numerous stories about top companies where they went overboard in providing service.   One example is the time that Xerox had a problem with their computer and IBM brought in eight experts from all over the world within twenty-four hours to help solve the problem. Someone was responsible for that decision, the costs involved, and the resulting favorable customer response.

4. Visit with important customers personally and develop a professional and personal relationship with them. Ask many questions and listen a lot. Learn the customers' business, how they think, and where are their problems and opportunities. Learn what is considered to be of value in the mind of the customer. This can help in a number of ways. It can help us to determine where to concentrate our resources and efforts. It does no good to solve a problem which the customer does not consider to be a problem. It also allows us to present the solutions, and their accompanying customer benefits, in a language and in a way that is acceptable and understandable to the customer.

5. Analyze all data received with a problem seeking as well as a problem solving mentality.   Be looking for customer-related problems we can solve, and thereby generate increased business (sales) and customer good will.

6. Apply creativity and innovative thinking to the customer's situation.   Develop new and better ways of serving the customer. Provide tailored solutions, products and services to serve customer needs. Sometimes entirely new solutions are required. At other times, solutions and products provided to other customers or industries can be modified or repackaged to be useful to this customer and this industry. Become an authority in your product line and in the customer's industry. This develops respect for you and your organization. Consider specializing in an industry or product area.

7. Make the customer feel dependent on you by becoming an authority. Learn his business. Think and plan ahead to provide so much value that he would not want to look elsewhere.

8. Provide the resources. Provide sufficient personnel, expenditures, time and effort, to effectively serve the customers and their needs.

9. Respond rapidly to customer requests and concerns. Frequently, a simple solution presented immediately is of considerably more value than a much better solution presented late.

10. Get others involved in serving the customer when appropriate. This includes experts and higher management. As a result, we not only will serve the customer more effectively, but will impresses him favorably as well.

11. Develop internal themes and slogans built around customer service. By its own words IBM is fanatic about its service beliefs. Everyone in IBM knows that the customer and customer service comes first at IBM. Quoting from the book, **A Business and Its Beliefs**, Thomas J. Watson, Jr., says, "In time, good service became almost a reflex in IBM . . . Years ago we ran an ad that said simply and in bold type, "IBM means service." I have often thought it was our very best ad. It stated clearly just exactly what we stand for. We want to give the best customer service of any company in the world . . . IBM's contacts have always offered, not machines for rent, but machine services, that is the equipment itself and the continuing advice and counsel of IBM's staff." Scandinavian Airlines' customer service theme is, "service, creativity, and finding a better way." This is discussed in more detail in the next section.

12. Establish service objectives. Objectives are targets for people to shoot at. If we work with our people to establish customer service objectives, they are going to be shooting at customer service targets. The same is true if we establish service objectives for ourselves.

13. Train our people and ourselves to perform effectively in the area of customer service. Many of the skills and areas of expertise presented later in this book apply. Effective training develops both confidence, and the skills to use that confidence to deliver effective service.

14. Monitor our effectiveness in providing customer service. People do what they are checked up on. When we inspect, they know we expect.

15. Reward customer service performance. People also do what they are rewarded for doing. When we reward performance in customer service we both bring attention to the area and demonstrate through our actions that it truly is important.

16. Continually evaluate customer satisfaction. Through contacts and visits with customers, from written and telephone surveys, and from comments heard in the industry we evaluate the level of satisfaction of our customers. We use this information to evaluate where we are doing well, where we are not doing so well, and how to improve our performance.

17. Consistently provide high quality and timely service. Through performing the practices listed above our quality of service and customer support will be that which puts us in the league with IBM, McDonalds, Scandinavian Airlines, and the other winning, successful organizations.

SOME CUSTOMER SUPPORT EXAMPLES

The Cross-Marketing philosophy of customer service and support has been successfully employed by only a small percentage of major and minor corporations. As would be expected, those few stand at the top in corporate performance and effectiveness. We have already discussed IBM, and the recent business turnarounds at Scandinavian Airlines and British Airways, and how their success depended on Cross-Marketing practices. As another example, Frito-Lay charges more for its potato chips than most other companies, and yet has a large percentage of the market because of its policy of *"excessive" customer service.* We all know how successful Disneyland and Disney World have been using the Cross-Marketing principles and practices. Procter & Gamble put in a toll free telephone number to allow its nation-wide customers to phone in with questions and concerns. Some of these are discussed in some detail by Peters and Waterman in their book, **In Search of Excellence.**

Caterpillar Tractor has out-performed its competition, such as International Harvester, using the Cross-Marketing principles. Caterpillar offers customers 48 hour guaranteed parts delivery service anywhere in the world. If it cannot fulfill that promise it provides the customer the parts for free. For years the theme of McDonalds has been, "quality, service, cleanliness, and value." Said founder Ray Kroc, "If I had a brick for every time I repeated the phrase, Q.S.C.&V., I think I'd probably be able to bridge the Atlantic Ocean with them." A study of the companies in the American Business Conference indicates that those companies have a strong tendency to apply Cross-Marketing practices. The American Business Conference is a coalition of 100 leaders of mid-size high growth companies which have grown at least 15% annually for the past five years. These companies represent all parts of the economy.

Cross-Marketing practices, likewise, have made the difference for many regional and smaller organizations. Some have turned their operations around, and substantially increased their business volume and profitability. Some local hospitals have been effective in employing Cross-Marketing practices. A newspaper went out of business because it did not effectively understand its market and its needs. Another has expanded substantially in the past few years. The second newspaper gave good customer support and used Cross-Marketing practices. Two contract cleaning companies more than doubled their business in four years while a number of competitors went out of business. In each case, Cross-Marketing practices, with effective customer support, made the difference.

Now let's look at one systematic way to apply these principles in organizations which directly serve the customer and the public.

CUSTOMER SERVICE MANAGEMENT

Organizations and industries which directly serve the public have the special opportunity to isolate and manage customer support and the customer service function. These include banks, savings associations, credit unions and other financial services institutions; transportation companies; hospitals and health care organizations; and other unskilled (as housekeeping), skilled (as maintenance), professional (as accounting), and mass consumer (as hotel and restaurant) services. Customer service management also applies to non-field sales, direct customer contact departments and people in manufacturing and sales service organizations (customer service, order departments, etc.).

The effective management of customer service is much more important than most of us realize. Chapters 1 and 2 address the importance of being customer driven and providing effective customer service. And nothing is done well, anywhere, if it is not managed properly; thus, this systematic look at customer service management.

Philip Crosby, author of the books, **Quality is Free** and **Quality Without Tears,** explains why management is so important for customer service with the statement, "Service people have the privilege of being sloppy and wasteful if they want to be. Because of this mentality, the price of nonconformance in these "service" operations is *twice* what it is in manufacturing." In other words, if we don't manage the customer service function we are both driving away customers and increasing our costs. As will be pointed out below, much of this management must be self management.

Customer service management consists of implementing the following nine steps.

STEPS TO CUSTOMER SERVICE MANAGEMENT

1. Perform Market Research
2. Perform An Internal Customer Service Audit
3. Develop a Customer Service Mentality
4. Develop a Service Theme
5. Analyze Existing Service Processes
6. Analyze and Improve Service Support Systems
7. Develop Service Specifications for each Service System
8. Establish Customer Service Audits
9. Establish a Feedback and Improvement System

Each of these steps could be the subject of an entire book or chapter. Some were discussed in the recent book, **Service America,** by Karl Albrecht and Ron Zemke. Our purpose here is to present each step briefly, but with enough explanation for you, the reader, to understand the results of each step.

1. Perform market research.   In order to understand what our customers want from us, and how we can satisfy their wants and needs, we need to ask them and analyze their answers. This can be accomplished in a number of ways including pre-arranged interviews, spot interviews at our places of business, telephone interviews, written surveys, focus groups, etc.

From the market research we are looking for answers to three basic questions:

(1)   What are our customers' judgements of our strengths and weaknesses, and as they compare to our competition,
(2)   Which service factors are important to the customer, and to which ones will they respond favorably, and
(3)   How well are we delivering those important service factors?

For example, British Airways performed market research with its customers, and was surprised to find that there were service factors which were very important to the customers that the company was almost totally unaware of.   *This is reported in the book, **Service America!** by Karl Albrecht and Ron Zemke, Dow Jones-Irwin, 1985. The four most important service factors found by British Airways were:

(1)   Care and concern (They were aware of this one)
(2)   Problem solving - handling travel schedules and complicated logistics (They were aware of this one)

(3) Spontaneity - the ability and willingness to think, and solve a problem that is not in the rule book (They had not thought much about this one)

(4) Recovery - the special effort to make amends when something goes wrong (They hadn't thought at all about this one).

In retrospect, these may make very good sense to us; but beforehand, British Airways was unaware of two of the four, and felt some other factors were more important than were these two. The lesson to be learned is that in our company or organization there may be very important service factors that we are unaware of, which we may be performing most unsatisfactorily, and thereby driving away customers. It would pay us to research the market and find out.

2. Perform an internal customer service audit. Through a combination of written surveys, focus groups, personal interviews, and reviews of records we can determining the following for our own organization:

(1) The administration's (top management's) present attitude toward customer service and the importance of being customer driven,

(2) The structure of existing customer service systems,

(3) Management policies and systems in support of customer service,

(4) The attitude of employees toward customer service, our organization and its management competency, other people and departments, the organization's products and services, and themselves and their jobs,

(5) The level of present employee effectiveness in the areas of job performance, leadership and teamwork, solving customer problems, providing customer wants and needs, and effective communications, and

(6) Company resources and strengths compared to customer and market needs, as related to customer service.

As a result of the internal audit, combined with the market research in step 1, we know where the company stands from the standpoint of recognizing the importance of, truly desiring to provide, and providing effective customer service. Almost always, in addition, we gain some specific useful ideas from customers and our people on operating and on serving customers more effectively.

3. Develop a customer service mentality. This is much easier said than done, especially if there is not already an orientation in this direction. Usually we are not as customer service oriented as we would like to believe.

Top management must commit itself to an internal mission of effective customer service, and then it personally must sell, motivate and inspire the rest of management and the front line employees to believe in and act on that mission. This requires the personal involvement of top management, and frequently starts with a campaign of contacts and meetings at all levels.

The service theme, step 4, along with the importance of that theme is what is communicated. One way of developing commitment at the front line is to involve those there deeply in defining, providing, measuring and improving customer service; and to involve them as intelligent adults who can make an important contribution. Some very successful companies have used the quality circle (service circle; productivity team) approach. This has been effective in generating employee commitment, in encouraging employees to think of and suggest new and better service ideas, and in effectively involving employees in the remainder of the customer service management process (steps 4-9). British Airways is one of the companies to have good results with quality circles.

A number of chapters in this book, especially 1 and 2, add additional insight to step 3.

4. Develop a service theme. The service theme is a short, clear statement of what our organization stands for from the standpoint of customer service. It is our focus, our rallying point, the guiding concept to which we address people's attention inside and outside the company.

As an example, the service theme for McDonalds restaurants is, "quality, service, cleanliness and value."

If possible, the service theme should clearly convey to our people and to the market what are our service objectives, how they will benefit the customer, and in what way they are different from and better than our competitors. It then can serve as the focal point for internal and external advertising. Scandinavian Airline System performed a total corporate turnaround based on a customer driven system with the service theme, "service, creativity, and finding a better way." It is a theme any of us could consider using, especially if the word cooperation were added to it; and it is supported by Cross-Marketing and this book.

5. Analyze existing service processes. Service processes are those chains of events in which something is done for the customer, from the time the customer is first encountered until the customer's needs are satisfied or the transaction is completed. Service processes in a bank would include signing someone up for a safe deposit box, helping them use their safe deposit box, depositing a check at the teller window, or signing them up for a new account. Service processes for an airline would include making reservations and purchasing tickets by phone, changing reservations for a canceled flight in person, and food service on board a flight. If we break our interactions with the customer into as many different service processes as possible, then analyzing and developing specifications for effective performance will be easier.

Each service process is diagrammed, and a listing is made of each event in the process. Again, the more it is broken down and the more the events are separated, the easier it will be to understand and improve. This can be done using conventional operations analysis techniques such as PERT or work flow diagrams. In addition, promising new techniques have recently been introduced.

After each service process is diagramed, or broken into as many parts as possible (eg., customer approaches desk, customer announces flight change is needed, customer hands ticket to representative, representative types information into reservation computer, etc.), then the customer contact points (ccp) are identified. The customer contact points are those where there is an interaction between the customer and a representative of our organization, and the way that interaction is handled by our representative will influence the customer favorably or unfavorably toward our organization.

The critical customer contact points (cccp) are those ccps which are identified, by market research and by discussions with our people who are involved, to be the most important and critical to the customer relationship.

We are now in a position to redesign the various service processes, in conjunction with the associated service systems (see step 6), to improve efficiency and productivity, reduce costs, and provide better customer service. We then can develop service specifications (see step 7) for combinations of service processes which go into the service systems. Also, a measurement and follow-up system can be designed with emphasis on the critical customer contact points (cccp).

6. Analyze and improve service systems. The service systems (SS) are those systems whereby our products, services and special customer service efforts are provided to the customer. They include the physical equipment and facilities and a combination of service processes. Examples for an airline would be the customer ticketing system, the baggage handling system, and the food service system. Examples for a bank would be the ATM system, the new customer handling system, and the loan processing system.

All service systems should be listed in order of their priority, based on their importance in affecting customer relationships and potential business volume. Then each in turn should be evaluated for modifications and improvements which would increase efficiency and productivity, reduce costs, and most importantly, provide better customer service and satisfaction. The resulting service systems (SS) should be customer friendly, and when possible emphasize customer service and convenience, as opposed to the convenience of our organization and our employees.

7. Develop service specifications for each service system. The service specifications (svs) define for each service system (SS) - such as baggage handling, ticketing, new customer handling - (a) the critical customer contact points (cccp), (b) the overall customer expectations (see market research, step 1), and (c) a definition of what our people should do to meet those expectations.

The service specifications provide the basis for measurement, feedback, performance modifications and rewards. As mentioned earlier, some companies have had excellent results with deeply involving front line people in establishing the service specifications, thereby utilizing their capabilities and gaining their commitment.

8. Establish customer service audits. A system is developed to contact customers on a continuing basis to determine if we are (a) meeting the important customer factors (see step 1) and (b) providing effective service at the cccp (critical customer contact points).

The resulting raw information is analyzed and fed both to management and back to the front line. This informs both of how we are doing.

9. Establish a feedback and improvement system. On a regular basis front line people review their level of performance (based on the customer service audits) as compared to the svs (specifications as to what that performance should be). Targets are established for performance levels. These generally are raised over time, as we become more experienced and more proficient in delivering effective customer service.

Rewards are provided to those persons and/or teams which generate acceptable or superior levels of performance. Guidance, training and/or transfers are provided to those who need to increase levels of customer service performance.

In a way these nine step should be listed in a continuing circle rather than in a straight line. Customer service management is a continuing function; just like operations management and sales management. As our business evolves and changes, and as our internal operations are modified and improved, we need to be continually and systematically upgrading our system of Cross-Marketing and customer service management.

SUMMARIZING THE CROSS-MARKETING™ CONCEPT

Cross-Marketing™ is an integration of good business practices which are employed in the most successful organizations and by the most effective people, plus some recently proven practices of customer support. The end result is the providing of customer-oriented business leadership through effectively communicating service, solutions and benefits from all parts of the organization, to other parts of that organization, and to the commercial customer. It consists of the following:

1. Everyone in the entire organization realizing they serve both commercial customers and personal customers, and providing effective service to every one of their customers, as if each were a major, corporate commercial customer.

2. Each employee in the organization, as appropriate, learning about and practicing the eight how-to concepts in the Cross-Marketing system:

1.	Business Leadership	5.	Group Performance
2.	Customer Driven	6.	Finding Solutions
3.	Teamwork Driven	7.	Communicating Solutions
4.	Personal Performance	8.	Implementation

3. And in addition, all employees in the organization providing effective customer support by following the seventeen customer support practices listed above, and by implementing customer service management as appropriate. How this all applies to individual front line workers is discussed in chapter 11.

4

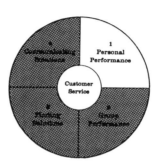

PERSONAL PERFORMANCE THROUGH SELF MANAGEMENT

A. IMPLEMENT A PLAN
B. USE MANAGEMENT PRINCIPLES
C. CONTROL YOUR BEHAVIOR
D. MANAGE YOUR TIME

The first of the four stages to *The Process of Cross-Marketing is Personal Performance*. Each member of the organization needs to perform his or her job with the highest possible effectivenesses and productivity. Each needs to be trained and to be led to use those personal performance practices which will yield high level results.

As has been stated, the leading corporations in most fields operate at twice or more the productivity of the average. This is even more true for individuals. The leading performers in any particular field (sales, customer service, marketing, business strategy, operations management, supervision, etc.) operate at many times the productivity and effectiveness of the average performers. This can be easily seen in the sales field for instance. Insurance salesperson Joe Gondolfo who wrote the book, **How to Make Big Money Selling**, sells 500 times the volume of insurance of the average insurance salesperson. He sells just under a billion dollars of insurance each year. He does this by being effective (doing the right things) rather by being efficient (doing what everyone else does better), although he is efficient also.

Whether you are a corporation president, a mid level manager or a first line performer, high performance comes from managing yourself to do the right things (often in an innovative way - see chapter 9) and to do them effectively.

In the classic work on management, **The Practice of Management**, Peter Drucker observed, "Management, in other words, is a practice, rather than a science or a profession, though containing elements of both." In this chapter those same management practices, which commonly have been applied to businesses and organizations, are turned inward and directed toward ourselves. Just as in a business, if we are going to achieve a high level of personal performance we must apply effective personal management, or self-management.

This chapter identifies forty practices of effective self-management and groups them under four categories:

    a. Implement a Plan (items 1-10)
    b. Use Management Principles (11-20)
    c. Control Your Behavior (21-30)
    d. Manage Your Time (31-40).

A. IMPLEMENT A PLAN

Setting goals, and establishing and implementing action plans to achieve those goals, is one of the fundamentals of effective management. We should be doing this on the job as well as at home. We would not build a house without a plan; but how many of us have a plan for our careers, or our day's or our week's activities? On the job we should establish, working with our superior if we have one, what most needs to be accomplished this week and this month, and what is the best utilization of available resources to accomplish that. We then stand an excellent chance of making a positive contribution to the overall objectives of the organization. If we undertake a special project or assignment we will want to implement a plan to accomplish that assignment effectively. As an illustration, chapter 12 demonstrates how to establish an action plan for the

Cross-Marketing system within our organization.

Steps 1-10 below discuss in logical order the practices required for effectivley implementing a plan to increase personal performance.

1. Research the environment. The first step in the planning process is to establish where we are now and what is going on around us.

As an illustration, regardless of our level or position, to research the environment in preparation for a job plan we might ask and obtain answers to questions like these:

- What is the primary mission of the total organization as it relates to our department? What current corporate goals and objectives does our department support?
- What is the primary mission of our department? What must our department do well, and how is "well" defined? What are the current major goals and objectives of our department?
- How does my job fit into the department mission and its goals and objectives? What specifically can I do to support the department in its most important areas of responsibility? What must I do well so as to not let the department down? What are the opportunities for me to make a major contribution which would be recognized by upper management?
- Where does my direct superior stand in the pecking order of the company? What can I do, if anything, to improve that standing?
- Is it advantageous to the company and to me for me to remain in my present job and department, or would a transfer be desirable?
- In what areas is my direct superior pleased with my performance and in what areas is my direct superior not pleased? Do I know how to improve my performance in those areas?
- Can I get help from my direct superior, my peers or other resources to perform my job more effectively? If so, how can I arrange for that help?
- What could I do to help my superior and others - peers and subordinates - to perform more effectively?
- What could I do to help others outside my department to perform more effectively?
- What could I do to help solve problems of our commercial customers, and to make them even more pleased with the services of our company?
- Do I need to improve my personal skills and knowledge in some way so I can perform more effectively, and how do I go about doing that?
- What trends inside and outside the company will alter our goals or job responsibilities? Am I preparing myself through training and education to remain effective or become even more effective as those trends become realities?

Through answers to these and similar questions we establish what is happening, how it affects us, and what we can do to be even more effective. We answer the six age old interrogative questions posed in verse by Rudyard Kipling:

> "I have six honest serving men,
> They taught me all I knew.
> Their names are what and where and when,
> And why and how and who."

2. Analyze for opportunities. The second step in implementing a plan is to list all the opportunities available for us to make a contribution in the area under consideration. These later will be compared with our strengths determined in step 3, and then selected from to establish goals in step 5.

Based on the results of our personal environmental analysis in step 1, we now look for opportunities to serve our customers and perform our jobs more effectively.

We ask questions such as these: What problems need solving which would increase the effectiveness and/or profitability of our company or our customers? Where is our department not quite fulfilling its mission? Where are other departments failing to perform, where we could fill the gap? Is there anything that I could do personally, or in conjunction with others, to serve our customers more effectively? Are we wasting money or resources anywhere? What could I do to finish my present work earlier, leaving additional time either to perform an additional responsibility, or to apply more time to a present important responsibility? Am I being as cooperative and as helpful as I can be to my peers, superiors and subordinates?

While asking these questions we are looking for problems to solve, and for opportunities to make increased contributions.

3. Learn our strengths and limitations. Each of us will be most effective if we are working on those tasks and projects which utilize our strengths, and avoid and refer to others those in which we have significant limitations. Consequently, we list our personal strengths and limitations, plus other resources which are available to us.

We should make an inventory of what we do well and what we do poorly, what we like and dislike to do, where we have experience and where we have none, and what are our strongest and weakest personal characteristics and skills. With this knowledge of ourselves we can more accurately judge the types of tasks and projects with which we will be most successful.

I performed such an analysis when I was a mid-level manager for a major corporation. I found that I was good at and enjoyed creative and innovative thinking, developing plans and looking at the big picture. I was not good at and disliked administering the details of carrying out those plans. Consequently, I hired an administrative assistant to administer the department programs. We worked together effectively, with the assistant supporting me in my areas of weakness, and vice versa.

4. Develop a mission. We determine what is the overall purpose of the task or assignment facing us.

Whatever our job - whether we are a division vice president, a department manager, a professional specialist, a clerk, a small business owner, a mechanic, a salesperson, whatever - we need to establish the overall "mission" of our job and for our work. To do this we can answer the question, "What is the overriding purpose of my job or position?" The mission of the job gives perspective to our decisions concerning goals and objectives, skills to be developed, and how time and resources should be allocated.

The mission of a department manager should include both the mission of the department and the mission of the manager's job within the department. The mission of an accounting department manager might be, "to manage the department in such a way that both the personnel of other departments, and those of our department, believe we are efficient, service-oriented, effective communicators, and that we provide accurate and well-designed operating data on a timely basis; and to accomplish those objectives in reality."

The mission of a customer service representative might be, "to establish such a high level of rapport with assigned customers, through knowing their concerns and their businesses, and responding rapidly and effectively to their requests, that our customers prefer to deal with us and our company as compared to dealing with anyone else."

The mission of a mechanic might be "to be, and become recognized as, the most skilled, effective and cooperative mechanic in the company."

Notice that the mission statements include two elements: (1) effective performance and (2) the perception of others that we are satisfying their needs. Each of us produces an output which is needed by someone else; either the commercial customer and/or one or more other persons or departments in our organization, our personal customers. We are being effective when we produce an output which is timely and in the form that it is conveniently and easily used by our customers.

Suppose three pieces of equipment break down. The effective mechanic is the one who determines which should be repaired first, communicates to all parties when each will be repaired and why, and proceeds to repair them in turn as quickly as possible, but being careful to do the job correctly the first time. The effective mechanic recognizes those types of jobs which are beyond his skill, and refers them to another, or arranges to receive training in that skill area. As a result, his performance supports his mission.

5. Set short term and long term goals. We ask ourselves, "What specifically should I do to accomplish by a specified time, those things which will help me most to accomplish my mission?"

In our jobs, while there are certain duties we must attend to, there is never enough time to do all the things we would like to do and do them well. So we should select those few things on which to concentrate, that by accomplishing them we will have made the largest contribution. These become our short term and long term goals. We perform the routine duties of the job satisfactorily, but as quickly as possible. We then concentrate our time and effort on achieving our established goals.

As a secretary there are many duties and activities which one must address. Just a few of these would include opening mail, sorting the mail, answering the telephone, stocking supplies, filing, taking dictation, composing letters, and assisting the manager to plan his days activities. In addition, the goals for today might be to get caught up on the filing and to type the three important letters which have been identified by the manager. A goal for the week might be to evaluate and select, with the help of the manager, a new dictating system.

In establishing and designing our goals we must make sure that they meet seven criteria. They should be:

1. Results-oriented; to accomplish something rather than just to take action.
2. Specific and concrete; rather then general and unclear. (Exactly what is to be accomplished, and by when?)
3. Measurable. We can clearly identify when and if they have been accomplished.
4. Realizable. Not impossible, nor so difficult that we easily get discouraged.
5. Meaningful. We understand their importance and are willing to sacrifice to accomplish them.
6. Compatible with other goals. We are not confused by conflicting goals.
7. Challenging. Large enough to make a meaningful contribution and to give us a motivational challenge.

A monthly goal statement for the new accounts representative of a bank, which is consistent with these criteria, could be: "to present an average of two additional bank products (savings account, safe deposit box, etc.) to each customer or prospect with which I meet; and to receive acceptance of (to sell) at least 0.8 additional products per contact, and at least 50 additional products per week." A half-year goal statement for an engineer which meets these seven criteria could be: "within the next six months to identify and solve at least one manufacturing problem which will reduce the cost of producing cyclohexylamine by at least one cent per pound."

A goal statement for a sales manager, which <u>violates</u> these seven criteria, might be: "to read some books on management so my people will sell better." This incorrect goal statement (1) is task oriented (to read), rather than results oriented, (2) is general, not specific (Which books? Increase sales where? By how much?), (3) cannot be measured, (4) is realizable, but who cares?, (5) is not really meaningful (Are you impressed?), (6) is compatible with other goals (but could be a waste of time if nothing happens as a result), and (7) presents no challenge or motivation.

6. Commit to the goals. It is one thing to establish a set of goals. It is another to see them through to completion. We should establish a few goals, and only those which are important to us and to our organization. This will make it easier for us to commit to their completion, and to do whatever is required to see that they are completed.

To assist us in carrying out that commitment we initially might review our goals with our superior or with someone else who is important to us, and then arrange periodic review meetings with that person to report progress. This will put pressure on us to complete them.

7. Make flexible action plans with timetables. The *action plan* defines the goal, lists the steps in chronological order that are required to achieve the goal, identifies what will occur when the goal has been accomplished, and specifies a date for the achievement of the goal. It may specify dates for completion of the individual steps of the plan. To make the action plan even more useful we can include a justification of why this goal is important, plus what is planned following the achievement of the goal. There are various methods which have been developed to present the steps involved in the action plan. Some of these include (a) a listing of steps in chronological order, (b) the critical path method (CPM), (c) PERT, and (d) the GANIT chart. These are described in books and articles on business and engineering planning. For our purposes, a listing of steps in chronological order is sufficient.

If we embark on a plan of action and that plan is not working, it is not achieving the goal; then we can change the plan. This does not mean we must change the goal, at least not until other plans have been tried and have failed.

Below is an example of an action plan for the engineer described in step 5 above.

Engineer's Action Plan

The Engineer's Goal Statement: Within the next six months to identify and solve at least one manufacturing problem which will reduce the cost of producing cyclohexylamine by at least one cent per pound.

Engineer's Action Plan Steps:

1. Review pertinent company literature.
2. Review pertinent outside literature, including magazine articles.
3. Obtain ideas from superiors and from other engineers in the department.
4. Interview the manufacturing department for ideas.
5. Interview major customers for ideas.
6. List all ideas obtained in order of their probability of success.
7. List all ideas obtained in order of the financial effect if they are successful.
8. Choose up to four ideas to test in the plant on a limited basis, based on the data in (6) and (7).
9. Test each idea in turn.
10. Choose the best idea.
11. Run a full scale plant test on the best idea or solution.
12. Prepare a cost justification report.
13. Obtain appropriate approvals for the change.

Note: Target dates can be listed for each of the steps.

Our goals can be very simple, such as writing a thank you letter today or showing some form of appreciation to each of our peers this week. Or they can be very complicated and extremely important, such as developing a market plan for establishing a new business, or devising a new hiring system to upgrade the level of our employees. A more comprehensive goal probably would generate a more complicated and comprehensive action plan. A simpler goal would have generated a shorter plan, perhaps with only one or two steps.

8. Force reasonable time pressure. We should spend enough time thinking about, planning and carrying out each step in our action plan to be effective, but we should not spend more time than can be cost-justified. If we have a tendency to be perfectionists, we may find ourselves spending much more time on a project or a step than is warranted. One way to avoid this is to set time-tables which establish time pressure. As a result, we spend enough time working on the project but not more than is justified.

Referring to the goal and the above action plan for the engineer; if a cost reduction of one cent per pound is a major accomplishment with significant profit implications, then the engineer might take this one goal as her entire assignment for the following six months. She then would be making decisions as to which of the thirteen steps warrants the most time, and which of the thirteen should be accomplished more quickly. On the other hand, if a cost reduction of one cent per pound is a rather minor accomplishment, and can be obtained rather easily; and if in addition the engineer has more important assignments to accomplish during the same time period; then the project would be allocated much less time, and much less time would be assigned to most of the steps involved. She would force herself to accomplish them more quickly.

9. Reward small successes. When we are working on an important goal, or one which is difficult to accomplish, there can be a long time span between the initiation of the action plan and its completion. In addition, if we are having difficulty accomplishing the goal and the associated action plan steps, we can become discouraged. Consequently, for a longer, more difficult project it is wise to divide the action plan into a number of steps, to consider each step to be an accomplishment in itself, and to reward ourselves in some way for completing each step. The nature and amount of the reward would depend on the situation.

10. Test and change. After commencement of the action plan, we often will determine that the plan is not working as we had anticipated. We then may test some alternative ideas and approaches, and, after gathering new information, change the plan. Consider the above action plan for the engineer. Suppose in step 4 of the plan, when she talked to a major customer she determined that a competitor already had instituted a cost reduction program which had reduced its cost by three cents per pound. Through discussions with the customer our engineer was able to understand the nature of that cost reduction. She then might skip steps 6 through 10, arrange for a full scale test on this new approach, and if successful, write a cost justification (step 12) around the results of that test.

As another example, as a part of the action plan for the banking new accounts representative (step 5), the representative may have been asking each customer-contact three specific questions, and as a result proposing up to three specific products for them to purchase. If this approach was not working, and was not benefiting either the customer or the bank, new approaches might be attempted. She might change or add to the questions. She might methodically present five different products using a flip chart. Or she might test out some new approaches, trying each approach with twenty different prospects. If none of the new approaches worked, she then might test a couple of additional approaches. When she found an approach that worked, she then would implement that approach for herself. When proven, the new approach might be implemented later for other customer service representatives in the company.

B. USE MANAGEMENT PRINCIPLES

During the time we are employing the above ten steps to accomplish our action plans, there are ten self-management principles we should be following to increase our personal effectiveness and performance. This is true whether we are high level managers or front line workers.

11. Focus on contribution. Many people come to work each day, work very hard all day, and go home tired and frustrated. They are frustrated because they worked so hard and yet cannot determine what they accomplished that was important. If this happens day after day, it may be because they are being efficient in their work, but not effective. Quoting Peter Drucker from his book, **The Effective Executive**, "Working on the right things is what makes knowledge work effective."

There are *two* very important words in the title to this section, *focus* and *contribution*.

One of Parkinson's Laws states, "Work expands to fill the time available." During the work week there are many calls on our time from numerous sources. These are not of equal importance. Some are very important, some are less important, and some are unimportant, as determined by our job responsibilities and our established goals. We should determine what job responsibilities and projects are most important to our making an effective contribution to the organization. We then should focus our attention, and attempt to spend as much productive time as we can accomplishing results and making contributions in those areas.

The following are a couple of quick examples. As company president you might observe that the local legislature is considering legislation which could substantially help your business, or could put you out of business, depending upon the results. In such a case you might almost totally delegate the operations of the company to your subordinates for a time, and spend almost full time working with the legislature, and with organizations which will influence the legislative decision.

As chief cost accountant, your superiors may be completely satisfied for you to continue analyzing and reporting accurate cost data, and to do nothing further. However, because of your specialized knowledge, you may suspect that a redesigned cost accounting system, employing the latest in related computer technology, could develop more accurate data, faster, and for a far lower cost. Without failing to continue providing *satisfactory* cost accounting reports, you might focus every available minute into evaluating a revised system, and then assuming positive findings, designing and implementing the new system.

12. Team up with competent performers. One version of Pareto's Rule states that "80% of the contribution in any organization comes from

20% of the people in that organization, in other words, the performers." At the opposite end of the performance spectrum are the negative employees; the lazy ones, the good-offs, the complainers, and those who hang around the perverbial water fountain to chat and complain. We want to make every effort to develop ourselves into one of the "performers," to associate with performers, and to stay away from complainers. Winners tend to pull us up to their performance level; losers tend to pull us down to theirs. We tend to think like, act like, and perform like the company we keep. We want to keep good company.

Another advantage of becoming business friends with performers, both inside and outside the company, is that it gives us our own private "board of directors" with which to discuss our projects, our problems and our opportunities. Other non-competing companies have performers whom we might meet through organizations and other outside activities. It would benefit us to meet with them occasionally, personally or in small groups, and to discuss what they are doing to achieve high performance and what they are avoiding. We could benefit substantially from regular conversations with performers, both from inside and outside our company.

13. Specialize. No one can be an expert in many things. While it gives us perspective to be well-rounded and to know a little about the entire business, the substantial accomplishments generally come from those who have specialized in important areas, and therefore have the specific knowledge to make meaningful contributions. We should determine in what areas of the company the largest contributions have been and can be made, and attempt to shape our career by specializing in one of these areas.

As an engineer, we could determine what type of engineering work this company and this industry will need most in the future. Is it market research? Product research? Product development? Process design? Computerization and instrumentation? As a clerical person what types of expertise can I develop to be of more value to the corporation and to myself. Should I improve my typing speed? Become efficient on a word processor? Start studying the totally computerized office? Take courses in management? Learn more about human relations and customer service? As a salesperson should I study sophisticated professional techniques in consultive selling? Learn computer operations? Study management and motivation of personnel? Become a technical expert in certain of our products and their applications in solving customer problems? Should I study selected customer industries to determine their technology and problems so I can provide guidelines to our company on development of new products and services? In what should I specialize? In what area should I direct my career?

14. Concentrate on essentials. Again referring to Pareto's Rule, approximately 80% of the results within an organization comes from 20%

of the activities employed to produce those results. Consequently, we need to concentrate our time and effort on those activities that will produce the largest results.

If you are a department manager, what is most important for you to accomplish during this time period? Should you really be spending all that time in meetings? Is it essential that you be there, or could one of your people represent you with equal results? Is it really important for your people to be spending so much time writing reports; and is it the best expenditure of your time to be reading them in detail and making corrections? Are there some major fundamental problems in your organization which cause recurring foul-ups? Are there some major opportunities to make a contribution which you are missing, because your time is being spent, or wasted, with less important activities? What is it that must be accomplished by your department for it to fulfill its mission during this time period? Answers to questions like these will direct us toward the essentials.

This easily can be demonstrated for a sales person. Generally, there are a few large customers and large potential customers which represent very large opportunities for profitable sales. If the sales person will concentrate his efforts on working with the larger accounts, and the larger potential accounts, without ignoring the smaller ones; when he gets a sale the sale will most probably be larger, with larger resulting benefit to the corporation.

It is known that some sales people out-perform their contemporaries by many times. The proper allocation of time to high potential accounts and industries is one reason. Quoting Joe Gondolfo, one of the highest producing sales people of all time, in his book, **How to Make Big Money Selling**, "I've always made it a point to call on the biggest people. It's easier to sell a 5 million dollar insurance policy to a multimillionaire than it is to sell a fifty thousand dollar policy to a person making twenty-five thousand dollars a year. And selling one five million dollar policy produces a hundred times greater volume and commissions!"

It can be difficult for a secretary to concentrate on essentials but it can be done. A secretary can ask both himself and his superior, "What can I do which will make a major contribution to my superiors and to the department's success, and what is it that if I don't do it at all, it will make very little difference?" If it is absolutely important that the correspondence leaving the office be well written and without error, then that deserves major concentration, even to the point of proof reading correspondence two or three times and thinking about better ways to phrase sentences. Filing is important, but in this case it deserves less concentration and time. On the other hand, if in this office the quality of correspondence is only moderately important, but it is extremely important to be able to find all documents quickly, and if one were lost it could be disastrous; then time and concentration should be spent on planning and implementing the filing system. The correspondence would be handled as well as possible, but with less special concentration.

15. Act on the important versus the urgent. Many of us find ourselves "putting out fires" a significant amount of the time. We have a tendency to respond to those problems and events which we consider to be urgent. If we are not careful, our jobs and our people will control us and manage us instead of us managing them.

If we will keep a record of what we spend our time on over an extended period of time (see step 31), we may find that a large amount of our time is being spent on activities which appear to be urgent but which are not very important. These are activities which could be done more quickly, could be delegated to others, or perhaps could be ignored or deleted entirely. This same analysis may show us that there are a number of very important activities which could make a major contribution to the organization and to our performance which we have not found the time to address because we were spinning our wheels working on the less important "urgent" activities. It is important for us to separate the important from the urgent and to spend our time on the important when possible.

A research director may find himself continually in meetings, and running down requests from officers of the company. He also may be getting involved in the details of most of the projects of the department, asking lots of questions, and causing department members to come to him for answers on a frequent basis; questions they should be answering for themselves.

An alternate procedure would be for the research director to send other members of the department to attend many of the meetings, absenting himself from the meetings when it is not imperative that he be present. He might ask that all requests from upper level officials for information be received in writing, to discourage unnecessary requests for information. He might schedule periodic planning and evaluation meetings with members of his department, and spend much less time interfering with or participating directly in day-to-day activities of the members of the department. Taking this action probably would be motivational to the department members, and would free up large amounts of his time for more important activities such as studying trends in the industry, visiting the technical facilities of important customers, recruiting specialized and high quality personnel, and planning the direction of the department and the resources required in future years.

16. Be creative and innovative. In the recent book by Clifford and Cavanagh, **The Winning Performance - How America's High-**

Growth Mid Sized Companies Succeed, an innovative approach to business was cited as one of the major reasons for the success of high growth companies. With a little imagination, we can look at our own jobs as businesses in themselves and approach them with the same creativity and innovativeness as would a corporation. We can look for new and better ways to provide output from our jobs, to our customers and to those within the company. We can ask how our jobs can be performed more effectively, and how they can be accomplished in a shorter period of time. Can equipment purchases reduce the time required to perform certain activities? Would a different department organization be more effective? Is there a way to get additional benefits from the work that our people are doing, or provide new outputs which would be helpful to people who are not now receiving benefits from our job or department?

The basic job of a nurse in a hospital is to provide superior patient care. However, she also could be participating as a sales person and customer relations representative in a number of ways. For instance, she could be especially friendly to patients and visitors, and point out to patients and visitors the excellent care we provide and the new equipment that has been acquired by the hospital She could even phone patients a few weeks after they leave to check up on them and to ask if everything is going okay. This certainly would be considered to be *innovative*. She also might make a contribution to improved patient care by asking each patient what they liked about the hospital stay and how the hospital stay could have been improved. If, for instance, there is a consistent comment that the coffee is not good, she might make this known to the dietary department. She might improve the perception of good patient care in her area by paying attention to the scratched paint, dirty corners and other aesthetic aspects in her area, and arrange for these to be reported and taken care of on a regular basis. Through this extra effort her area might be maintained at a higher level of appearance than other areas.

If every nurse in every area did the same, then the entire institution would be more effective and more attractive to customers. If every employee in every department did just a little extra, and applied creativity and innovativeness to their jobs, the entire institution would be significantly more attractive to customers, and more effective in many little ways, as compared to competitive institutions. This would benefit the customers, the employees and the organization itself.

We might pause for a moment to answer a thought which could be in your, the reader's, mind. You could be thinking, "The above is basic; everyone knows and does this." There are two responses to this line of thinking. First, much of this is basic, but it is not performed even close to effectively in most companies and institutions. Second, if you feel your organization is performing effectively in this area then either (a) your organization deserves congratulations, or (b) you are deluded, and what you think is happening is not happening nearly to the extent you think it is.

Chapter 9 discusses the subject of innovation in more detail.

17. A place for everything and everything in it's place. This is the battle cry of the organized worker. For some people organization comes easy, and in fact they are upset if they are not living in an organized world. For others, organization is difficult, and they need crutches and helps in their efforts to be more organized. The following are some suggestions for organizing jobs and work more effectively.

1. Take the time, perhaps a full uninterrupted day, to decide what your organization system should be and where every major item and file should be located.
2. Design a filing system that you can live with. You may have a system which includes a series of folders to contain the various projects or activities on which you are working. These could be numbered and kept in order so that all the material concerning any project or activity would be kept in that folder. These then could be brought out on your desk one at a time while you work on a specific project.
3. Make it a habit to put things away when you are finished with them. Then they will always be where they belong.
4. If you are a manager, consider hiring an organized assistant, someone who already is well organized, and does not have to learn how to become organized.
5. Have one person be responsible for any specific area of filing, or any specific area of anything.
6. Organize your desk. Clear the desk drawers of unnecessary items and have a place for everything within the desk.
7. Clear the top of the desk except for the one project on which you are working at a time.
8. Establish a daily and monthly planning system. There are a number of good commercial systems available.
9. Maintain a "to do" list, containing everything of importance which you have to do, coded by its importance.
10. Each day select the most important projects from the "to do" list which will not automatically be accomplished within the next two days. Schedule time each day, or at least each week, toward their completion. Take into account your energy cycle when scheduling the projects.
11. Create and keep handy an idea notebook for ideas which come into your mind at odd hours, especially those related to solving problems and improving performance.
12. Initiate a "miscellaneous notebook" in which to put miscellaneous names, dates, phone numbers, and other pieces of information which do not have another logical place in your filing system.

Personal organization is further discussed in chapter 5 of the book, **Build A Better You Starting Now! 12**, Michael Baber, et. al.

In addition, we need to get organized to address any specific goal or project, such as discussed in sections 1-10. In doing so we should think through, probably on paper, the people who will be involved, the resources which will be required, and the location for each.

18. Make fundamental decisions based on accurate knowledge. As discussed earlier, we frequently find ourselves being controlled by our jobs and our people instead of us managing our jobs and our people. We find ourselves solving problems and then having them recur. We find ourselves continually putting out fires, and not finding the time to do the important jobs such as planning, organization, fact finding, etc. To solve dilemmas such as these there are two specific questions concerning decision making which we need to address. These questions will be discussed in the following paragraphs.

The first question is, "What decisions can I make which will have a profound influence on the company, the department, our workers, and myself?" The answer to this question addresses some of the concerns we already have discussed; questions such as, "Where can we make a major contribution; where should we specialize; where should we concentrate; what is important versus what is urgent; and where do we need to be creative and innovative?" Through first answering these questions, we can identify the areas we need to address, and where the decisions that we make will make a major difference in our performance and our accomplishment. We then can go about gathering all of the information which is required to answer the first question sensibly.

The second question we need to answer is, "What problems continue to recur even after they apparently have been solved?" Generally if a problem or a class of problems keeps popping back up, then it has not really been solved in the first place. In other words, we have addressed and perhaps solved the symptoms, but not the underlying disease. We need to spend the time to determine the underlying cause of the recurring problem, and then solve that cause so that the problem will not recur.

A plant manager was attempting to increase the productivity in his plant. He decided on a system of incentive pay in which if the workers were more productive they would be paid more. No matter what he did with the pay system he was not able to improve productivity. Upon analyzing the situation he found that the workers in that particular plant came from a general ethnic group in which the custom was for the families to pool the moneys received, and then be given for expenses whatever they required. What was happening was that money was not a motivator for these workers, because they were required to take their money home and give it to their parents. When the manager determined this to be the underlying problem, he then switched to a motivational system in which the workers were given time off for increased productivity, and productivity immediately increased substantially.

In another example, tardiness, absenteeism and turnover was excessively high in one department. The manager of that department had instituted a series of disciplinary and motivational actions for turning this around with no effective results. Upon analysis by upper management, it was determined that the problem was in first level supervision. Some persons had been selected as supervisors who did not have the ability to perform. In addition, the supervisors were poorly managed and were poorly trained. This resulted in unhappiness at the first line employee level. To solve this problem, the department manager himself was replaced. The new department manager replaced some of the supervisors and instituted a supervisory training program. As a result, over time the tardiness, absenteeism and turnover was reduced to below the average level for the entire organization.

19. Delegate but do not abdicate. Most good employees, those who stretch themselves, find themselves with more work that they would like to do than time to do it. One way of handling the dilemma is to concentrate on essentials. A second way is to delegate some of the important, but less critical, activities to someone else.

When a manager, sales person or professional already is being effective, they frequently can even further increase their effectiveness and productivity by delegating some of their less critical activities to someone else, thereby freeing up time to spend on the more important activities. Many highly paid direct commission salespersons have hired assistants, and paid for them out of their own pockets; and as a result have earned far more with the time saved than the amount paid to the assistant.

When we delegate a task to someone else, we need to make sure that the person is interested in and motivated to accomplish that task. One way to encourage this is to make sure the task is important and challenging, and not just busy work we don't want to do ourselves. We also need to make sure that the delegatee clearly understands both what is expected of him, and what are the guiding principles involved. We need to remember that delegation is not abdication, and while we do not want to be looking over someone's shoulder all the time, we still ultimately are responsible for their success or failure in properly carrying out the delegated tasks.

20. Follow-Up. There is an old bromide in management, "Inspect what you expect." People do what is expected, what is checked-up on. (They also do what is rewarded, but that is a different subject.) For that reason, whenever we assign a task it is important that we follow-up on and check the performance of that task. In addition, this action is motivational to the other person, because they get the opportunity to show us what a fine job they have done. It also is motivational because they do not want to be found to have failed a task which was requested. In our management consulting we have found that failure to follow up on instructions given was one of the mistakes most frequently made by ineffective managers and supervisors.

When we decide to take a certain action or accomplish a certain goal, we also need to follow-up on ourselves. We can do this by establishing checkpoints, checking up on our progress, and recommitting to action and accomplishment whenever we fail to act or fall behind schedule.

C. CONTROL YOUR BEHAVIOR

Our effectiveness and productivity are dependent upon the thoughts we think as well as the actions we take. In this section we discuss ten different ways to control our behavior to make us more effective and more productive.

21. Influence your mind and attitude positively.

"If you think you're beaten, you are.
If you think you dare not, you don't.
If you like to win, but think you can't,
it's almost certain you won't."
"Life's battles don't always go,
to the stronger or faster man.
But soon or late the one who wins,
is the one WHO THINKS HE CAN."

These two verses from a well known poem express the view that the thoughts we put into our mind control both the way we think and the way we act. Ralph Waldo Emerson once said, "A person is what he thinks about all day long." William James, well known philosopher of the first half of this century, said, "The greatest discovery of my generation is that human beings can alter their lives by altering their attitudes of mind." The Holy Bible says, "As a man thinketh in his heart so is he." In addition there have been a number of scientific studies and numerous books written which conclude that if we influence our minds and attitudes positively we will think more positively, act more positively, and live more positively and effectively.

22. Believe in yourself and your mission. In Chapters 5 and 9 we discuss the subject of "believing" in considerable detail. If we believe in ourselves; if we believe that our mission and our objectives are worthwhile and that they can be accomplished, we stand a much better chance of being successful. We need to control our behavior by causing ourselves to believe in ourselves and in our mission.

23. Purposefully remove negative influences. This is the counterpart to Sections 21 and 22 above. It is so important that we think positively and believe in what we are doing, that we should make every effort to purposely remove negative thoughts and influences from our minds, and replace them with positive thoughts and influences. This is not a book on positive thinking and self confidence building. However, because of their importance, the following is a brief list of some of the techniques which can be used for replacing negative thinking patterns with positive thinking patterns, resulting in more self confidence.

- Positive self talk; telling ourselves good things about ourselves and that we can accomplish what we set out to do.
- Mental imagery; visualizing in our minds positive things about ourselves and the happening of positive events, thereby driving these positive thoughts into our subconscious minds.
- Developing specific expertise in product technology, or in process technology, such as accounting, sales or public relations. This develops in us the self confidence that we can be effective in these areas.
- Dressing successfully and stylishly, thereby making us feel good about ourselves.
- Looking for and cultivating supportive friends who say positive things about us.
- Learning, and incorporating into our habits, the winning image characteristics explained in chapter 5.
- Making a list of our past successes, thinking on them, and feeling good about them. And likewise, keeping our minds off of past failures.
- Reading and listening to positive, uplifting material such as books and tapes.
- Making every effort to be as productive and as effective as we can, thereby making ourselves feel better about ourselves, and increasing our confidence that our superiors will be pleased with our work.
- In addition, there are certain religions and philosophies which have built into them positive or negative views of mankind. If we hold those beliefs we will be affected by them. For instance, Biblical Christianity teaches that mankind is born in sin (a negative view), but that through belief in Jesus Christ that sin is removed, and God (The Father) sees us as perfect, loves us, will help us to be healthy, happy, and successful in this life, and upon death will take us to live with Him in glory forever (a positive view).

24. Set priorities. There is a classic, true story about a professor and consultant by the name of Ivy Lee. He was retained by the great steel industrialist, Andrew Carnegie, during the early part of the century. After performing a consulting project for Mr. Carnige, Ivy Lee was asked what were his recommendations for increased performance. He wrote them on a slip of paper and handed it to Mr. Carnegie. All it said was, "Make a list of everything that you have to do; list them in order of priority; start working on the most important item and continue working on it until you are finished, and then start on item two." Mr. Carnegie was surprised at the simplicity of this recommendation and asked Mr. Lee what he owed him. Ivy Lee replied, "Follow this recommendation for six weeks and when I return pay me what it is worth." When Ivy Lee returned Mr. Carnegie had waiting for him a tremendously large check worth by today's standards well over $100,000. Mr. Carnegie said, "This is the single most valuable suggestion I have ever received." Mr. Carnegie then proceeded to institute the practice throughout his company.

The point of this story, of course, is that we need to set priorities. We need to determine what are the most important things for us to do and then proceed to do them. Again, quoting Peter Drucker from his book **The Effective Executive**, "Effective executives...... know that they have no choice but to do first things first and second things not at all. The alternative is to get nothing done."

25. Use self discipline. Most of us, if we would take the time to think it out, know most of the things we should do to be effective and successful. The secret is in making ourselves do what we know we should be doing. This is the secret of successful dieting; it is the secret of good study habits; and it is the secret of good work habits. In fact, habits are the answer. There is a saying that "Winners make the habit of doing what losers hate to do." We need to form good work habits and become their slaves.

We need to develop the capability to decide what we should do, and then make ourselves do that, whether we like it or not, and with dogged determination. There are two ways to accomplish this. The more difficult is to just force ourselves to do what we should do; to decide what we should do, and then with blinders on just do it. The second way is to develop the habit of self discipline by each day deciding on one thing to do, that we know we should do, that we would really rather not do, and then doing that one thing. The first day we would pick something rather simple and neither very difficult nor distasteful. The second day, we would choose something slightly more difficult and more distasteful; increasing each day until at the end of a few weeks we have developed the habit of being decisive and using effective self discipline.

A third way to help ourselves to have self discipline is to structure our tasks in such a way that they are easier to accomplish. For instance, one of my clients, a banking officer, decided that he wanted to make enough cold phone sales contacts each week to set up at least two appointments. This was difficult to arrange in light of his copious bank duties. At my suggestion, he took a half day and made a list in a notebook of over one hundred prospects who he might contact, together with phone numbers and other pertinent information. Each day, as he could find a few minutes, he would refer to the notebook in which he had listed all the information needed for making the phone contacts. He then would dial a few phone numbers. In other words, he had made it easy for himself to carry out the task.

26. Develop determination and persistence. There is an apocryphal story of a man who developed a soft drink and named it One-Up. When it was unsuccessful on the market he reformulated it and named the drink Two-Up. It to was unsuccessful. He developed Three-Up, Four-Up, Five-Up, and Six-Up, all without success. He then became discouraged and stopped. There are those who feel that if he had tried one more time he would have become very wealthy, having developed the soft drink, Seven-Up.

There is the true story of the old time prospector who had been prospecting for gold for many years in a certain mine. Finally, he gave up and sold his gold mine. The purchaser of the gold mine started mining and dug just one more foot before he struck a very valuable vein of gold, and became very wealthy.

The points of these stories are obvious. There are many times in our lives in which if we will continue with persistence and determination we will achieve success, and if we don't we won't. This is particularly true in the sales field. A study was performed at Notre Dame University in the area of selling. In this particular study it was determined that the average sale was made on the fifth closing attempt. Those who attempted to close a sale less often than five times generally did not get an order. Because we are all sales people, in that we are selling our ideas to others, we must develop determination and persistence whenever we believe we are right, and whenever we believe that we have something of value to offer to the department, to the company, or to the customer.

How do we develop determination and persistence if it is not in our innate nature? Probably the best way is to study our idea sufficiently, so that we develop a strong belief that we are right, and that we have something of considerable value to offer.

Suppose, through some unusual circumstances, you had discovered an unusual cure for cancer and a number of your relatives had been totally cured from this form of cancer by this unusual process. You would have very little problem being persistent and determined in attempting to communicate to a friend or an acquaintance who had this form of cancer that they should attempt this new treatment. In the same way, if we become totally convinced that we are right, then determination and persistence will grow within us.

How do we become convinced that we are right? How do we develop this belief? The answer is to do what outstanding sales persons do. List all the features and advantages of our idea, along with how they will benefit others; and then list the evidence to back that up. If we really have something to believe in, and if we will study it intensely, we will become so convinced that it is of value, that persistence and determination will grow within us like a seed grows within the ground. As an oak seed grows into a great oak tree, so the seed of our idea will grow to a strong conviction and belief.

27. Develop a pleasing personality. What type of person do you enjoy being around? What type of person draws you to them. Isn't it the person who is smiling, who is friendly and happy? If we develop ourselves in the following four ways we will have a more pleasing personality.

1. Think positive and happy thoughts about yourself and others. Make a list of all of the good points about yourself and about others, and concentrate on those.
2. Smile. Practice smiling and use that smile whenever possible. Frequently look in a mirror to see if you are smiling and have a pleasant expression. Remember to put a smile in your eyes. People love to be around a smiling person.
3. Remember and use names. Remember what Dale Carnegie said, "A person's name is to that person the sweetest and most important sound in any language." The most important principle in remembering names is to pay attention to the name when it is first heard. There are a number of techniques for remembering names. These include relating the name to someone else of that same name, making a rhyme with the name, and developing a mental picture of the person in some way tied to the name.
4. Show a genuine interest in others and be helpful to them. Ask yourself what is important about this person and what are they interested in? Talk to others in terms of their interests.

28. Delete harmful habits and actions. To delete harmful habits and actions we can make a list of any habits we have, and actions we take, that we consider to be harmful to ourselves, to others, or to our work objectives. Then, one by one, we can remove these habits, either by sheer determination or by replacing them with better habits.

If we will force ourselves to take a certain action repeatedly, over time it will become a habit. As it becomes more familiar and more a part of us, it also becomes more enjoyable in most cases.

The president of a company with which I was consulting had a habit of interrupting his subordinates, and asking penetrating questions throughout their presentations. This so intimidated many of his people that they failed to express their real opinions, and attempted to tell the president what he wanted to know. When this was pointed out to him, he developed a new habit of making notes during the presentations, and then holding his questions to the end. This was less intimidating, and over time he obtained better results.

29. Have a self-development plan. Each of us should have both job and personal objectives. Your job objective may be to become president of your division, or to become the world's expert in a certain area of technology. Your personal objective may be to develop a better relationship with your children or take a leadership role in a local civic organization. Having established objectives, you then can develop self-development plans, using the steps in sections 1-10 above.

For instance, if your objective is to become president of your division, you can determine what types of knowledge and experience would be of most value in performing effectively in that position, and in helping you to be chosen for that position. You then can develop a plan to obtain that knowledge and that experience.

30. Be a person of action. Aldous Huxley once said, "The great end of life is not knowledge but action." Quoting Thomas Edison, "Success is one percent inspiration, ninety-nine percent perspiration." And quoting George Bernard Shaw, "People are always blaming their circumstances for what they are. I don't believe in circumstances. The people who get on in this world are the ones who get up and look for the circumstances they want, and if they can't find them, make them." If we have a tendency to procrastinate; if we have a tendency to make grand and glorious plans but not to act on them, how can we change this? One way is to make it easier and less painful for us to take action than to avoid action. We can announce our plans to others, then if we don't act we will be embarrassed. We can make it impossible not to take action. Julius Caesar burned his ships when his army entered Britian. His army had no choice but to conquer Britian. Perhaps the best way is to ask at the beginning of each day, "What is it that I should take action on today?" And then have the decisiveness to take that action. In other words, form the habit of being an action-oriented person.

D. MANAGE YOUR TIME

Time is the one commodity which has been shared with us all equally. None of us have enough time to do what we would like to do, and yet we all have all the time there is. Time is the resource we use to accomplish our objectives and to become productive. It is important to manage our time effectively. Listed below are ten steps to effective time management.

31. Record where your time goes. Most people believe they know fairly accurately where their time is being spent, but this has been found through years of study to be inaccurate. I have recommended to numerous managers and executives at all levels that they perform a two week study on where their time goes, recording every one to two hours the allocation of their time down to at least fifteen minute segments. Most people who have done this have learned a tremendous amount about where their time was going, and how to spend it more productively. This activity is difficult for the first couple of days but then it becomes quite easy as we get used to it. After keeping the time record for two weeks we then should analyze where the time went by category or activity. Time expenditures can be analyzed by the type of work we are working on, by the people that we are dealing with, and by the relative importance and urgency of the work.

32. Delete less important activities and watch out for wasted minutes. Upon analyzing the time record most people find that they are spending much too much time on less important activities and not nearly enough time on more important activities. Also, they usually find that they're spending a considerable amount of time on activities which don't need to be done at all or which can be delegated. Some people identify a large number of wasted minutes, such as time wasted between meetings, and time spent talking to unproductive people, that could be used for more productive purposes.

33. Reduce interruptions and distractions. It can be very difficult for some people to reduce interruptions and distractions because these are actually part of their job. A bank teller or a hospital nurse could be in this position. Through creative thinking, even these people can either reduce interruptions and distractions somewhat, or make better use of the time in-between. The rest of us can take very effective measures. We can position our furniture properly. We can meet and talk to visitors outside of the office. We can converse standing up. We can close the door to our office. We can arrange to meet in the other person's office. We can keep the interruptions or meetings short. We can arrange for a visit to be interrupted after a short time period.

We can plan to reduce distractions by facing our desks away from the door; keeping our draperies shut; drowning out noise distractions with a miscellaneous noise machine; keeping our desks clear with distracting objects out of our sight; taking our phone off the hook; or removing ourselves to a quiet place such as a library for a period of time.

34. Consolidate time for major projects. There are types of work and projects which require longer stretches of uninterrupted time for productive accomplishment to occur. We need to manage and plan our time so as to consolidate uninterrupted time periods to spend on these types of projects.

35. Stop wasting others' time. Realize that those around us, especially our subordinates, are affected by our attitudes and actions. Be careful to not waste the time of others by continually interrupting them, or by making unneeded requests. We can waste others' time by interrupting them, by taking to them one question or project at a time instead of accumulating questions and projects for a short meeting, by holding inefficient meetings, and by being generally impolite and disrespectful of their time.

36. Use time-saving practices. To find blocks of uninterrupted time we can take certain time saving measures such as reviewing all of our mail efficiently and at one time, grouping our outgoing phone calls, delegating appropriate work, deleting unnecessary activities, reducing interruptions and distractions, dictating instead of writing correspondence, reading during commuting time, handling each piece of paper only once, having our telephone calls screened, holding stand up meetings, getting to the the point quickly in meetings and phone calls, planning efficient meetings, and scanning non critical material instead of reading it thoroughly.

We can schedule these blocks of time at a time when we are likely to be uninterrupted, such as early in the morning, later in the evening, or during the lunch periods of others.

We can remove ourselves physically, by going to a quite spot such as the library; or we can remove ourselves psychologically by shutting down the phone, closing the door, putting a note on the door and turning up a random noise machine.

Once we have established our priorities we can schedule on our daily and weekly planners set-aside time to accomplish any necessary projects. Generally, we should not totally fill the day's schedule, because we need to leave approximately one third of our time available for necessary interruptions.

37. Make check lists and pay proper attention to details. An airline pilot saves time, not wastes time, by going through a check list before taking off. Likewise, we can prepare check lists of items we need to accomplish for various tasks, and then review those check lists as appropriate. This prevents the need to be continually rethinking our jobs.

One of the reasons the Japanese companies have been so very successful has been their near obsession for paying attention to detail. You may have heard the statement, "There's never time to do things right, but there's always time to do them over." Studies by Philip Crosby and others have shown that paying attention to details, and thereby performing work of high quality, actually saves time and reduces costs. How does one pay attention to detail if they are not a detail-oriented person? One way is to set aside some time at the beginning of each project to completely think it through from beginning to end, listing chronologically every activity that needs to occur and every subactivity under that activity. As a result we will have produced a checklist. Then we can refer to the checklist, to make sure that we have taken care of every important detail.

38. Use time-saving equipment. Much time can be saved by using time-saving equipment and instruments. Proper use of the telephone can save much time as compared to writing correspondence or holding face-to-face meetings. Proper use of a dictaphone, as compared to writing by hand, can reduce correspondence time by more than 50%. This book is being written with a computer programed as a word processor. As a result, words, sentences and format can be changed swiftly without retyping entire pages.

39. Expand yourself through delegation. Many managers and professionals can expand their productivity substantially by delegating properly and/or by hiring a competent but lower paid assistant. Such a person, at a lower salary level, can relieve us of some of the more time-consuming duties and allow us time to concentrate on problems and opportunities which can have a higher impact on corporate and department performance.

40. Manage yourself and your time. By employing together the prior nine principles of time management, along with the other thirty principles of self management, we can more effectively manage ourselves and our time. We should continually remember that if we do not actively manage people, projects and activities; people, projects and activities will manage us, and our productivity and effectiveness will be less than it should be.

5

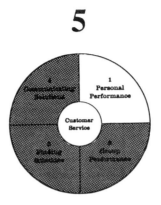

MORE ON PERSONAL PERFORMANCE

THE WINNING IMAGE
THE DECIDING DOZEN
BEFORE AND AFTER

Chapter 4 shows us how to increase personal performance through effective self management. Chapter 9 addresses increasing performance through the BICTCS formula; believing, innovating, concentrating our efforts, touching others with good human relations, communicating, and serving the needs of others. Chapter 5 discusses the importance of personal image and how to project a winning image. It then presents a summary checklist, listing a dozen ways to become a superior performer, and then how to implement those ways.

THE WINNING IMAGE

It doesn't matter what we know or how well we can perform; if the right people (customers, superiors, decision makers, etc.) do not respect us and our views, we will not get the opportunity to demonstrate our knowledge and expertise. Alternately, if we project a winning image and others respond positively to us, our self confidence is increased and we will more assertively do the things we know we should do to achieve superior results.

So, we are dealing with a chicken and egg situation. We do things which make us appear to others as competent winners. Others then respect us, treat us with respect and give us the opportunity to perform. We perform using the principles and practices presented in "The Deciding Dozen" and in chapters 4 and 9. As a result, we achieve effective results and these results further enhance our reputation, our self respect and our self image.

There are four ways we project our image to other people, and these are discussed briefly in the sections below. First, other people consciously or unconsciously observe our body signals, as to whether they are positive or negative, high class or low class, etc. Second, they consciously or unconsciously hear our verbal patterns, how we speak. Third, they observe how we dress. And fourth, they observe how we communicate - our skills, methods and attitudes. John Molloy in his book **Molloy's Live for Success**, presents some valuable research on self image. Some of this chapter is based on that research.

The first four sections below outline how we should behave and what we can do if we want to project to others the image of a winner, a can-do person, a competent business executive or its equivalent. The fifth section presents guidelines for making a good first impression.

If we are business executives and act in opposition to these principles we may reduce the consideration others give to our knowledge and views. This may be true even if we have a formal title and even after they get to know us well. Alternately, even if we are in a lower status position, by incorporating these behaviors and taking these actions, we will increase our status and intelligence in the eyes of others. Some of the attendees of our seminars have considered these conclusions to be unfair. Nevertheless, test results have shown them to be true.

BODY SIGNALS

1. Facial expression. To project a winning image we should carry a confident, serious but relaxed expression on our face; an expression such as we might visualize on a judge or a famous surgeon. This gives the impression of success, self confidence and intelligence. We should not frown or look stuck up, but smile with a mature, understanding smile. To judge our expression we can look in the mirror and ask ourselves, would this expression on someone else inspire in us confidence and respect?

2. Shoulders and head erect. We have been bred to believe that men and women of "class" walk with an upright posture. I remember as a child seeing my mother walking around the house with a book on her head, training herself to walk with a correct posture. When someone observes an upright posture, they tend judge the person to have breeding, class and self confidence. This is true whether the observer was brought up in a high class or a working class home.

3. **Body movements.** Unhurried and controlled body movements, rather than jerking and fast moving body movements, give the impression that the person has class and self control.

4. **Style of walk.** If someone appears to have upper class or upper middle class breeding as compared to lower middle class or lower class breeding, our society is conditioned to give them more respect. Upper class people have a tendency to walk erectly, and without hips or arms swinging extensively. On the other hand, we think of the lower or working class person as being slightly bent over, and with their arms swinging rather substantially, almost slightly ape style. If we will imitate the former rather than the latter, our image as perceived by others will be higher.

5. **Smiling versus grinning.** A pleasant smile makes us appear to be friendly, and this is positive. However, a forced grin makes us look silly at best, and deceitful at worst. Unfortunately, smiling can get us into trouble if we smile at the wrong time, as when the other person is upset. In such a case we should appear to be taking the matter very seriously. Otherwise, we may appear to be acting inappropriately and not giving proper respect to the situation.

VERBAL PATTERNS

The other person makes a judgement as to our social and business standing, our intelligence, and our mental capabilities, from observing our verbal patterns.

1. **Grammar.** Good grammar is a sign of education and good breeding. Statements like, "He shouldn't otta do it," or "she ain't got none," do not build respect in the listener's mind.

2. **Colloquialisms.** We should avoid slang expressions such as "Hot Dog" and "Oh Boy." In addition, we should attempt to pronounce words correctly. Dropping the "ing" from the end of words is a common mistake, such as saying "doin" instead of "doing." A heavy southern or mountain accent can be judged as an indication of poor education and breeding in certain parts of the country.

3. **Vocabulary size.** We are perceived as being more educated and more intelligent if we properly use a larger vocabulary and more "college level" words. Tests have indicated that vocabulary size is directly proportional both to educational level and to position level in major corporations. There are two ways to address this challenge. First, we can increase our vocabulary by studying vocabulary words from vocabulary books, the *Readers Digest*, etc. A second option is for us to carefully

select only a couple of hundred high quality, college level words (such as paroxysm, lugubrious and assuage); clearly learn their definitions and pronunciations; and incorporate them into our vocabulary. If we unconsciously and properly use these words in our conversation, when we otherwise would not, we will be perceived by the listener as having four additional years of formal education.

There are situations where using sophisticated words will not be helpful to us, and could even be harmful. However, there are numerous business situations where the listener will hold us in higher regard, and will want to associate with us and do business with us, if we are perceived as having the educational and status level of a college graduate or above.

4.   Voice Rhythm. An even, relaxed rhythm to our voice will cause us to be perceived as being more intelligent, and at a higher social level than if we have an erratic rhythm. It gives us the appearance of being intelligently controlled, rather than excitable and/or confused.

5.   Voice. A deeper, relaxed and smoother voice builds confidence within the listener. One way to accomplish this type of voice is to open our throat, expand our rib cage to tighten our diaphragm, stand erect, and direct our voice to an imaginary microphone in our tailbone, or in the pit of our stomach. This will have a tendency to drive our voice to a lower, deeper and smoother level. Practice, under a competent voice coach, can be effective in changing the sound and impact of the voice.

DRESS

To be considered as a high status and thinking person we should dress as would such a person. For instance, most corporate presidents and judges are rather conservative both in grooming and dress. Some dress rules from the book, **Dress For Success**, by John Molloy, which seem to make sense are as follows:

- Dress affluently and conservatively.
- Always be clean.
- Always dress as well as the people with whom you are dealing.
- Never wear sun glasses. Looking people in the eye builds confidence.
- Carry quality accompanying items such as attache case, pen and pencil, etc.
- If you are a man, never wear any item that might be considered feminine.
- If you are a woman, stay away from sexy looking or frilly clothing and styles.

Recent data indicate that we all fall into one of four color ranges, as far as complexion and skin tone, which have been named, "spring," "summer," "fall," and "winter." We look more healthy and attractive when we are wearing clothes and accessories in our own "colors." Color specialists are in major cities, and are available to assist in this area.

COMMUNICATIONS AND ATTITUDE

Our attitudes, and how we communicate with others, has an obvious effect on the image we project.

1. Eye Contact. Look other people directly in the eye whenever appropriate. Good eye contact builds an image of self confidence and honesty.

2. Attitude. A positive, can do, non-critical attitude builds confidence in the other person. Develop such an attitude.

3. Energy level. Tests have indicated that a high energy level is the single most important indicator of successful and happy people. Consequently, if we come across to other persons as being alert, forceful and energetic they will perceive us as being self confident and having a high self image.

4. Listening. If we are perceived by others as listening effectively, we will be showing them respect by demonstrating concern for their views and opinions. This builds a reservoir of good will in addition to making us appear patient, interested and intelligent.

5. Personal sensitivity. A sensitive person listens to others, is polite, does not interrupt, talks in terms of their interests, and is understanding and sympathetic. If we are sensitive to the opinions and reactions of others we will be showing them respect, and at the same time we will be demonstrating a level of maturity rather than immaturity. An appearance of maturity helps us to have a winning image. The HULRAH formula in chapter 8 relates to personal sensitivity.

PERSONAL IMPRESSION

You have heard the expression, "We only have one chance to make a good first impression." What kind of first impression do we want to make on the other person? Certainly one that is compatible with a "winning image." Figure 5-1 on the following page lists ten important aspects of a positive first impression. You can have some productive fun by making a copy of this sheet, and having a few of your friends rate you from one to ten in each of these areas. The chart is set up so a rating of "five" is the best rating.

To make a good first impression we want to have an upright posture, a warm smile, a firm hand shake that is alive, a good medium pitched voice, a friendly personality showing warmth, good eye contact, a mature and relaxed manner, and a neat and stylish style of dress. There are other characteristics which would go into making a good first impression. Another game to play with your friends would be to have each person develop their own "first impression" chart, and then compare charts.

Figure 5-1

PERSONAL IMPRESSION RATING

	1	5	10
1. POSTURE	STOOPED	UPRIGHT	STIFF
COMMENTS:			
2. SMILE	FROWN	WARM SMILE	GRIN
COMMENTS:			
3. HANDSHAKE	SOFT	FIRM	HARD
COMMENTS:			
4. HANDSHAKE LIFE	DEAD	ALIVE	PUMP HANDLE
COMMENTS:			
5. VOICE	HIGH	GOOD	LOW
COMMENTS:			
6. FRIENDLINESS	SOURPUSS	FRIENDLY	SUPER JOLLY
COMMENTS:			
7. WARMTH	COLD	WARM	OOZING
COMMENTS:			
8. EYE CONTACT	NONE	GOOD	COLD STARE
COMMENTS:			
9. STYLE OF DRESS	SLOPPY & UNSTYLISH	NEAT & STYLISH	OVERDRESSED
COMMENTS:			
10. MANNER	IMMATURE & EAGER	MATURE & RELAXED	UNINTERESTED & LAZY
COMMENTS:			

THE DECIDING DOZEN

In summary, what is it that the super-effective performers do which makes them achieve far more than average or even good performers? What is it that Joe Gondolfo in insurance sales, Joe Girard in automotive sales, Lee Iacocca in business leadership, Jimmy Sweigert in religious broadcasting, and John F Kennedy in politics did which yielded extraordinary success? A study by the author of highly successful performers in many industries and areas of life; indicate that there are twelve sets of practices the top performers follow. These have been named "The Deciding Dozen."

THE DECIDING DOZEN

1. Be a professional expert with the bearing of success.
2. Have strong convictions.
3. Be a consultant.
4. Be a student of human behavior.
5. Provide consummate satisfaction and service.
6. Have supreme confidence resulting from a purposeful positive attitude and being a student of communications and motivation.
7. Market and sell yourself.
8. Develop physical, mental and spiritual health and energy.
9. Develop a burning desire to achieve.
10. Implement a program for success.
11. Pay the price in time and effort.
12. Be decisive, with consummate self-discipline.

Figure 5-2 on the following pages further explains these twelve practices, and gives a checklist of actions which can be taken to achieve competency in each practice.

Figure 5-2

THE DECIDING DOZEN

1. BE A PROFESSIONAL EXPERT WITH THE BEARING OF SUCCESS
(KNOW YOUR BUSINESS AND LOOK LIKE YOU KNOW YOUR BUSINESS)

A. DRESS AND GROOM SUCCESSFULLY AND CONSERVATIVELY.
B. CARRY YOURSELF CONFIDENTLY, ERECT, UNHURRIED, AND SUCCESSFULLY. CONSISTENTLY LOOK THE OTHER PERSON IN THE EYE TO GENERATE TRUST AND CONFIDENCE.
C. BE A PERSON OF BUSINESS, WITH SOMETHING IMPORTANT AND HELPFUL TO DISCUSS. BE FRIENDLY WITH RESERVE.
D. GIVE THE (TRUE) APPEARANCE OF BEING BUSY.
E. PRESENT EDUCATED VERBAL PATTERNS OF GOOD GRAMMAR, NO SLANG, GOOD VOCABULARY, AND A DEEPER, RELAXED, SMOOTHER VOICE.
F. STUDY AND KNOW THOROUGHLY YOUR JOB, YOUR PROFESSION AND BUSINESS, AND THEIR SURROUNDING TECHNOLOGIES. BECOME AN EXPERT AND AN ADVISOR.
G. STUDY AND KNOW THE BUSINESS OF YOUR CUSTOMER OR BUSINESS ASSOCIATE AS IT RELATES TO YOUR PROFESSION AND JOB.
H. STUDY, LEARN FROM, AND COMMUNICATE WITH THE SUCCESSFUL PEOPLE IN YOUR FIELD.
I. SPECIALIZE IN A TECHNOLOGY OR AN INDUSTRY, AND BECOME WELL KNOWN AND AN AUTHORITY.
J. STUDY AND KNOW YOUR COMPETITORS' PRODUCTS AND SERVICES, THE RELATIVE ADVANTAGES AND BENEFITS OF THE PRODUCTS AND SERVICES OF YOUR COMPANY OR DEPARTMENT, EVIDENCE TO BACK UP THOSE ADVANTAGES AND BENEFITS, AND ANSWERS TO MAJOR QUESTIONS ANTICIPATED. THIS HELPS YOU TO BE MORE CUSTOMER OR CLIENT ORIENTED.

2. HAVE STRONG CONVICTIONS
(DEEPLY BELIEVE IN WHAT YOU ARE REPRESENTING AND HOW TO BEST COMMUNICATE IT)

A. BELIEVE IN, HAVE FAITH AND STRONG CONFIDENCE IN -
  - YOUR INDUSTRY
  - YOUR COMPANY OR INSTITUTION
  - YOUR PRODUCT OR SERVICE AND HOW IT BENEFITS THE CUSTOMER
  - YOUR PROFESSION
  - THE BENEFITS TO YOU OF BEING SUCCESSFUL IN YOUR JOB OR PROFESSION
  - YOURSELF AND YOUR ABILITY TO ACCOMPLISH YOUR JOB.
B. FIND WHAT ABOUT YOUR JOB REALLY TURNS YOU ON.

C.   BELIEVE IN AND HAVE CONVICTION IN YOUR WORK. THIS GENERATES ENTHUSIASM AND EXCITEMENT IN YOU, WHICH IS PERCEIVED BY THE CUSTOMER AND OTHERS IN THE COMPANY.

D.   OWN WHAT YOUR COMPANY PRODUCES, WHEN APPROPRIATE.

E.   BE PERSISTENT AND ENTHUSIASTIC, BASED ON YOUR CONVICTIONS.

F.   DEVELOP A STRONG CONVICTION TO A WORKING PHILOSOPHY OR CONCEPT.

G.   ENJOY YOUR WORK.

3. BE A CONSULTANT
(BE SKILLED AT DETERMINING NEEDS AND PROBLEMS, AND AT SOLVING PROBLEMS)

A.   BE PROFICIENT AT ASKING MANY AND PENETRATING QUESTIONS, LISTENING, ANALYZING, AND DETERMINING OTHERS' PROBLEMS, OPPORTUNITIES, WANT AND NEEDS.

B.   BE PROFICIENT AT THE SKILLS OF QUESTION-ASKING, LISTENING AND PERSONAL OBSERVATION.

C.   USE CREATIVITY; MATCH PRODUCTS AND SERVICES AVAILABLE TO PROBLEMS AND NEEDS; AND PROVIDE SOLUTIONS TO PROBLEMS. KNOW THE OTHER PERSON'S WANTS AND NEEDS BEFORE PRESENTING PRODUCTS OR SOLUTIONS.

D.   MAINTAIN CONTROL AND PREVENT UNNECESSARY INTERRUPTIONS OR DEVIATIONS.

E.   LEARN AND USE THE "TRADE TALK" OF THE INDUSTRY.

F.   WHEN APPROPRIATE, EVALUATE AND ADVISE YOUR CUSTOMER BASED ON THE NEEDS OF YOUR CUSTOMER'S CUSTOMER-INDUSTRY.

4. BE A STUDENT OF HUMAN BEHAVIOR
(UNDERSTAND PEOPLE AND HOW TO RELATE TO THEM AND MOTIVATE THEM, AND CONTINUE TO STUDY HUMAN NATURE)

A.   PRESENT YOURSELF TO OTHERS AS A FRIENDLY, THOUGHTFUL, CARING PERSON WHO IS GENUINELY INTERESTED IN HELPING.

B.   BE SOFTSPOKEN AND DISARMING, BUT WITH AN INNER ENTHUSIASM AND EXCITEMENT.

C.   KNOW AND USE THE BASIC PRINCIPLES OF HUMAN RELATIONS.

D.   REMEMBER AND USE NAMES OFTEN.

E.   BE SENSITIVE TO THE PERSONALITY AND PERSONAL NEEDS OF THE OTHER PERSON; BE RESPECTFUL OF HIM AND HIS "SPACE"; NEVER MAKE HIM FEEL UNCOMFORTABLE, EMBARRASSED OR UNFAIRLY PRESSURED; ADJUST YOUR DRESS AND STYLE TO HIM; BE RESPECTFUL OF HIS TIME; AND DO NOT SMOKE IN HIS OFFICE OR IN AN OFFICIAL MEETING.

F.   BE SINCERE AND HONEST. THIS BUILDS TRUST.

G.   BE INTERESTED IN THE OTHER PERSON AS A PERSON, AND MAKE HIM FEEL IMPORTANT.

H.   BE EMPATHETIC WITH HIS OPINIONS, NEEDS AND DESIRES.

I. UNDERSTAND AND BE ABLE TO READ AND PORTRAY POSITIVE (AND NEGATIVE) BODY SIGNALS.

J. PROJECT YOUR CONVICTION AND SINCERITY WITH CONSISTENT EYE CONTACT.

K. BE A SMILING, HAPPY PERSON WITH INNER PEACE AND A SENSE OF HUMOR. BUT DO NOT PORTRAY A CONSTANT GRIN OR INSINCERE SMILE.

L. LISTEN EFFECTIVELY, AND DEVELOP ADVANCED LISTENING SKILLS.

M. PURPOSE TO LIKE, RESPECT AND BE AGREEABLE WITH EVERYONE, REGARDLESS OF CIRCUMSTANCES.

5. PROVIDE CONSUMMATE SATISFACTION AND SERVICE
(MAKE YOUR PRIME CONSIDERATION EFFECTIVELY SERVICING, COMMUNICATING WITH AND PLEASING THOSE YOU SERVE, ESPECIALLY THE COMMERCIAL CUSTOMER)

A. TRY ALWAYS TO SOLVE THE OTHER PERSON'S OR ORGANIZATION'S PROBLEMS, AND TO GENUINELY HELP THEM.

B. FOLLOW-UP AFTER PERFORMING ANY SERVICE, IN AN ORGANIZED WAY, TO INSURE SATISFACTION.

C. COMMUNICATE OFTEN WITH THOSE YOU ARE SERVING; KEEPING THEM UPDATED; AND BOTH SUBTLY AND NOT SO SUBTLY INFORMING THEM OF THE MANY SERVICES YOU ARE PERFORMING FOR THEM.

D. WORK AT, AND EVEN FIGHT WITHIN YOUR ORGANIZATION TO PROVIDE CUSTOMER SATISFACTION, AND THEREBY BECOME PERCEIVED BY OTHERS, ESPECIALLY CUSTOMERS, AS A GENUINE ADVOCATE OF THEIR INTERESTS.

E. PROMISE A LOT. DELIVER MORE.

F. DON'T HESITATE NOT TO SELL IF IT IS IN THE CUSTOMER'S BEST INTEREST.

G. EARN THE CONTINUING GRATITUDE AND TRUST OF OTHERS BY BEING SERVICE ORIENTED, HONEST, TRUSTWORTHY AND DEPENDABLE.

H. PAY CONTINUING LITTLE ATTENTIONS SUCH AS THANK YOU NOTES AND BIRTHDAY CARDS.

I. AS A RESULT OF THE ABOVE, THE OTHER PERSON WILL FEEL APPRECIATIVE AND OBLIGATED TO YOU, AND WILL WANT TO PROVIDE YOU WITH COOPERATION AND RETURNED SERVICE.

6. HAVE SUPREME CONFIDENCE RESULTING FROM A PURPOSEFUL POSITIVE ATTITUDE AND BEING A STUDENT OF COMMUNICATIONS AND MOTIVATION
(THOROUGHLY BELIEVE IN YOURSELF AND YOUR ABILITY TO COMMUNICATE AND SELL, AND CONTINUE TO IMPROVE THOSE ABILITIES)

A. LOVE BEING WITH AND HELPING PEOPLE.

B. FILL YOUR MIND WITH THOUGHTS OF SUCCESS AND HAPPINESS.

C. USE MENTAL IMAGERY TO VISUALIZE SUCCESSFUL SITUATIONS.

D. CONTINUALLY GIVE YOURSELF POSITIVE SELF TALKS.

E. CONTINUE TO STUDY, KNOW AND PRACTICE THE PRINCIPLES AND TECHNIQUES OF YOUR PROFESSION.

F.   CONTINUE TO READ BOOKS AND LISTEN TO TAPES FROM AUTHORITIES AND SUCCESSFUL PERFORMERS IN YOUR PROFESSION, AND CONCERNING POSITIVE MOTIVATION, SUCCESS AND HUMAN RELATIONS.

G.   KEEP DEVELOPING NEW CONTACTS AND NEW IDEAS. THAT GIVES MOMENTUM TO YOUR THINKING AND ACTIONS.

H.   DEVELOP AND IMPLEMENT A PERSONAL SUCCESS STRATEGY.

I.   SELL IDEAS AND CONCEPTS RATHER THAN SIMPLY TALKING ABOUT PRODUCTS OR SERVICES. DO THIS BOTH INSIDE AND OUTSIDE THE COMPANY.

J.   ASSUME THAT YOU WILL BE SUCCESSFUL, AND CARRY THAT CONFIDENCE INTO EVERY SITUATION.

K.   USE PRESSURE ON OTHERS ONLY AT THE RIGHT TIME, CAREFULLY, AND IN THE RIGHT WAY.

L.   USE THE THEORY OF RATIOS, KNOWING THAT MOST SUCCESS IS A NUMBERS GAME, AND THAT MORE TRIES RESULTS IN MORE ACHIEVEMENTS.

M.   USE THE TELEPHONE AS AN IMAGE-BUILDING AND TIME-SAVING TOOL.

N.   NEVER ASSUME THAT THE IMPORTANT PERSON HAS ALREADY BEEN CONTACTED, INFORMED AND SATISFIED.

O.   WORK WITH THE DECISION MAKER, AND AT A HIGH ENOUGH LEVEL.

P.   INCLUDE ANYONE IN A MEETING YOU BELIEVE IS NECESSARY TO MAKE A DECISION.

Q.   MAKE CONTACT WITH IMPORTANT AND BUSY EXECUTIVES BY APPROACHING THEM AT UNUSUAL TIMES AND IN INNOVATIVE WAYS.

R.   BECOME EXTREMELY COMPETENT AT UNDERSTANDING, DIGGING OUT AND HANDLING THE DELAYING TYPES OF QUESTIONS AND OBJECTIONS.

S.   DO WHAT YOU CAN TO PREVENT DISTRACTIONS DURING ANY PRESENTATION. DISTRACTIONS COOL-OFF INTERESTED CONTACTS.

7. MARKET AND SELL YOURSELF
(MARKET AND SELL YOURSELF TO BECOME RECOGNIZED, RESPECTED AND APPRECIATED BY OTHERS)

A.   DO THOSE THINGS WHICH BUILD FOR YOURSELF PERSONAL RECOGNITION AND A GOOD REPUTATION. THIS SUPPORTS YOUR POSITION AS AN AUTHORITY, AND ENCOURAGES PEOPLE TO CONTACT YOU AND TO BE RESPONSIVE TO YOU.

B.   PRESENT YOUR OWN AND YOUR COMPANY'S CREDENTIALS IN A HUMBLE BUT UNAPOLOGETIC WAY EARLY IN A PRESENTATION, TO ESTABLISH WITH A NEW CONTACT WHY HE SHOULD WORK WITH YOU AND YOUR COMPANY.

C.   DESIGN YOUR OFFICE, YOUR DRESS AND YOUR PRESENTATION MATERIALS TO SELL YOU.

D.   TAKE A NUMBER OF ACTIONS TO DEVELOP A POSITIVE RELATIONSHIP WITH OTHERS, INCLUDING SENDING THANK YOU NOTES; SENDING BIRTHDAY, ANNIVERSARY AND HOLIDAY CARDS; MAKING OCCASIONAL VISITS OR PHONE CALLS WITH A PURPOSE; SENDING CLIPPINGS OF INTEREST FROM THE NEWSPAPER; AND PRESENTING NEW AND STIMULATING IDEAS.

E. MAINTAIN AND DEVELOP NUMEROUS RELATIONSHIPS THROUGH ACTIVE PARTICIPATION IN ASSOCIATIONS, ORGANIZATIONS AND THE COMMUNITY. FOLLOW UP ON THESE RELATIONSHIPS IN A CAREFUL AND NON-OFFENSIVE WAY.

F. TAKE ANY OF A NUMBER OF PUBLIC RELATIONS ACTIONS SUCH AS WRITING ARTICLES, ARRANGING TO HAVE ARTICLES WRITTEN ABOUT YOU, DEVELOPING A BROCHURE, GIVING SEMINARS, SENDING OUT A NEWSLETTER, OR BECOMING A CELEBRITY IN SOME WAY. THESE INCREASE YOUR RECOGNITION AND REPUTATION.

8. DEVELOP PHYSICAL, MENTAL AND SPIRITUAL HEALTH AND ENERGY

(DO WHAT IS NECESSARY TO LOOK AND FEEL HEALTHY, ENERGETIC AND HAPPY, AND MAKE THOSE AROUND YOU FEEL THE SAME WAY)

A. SINCE HOW YOU LOOK AND HOW YOU FEEL DIRECTLY AFFECTS YOUR PERFORMANCE AND HOW YOU ARE PERCEIVED BY OTHERS, WORK AT IMPROVING BOTH.

B. BE ALERT, FORCEFUL AND ENERGETIC.

C. KNOW YOUR NEEDS FOR PROPER NUTRITION, EXERCISE, RELAXATION AND SLEEP, AND FOLLOW THEM.

D. STUDY NUTRITION, EXERCISE AND RELAXATION TECHNIQUES ENOUGH TO KNOW WHAT IS BEST FOR YOU, OR FIND A COMPETENT CONSULTANT.

E. FILL YOUR MIND WITH THOUGHTS OF PEACE, HOPE, JOY, SUCCESS, ENERGY, HEALTH AND HAPPINESS.

F. GET RIGHT WITH YOURSELF AND YOUR MAKER.

G. DEVELOP PERSPECTIVE CONCERNING WHAT REALLY IS IMPORTANT TO YOU AND YOUR FAMILY BOTH NOW AND OVER THE LONG TERM.

H. COMMUNICATE WITH AND DEVELOP A POSITIVE RELATIONSHIP WITH YOUR SPOUSE AND FAMILY. SPEND QUALITY TIME WITH THEM. A GOOD SUPPORT SYSTEM AT HOME IS IMPORTANT.

9. DEVELOP A BURNING DESIRE TO ACHIEVE

(WANT TO ACHIEVE SO MUCH THAT YOU ARE WILLING TO DO WHATEVER IS REQUIRED TO ACCOMPLISH YOUR MISSION)

A. EITHER YOU HAVE A BURNING DESIRE TO ACHIEVE OR YOU DO NOT. IF YOU DO, GOOD. IF YOU DON'T, CULTIVATE IT.

B. AN ACHIEVER GENERALLY IS SELF MOTIVATED, COMPETITIVE, HAS A HEALTHY FEAR OF FAILURE, IS MOTIVATED BY PEER RECOGNITION, HAS INNER PRIDE, HAS A SENSE OF URGENCY, AND HAS A DESIRE TO EXCEL AND TO BE THE BEST.

C. CULTIVATE YOUR DESIRE TO ACHIEVE BY VISUALIZING YOUR GOAL IN LIFE, AND HOW THAT GOAL CAN BE BETTER FULFILLED BY YOUR TAKING ACTIONS TO ACHIEVE RESULTS NOW. GET HUNGRY FOR THE RESULTS.

D. A LACK OF DESIRE TO ACHIEVE MAY COME FROM A NEGATIVE SELF IMAGE AND THE BELIEF THAT "I CAN'T ACHIEVE, SO WHY BOTHER?" THIS CAN BE OVERCOME THROUGH THOROUGHLY LEARNING JOB SKILLS, POSITIVE MENTAL IMAGERY AND SELF TALK, AND

PROGRAMMING YOURSELF FOR SUCCESS.

10. IMPLEMENT A PROGRAM FOR SUCCESS
(MANAGE AND CONTROL YOURSELF AND YOUR TIME EFFECTIVELY SO YOU ARE ACCOMPLISHING EXACTLY WHAT YOU SHOULD TO ACHIEVE YOUR GOALS)

A.   KNOW WHAT YOUR FIRST PRIORITY IS, AND CONCENTRATE YOUR TIME ON THAT.

B.   DO YOUR HOMEWORK AND PLANNING OUTSIDE OF NORMAL WORK HOURS WHEN POSSIBLE.

C.   PLAN TO "BE AT THE RIGHT PLACE AT THE RIGHT TIME." EVALUATE WHICH PRODUCTS, TECHNOLOGIES, BUSINESSES, INDUSTRIES, AND AREAS ARE GROWING OR CHANGING, AND WHICH OFFER THE BEST CAREER OPPORTUNITY.

D.   BE PROPERLY PREPARED FOR EACH PRESENTATION AND DECISION MEETING.

E.   KEEP ACCURATE RECORDS AND ANALYZE THEM.

F.   MANAGE YOUR JOB SO AS TO INCREASE THE TIME SPENT ON THE MOST IMPORTANT PROJECTS (REMEMBER THE 80/20 RULE) AND TO MINIMIZE WASTED AND TRAVEL TIME.

G.   MANAGE YOUR TIME BY -
- RECORDING WHERE YOUR TIME GOES
- DELETING LESS IMPORTANT ACTIVITIES
- REDUCING INTERRUPTIONS AND DISTRACTIONS
- CONSOLIDATING TIME FOR MAJOR PROJECTS
- SETTING PRIORITIES
- STOPPING WASTING OTHERS' TIME
- MANAGING YOURSELF AND YOUR TIME
- SCHEDULING TIME TO DO WHAT NEEDS TO BE DONE
- MAKING CHECKLISTS AND PAYING PROPER ATTENTION TO DETAILS
- USING THE TELEPHONE
- EXPANDING YOURSELF WITH ASSISTANTS
- WATCHING OUT FOR WASTED MINUTES.

H.   CONSIDER TEAMING UP WITH ONE OR TWO OTHER COMPETENT PERFORMERS, FOR THE PURPOSE OF THINKING, PLANNING, AND EVALUATING PERFORMANCE.

I.   BE A CREATIVE, RESOURCEFUL IDEA-PERSON.

J.   INFLUENCE YOUR MIND WITH POSITIVE AND SUPPORTIVE BOOKS, TAPES, MOVIES AND PEOPLE.

K.   SET LONG TERM AND SHORT TERM PERFORMANCE GOALS, WHICH CAN BE MEASURED, AND ANNOUNCE THEM.

L.   MAKE PLANS WITH TIMETABLES TO ACCOMPLISH THOSE GOALS.

M.   BE ORGANIZED IN YOUR PERSONAL AND PROFESSIONAL LIFE. HAVE A PLACE FOR EVERYTHING.

N.   HAVE A PURPOSE FOR EACH USE OF YOUR TIME. ASK OVER AND OVER - IS THIS ESSENTIAL? AND - IS WHAT I AM DOING NOW MOVING ME FORWARD TOWARD ACHIEVING MY GOALS?

O.   WORK UNDER CONSTANT TIME PRESSURE. AND THEN RELAX DURING OFF-HOURS.

P.   REWARD YOURSELF FOR SMALL SUCCESSES.

11. PAY THE PRICE IN TIME AND EFFORT
(BE WILLING TO DO WHATEVER IS REQUIRED AND WHENEVER AND WHEREVER IT IS REQUIRED TO GET THE JOB DONE, REGARDLESS OF THE RESULTING INCONVENIENCE AND DISCOMFORT)

A.   BE WILLING TO SPEND WHATEVER AMOUNT OF TIME IS REQUIRED, AND WHEN AND WHERE IT IS REQUIRED TO GET THE JOB DONE.

B.   MAKE THE EFFORT TO SCHEDULE YOUR ACTIVITIES, SO IMPORTANT WORK PROJECTS GET ACCOMPLISHED, AND SO IMPORTANT HOME ACTIVITIES GET ACCOMPLISHED.

C.   SELL THE FAMILY ON THE VALUE OF QUALITY OF TIME VS QUANTITY OF TIME.

D.   REALIZE THAT RESULTS ARE OFTEN PROPORTIONAL TO THE NUMBER OF EFFECTIVE EFFORTS.

E.   SPEND TIME DURING NON WORKING HOURS TO STUDY AND BECOME AN EXPERT IN YOUR PROFESSION AND YOUR BUSINESS.

12. BE DECISIVE, WITH CONSUMMATE SELF-DISCIPLINE
(MAKE THE RIGHT DECISIONS AND MAKE YOURSELF CARRY THEM OUT TO COMPLETION)

A.   MAKE YOURSELF DO WHAT YOU SHOULD DO; INCLUDING PLANNING YOUR WORK, PRACTICING NEW SKILLS, HAVING A POSITIVE ATTITUDE, KEEPING RECORDS, AND ANALYZING RECORDS TO IMPROVE EFFECTIVENESS, EVEN IF AND WHEN YOU DON'T FEEL LIKE IT.

B.   DECIDE TO REFRAIN FROM EXCESSIVE DRINKING, WASTED CONVERSATION, OR ANYTHING ELSE WHICH INTERFERES WITH GOAL ACHIEVEMENT.

C.   DETERMINE WHAT IS REQUIRED TO ACHIEVE, TO MEET YOUR OBJECTIVES; DECIDE FIRMLY AND RESOLUTELY TO DO THAT; AND THEN DO IT WITH DOGGED DETERMINATION, MAKING YOURSELF DO WHATEVER IS REQUIRED, WHETHER YOU LIKE IT OR NOT.

BEFORE AND AFTER

After spending two chapters on the subject of improving personal performance, it's time to stop and reflect. Figure 5-3 provides space at the top for you to describe yourself as you are now, emphasizing those areas where you would like to improve. Then space is provided at the bottom to write down who you would like to become from a personal effectiveness standpoint, after you employ the principles and practices we have been discussing in these two chapters. This will give you a guideline to choose which personal performance improvement practices to first start employing on your path to becoming an even more effective "winning" performer.

Figure 5-3

BEFORE AND AFTER

BEFORE

1. _____
2. _____
3. _____
4. _____
5. _____
6. _____
7. _____
8. _____
9. _____
10. _____

AFTER

1. _____
2. _____
3. _____
4. _____
5. _____
6. _____
7. _____
8. _____
9. _____
10. _____

6

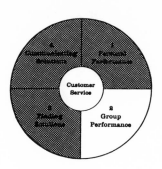

LEADERSHIP THROUGH MOTIVATION

MOTIVATIONAL BELIEFS WHICH INSPIRE PEOPLE TO HIGH PERFORMANCE
"Beliefs In" Which Inspire and Motivate
"Beliefs That" Which Inspire and Motivate
PERSUASION TO BELIEVE
Persuasion Steps
MOTIVATIONAL INFLUENCES
A. The Leadership
B. Peer Motivation
C. Self Motivation
D. Task Or Mission Motivation

It is inherent in the Cross-Marketing (eg.-Integrated Business Leadership Through Cross-Marketing™) system that all employees in the organization, at all levels, work together in effective teamwork, with the objective of effectively serving the customer. This requires that all the people follow the lead of their superiors, communicate effectively with everyone with whom they work, apply creativity and innovation to their assignments, and work as productively and effectively as they can, regardless of whether anyone is watching.

Our people will do this, or attempt to do it, only if they are motivated to do so. One of our important tasks in management is to step out in leadership, to set policies and make decisions which will encourage self motivation, and to say and do those things which will cause a constant and continual positive motivational influence on our people. The purpose of this chapter is to provide the insight for making the correct decisions and taking the correct actions.

This chapter contains three major sections:

a. Motivational beliefs which inspire people to high performance,

b. Persuasion to believe - how to persuade our people to hold the beliefs which will cause them to be motivated to perform effectively and productively, and

c. Motivational influences - those influences, which encourage our people to be motivated or not to be motivated. These influences can be affected by us as managers and leaders.

MOTIVATIONAL BELIEFS WHICH INSPIRE PEOPLE TO HIGH PERFORMANCE

There are specific motivational beliefs, which when held by a person, will inspire him to take positive action. Twenty such beliefs are discussed in this section.

The secret to motivation, whether it be self motivation or motivation of others, is to affect the belief system of the person. If we truly (100%) believe in anything, then we are going to be truly (100%) behind it, and do whatever is supported by that belief. Two tasks face us in motivational leadership, and they are discussed in this and the next section, respectively. **The first task** is to determine what the person needs to believe to be sufficiently motivated to take the action which is desired. **The second task**, covered in the next section, is to persuade the person to believe those things.

For perspective, let's first discuss an incident which explains the importance of convincing others to believe.

The action which seems to frighten more business people than any other, with the possible exception of speaking in public, is that of making cold sales calls. This is not a sales book. However, it is a book about communicating and selling to those inside and outside the company our beliefs; the beliefs that we, our department and our company possess valuable products and services to provide to others. That makes this example even more appropriate.

Consider the following situation. Suppose you had a very good friend who had a rare and incurable form of cancer. You and your friend had visited all of the major health care institutions in the country which specialize in cancer. Each one in turn had informed you with total certainty that there was no cure for this cancer and that your friend would die within the next six months. One day, by accident, you happened to be reading a magazine such as the National Enquirer, and you read about a physician in Europe who had discovered an unusual cure for cancer. This physician ground up the bark of a certain tree in Europe and had his patients drink it mixed with goat's milk. Grasping at any possibility you approached a number of the important health care institutions concerning this supposed cure and was told that this physician was a quack and you should forget about it entirely. In your desperation you contacted the physician, carried your friend to Europe and had her treated by this unusual treatment. Five years later you and your friend returned for her final check up. She had been totally cured of the cancer to the astonishment of the doctors in the United States, and when you entered the physician's office in Europe you discovered that there were twenty other people sitting there, all of whom had had this rare form of cancer, all of whom had been told not to come to this physician, and all of whom had been cured.

Now here is the question. If you were back in this country and you discovered that the owner of the local service station where you purchase gas had this form of cancer, would you hesitate to approach him and suggest that he go to Europe and take this cure (which would be a cold sales call)? If he refused, would you hesitate to talk to his wife and strongly encourage her to take him to Europe to take this treatment (thereby demonstrating your selling persistence)? Wouldn't you be forceful and assertive in attempting to "sell" this husband and wife to take this action that you strongly <u>believed</u> in?

The point of the story is this. If we truly believe; if we are absolutely convinced that something important is true, **we will be motivated** to take action on it. Now back to the question. How do we become so motivated? How do our people become so motivated? The answer is for us to truly believe in something which needs to be done. And how do we truly believe in that something? We truly believe, and we cause others to truly believe a certain major truth by helping them to believe in a number of supporting truths. What these truths are, and how to affect belief in those truths, are covered in the sections which follow.

"BELIEFS IN" WHICH INSPIRE AND MOTIVATE

As leaders we are attempting to motivate our people to think certain ways and to take certain actions. Regarding any particular situation or decision there are ten factors which we need to persuade our people to believe in, if they are going to be motivated to think or act positively. The ten things we need to encourage or persuade our people to believe in are covered in this section.

Sometimes for our people to be motivated sufficiently to take action they will need to believe in all ten of these things. At other times, belief in only one is sufficient to cause action because of its particular importance to the person. If a person is not yet motivated, it is our responsibility as leaders to determine which of the ten "beliefs in" (and/or which of the ten "beliefs that" which follow in the next section) are the problem. We then can use the tactics discussed in the next major section on persuasion, in an attempt to solve the problem; in other words, to persuade the person to believe in or to believe that the item in question is true.

The ten "beliefs in" are listed below with some accompanying explanations and illustrations.

"BELIEFS IN"
WHICH INSPIRE AND MOTIVATE

1. The industry
2. The institution or organization
3. The management
4. The job or profession
5. The program and purpose
6. The quality, product and purpose
7. The benefits to the customer
8. The benefits to the company
9. The personal benefits
10. Myself - that I can do it

1. The industry. Our people need to believe in their industry, the industry their company is a part of. For instance, if we are in the banking industry, and our people believe that banks rip people off, and that people are better off dealing with a savings and loan or a credit union, then we are in trouble. It is going to be difficult for them to become motivated to work hard for our bank and to sell our bank and its products. As another illustration, what if a credit union's staff believed that credit unions are only for people with small amounts of resources? Then they are not going to be motivated to try to do business with people who have substantial resources. If the staff of a hospital believes that hospitals in general provide a wonderful service to the community, then this in itself is going to be an inspiration and a motivation to them to work effectively in and for their hospital.

2. The institution or organization. If our people are proud of the history of our organization, if they are inspired by the values of our company or institution, this will help to motivate them. On the other hand, if they consider our organization to be unethical, or to have a history of being poorly run, then they might be thinking more of working somewhere else rather than working hard for this particular organization. A distinction should be drawn between the institution itself and the current management of the institution. Our people can believe that our organization - our company, our hospital, our bank, our university - is a worthwhile organization with a purpose, and at the same time either believe in or not believe in the current management of that organization. This especially is true if we are in a division or a large department, and if our people relate more to our division or department than to the overall organization.

3. The management. If our people believe that their management knows what it is doing, has proper values and goals, and is effectively managing the organization; if they believe management is making the correct decisions to benefit the customer, the company and the employees; then this inspires and motivates them. In the final section to this chapter numerous items are presented which management can address to cause its people to believe that management is managing properly. This will help them to be motivated.

4. The job or profession. Our people need to believe in the department and/or the job or the profession in which they are involved. They need to be proud of what they are doing, and believe that it holds importance within the organization. For instance, if we are in the research department and the company seems to ignore the director of research, and provides very little money for research as compared to other companies of our type this would be demotivational. On the other hand if we are in the accounting department and the accounting department historically has been a weak sister; but just recently we've hired a controller from a major corporation and it has been made very clear that accounting now is going to have an important position within the organization, this motivates the members of that department. If a sales person considers sales to be the rip off function, with the purpose of cramming unworthy products down people's throats, and stealing money from their pockets, then that sales person is going to be much less motivated than if she believes that sales is an important and worthy occupation, that sales is the machine which solves customer problems and creates jobs for those in our company.

5. The program and purpose. Regardless of the department a person is in, or the job or the profession that he holds, it is important for him to believe in the particular program that he is involved in, and the purpose of that program. If you are a marketing manager for a high tech company, and have been put in charge of a program which seems to be failing and that you personally don't believe in, then you are going to be less motivated than if you were put in charge of a program that you really did believe in. If you are a hospital housekeeping supervisor and have been asked to implement a sophisticated odor control program within your hospital, you will be much more motivated to do so properly if you believe that odor control is important, than if you believe that odor control is a waste of time and expense.

6. The quality, product and purpose. No matter what is your job or department within an organization, your job produces a product or a service which is used by someone else within or outside the organization. Sales people normally believe in the value and the quality of some products more than others, and they often find themselves motivated to sell the products they believe in and avoiding selling the products they do not believe in. Likewise, a housekeeping scrub team may produce a shiny, beautiful floor as its product. If the team is proud of its product, the shiny beautiful floors, then the team will be more motivated to work hard to perform its job. If a nurse is proud of the quality of the nursing service provided, not only by herself but by the entire hospital, she will be more motivated to stay at the hospital and to work hard for long hours to provide exceptional nursing service.

7. The benefits to the customer. It is important that our people believe that their customer will benefit from what they are doing. If bank tellers are asked to market or sell new banking services to present customers, they will be more motivated to do so if they believe that these services will benefit the customers. In support of this, our consulting and surveys indicate that bank tellers and associates specifically are more concerned with customers receiving benefits than they are with the bank being profitable. A savings and loan manager will be more motivated to phone present customers and make appointments for a sales specialist to call on them if she believes that the services and products which are going to be offered truly will benefit the customers.

How do we convince our people that our products and services will benefit the customers? One way is to sit down with them, explain the products and services, explain what the benefits to the customers are, and what evidence we have to back up what we say. Another is to take them to visit some present customers who are very happy with these products and services to see first hand just how our customers are benefitting from the specific products and services.

If a nursing home maintenance staff is asked to work very rapidly for a few weeks to install humidifiers throughout the nursing home, they will be more motivated to do so if they believe that installing the humidifiers will really benefit the patients, and that it is important to do so quickly. In this case, the product which will benefit the customers is the installation of the humidifiers. The customers are the nursing home patients.

8. The benefits to the company. Suppose the nursing and other supporting staff of a nursing home are asked to go out of their way to be friendly to and cooperative with both the patients and the visitors to the institution. They are asked to do this in spite of the fact that they are overloaded with work, and others frequently do not return the friendliness. It is important that they believe that the institution will benefit from their actions, perhaps through more patients and more income. On the other hand, if they believe they are in a monopoly situation, and how they behave will not influence sales or the number of patients at the home, then they will be less motivated to go out of their way to give friendly service.

Suppose a machine lathe operator, who is being managed properly, is asked to change his procedure to pay particular attention to every item that is manufactured so as to produce an extremely high tolerance and no defects. If the operator believes that by doing so the company will receive increased business he may be inclined to comply. If on the other hand, he feels that he is being asked to produce quality that isn't required, that there is no special benefit to the customer, and the company isn't really going to benefit through increased sales, then he is going to be inclined to continue to operate by his former, easier standards.

9. The personal benefits. Have you heard of the word **WIIFM?** When we are asked to stretch ourselves and to perform to high standards, consciously or unconsciously we ask the question, **"What's in it for me?"** What's in it for me to go out of my way to cooperate with, communicate with, and be friendly to others, both my peers and our customers? What's in it for me to have a smile in my voice when I answer the telephone? What's in it for me to come back from lunch a little early and get to work on that important project rather than taking an extra long lunch hour if I can get by with it? What's in it for me to talk positively about the organization and its products to my friends and acquaintances in the community? WIIFM is one of the fundamental questions of motivation. And it must be answered positively if we expect others to be motivated, to perform to high standards. There are many ways of answering this question and many of the answers are provided in the final section of this chapter.

There is another very basic factor related to personal benefits. The task or assignment (let's say cold call sales as compared to intricate mechanical drawing) will require certain personal characteristics and skills (in this case - enthusiasm, persistence, competitiveness, listening and problem solving, as compared to - attention to detail, a steady hand, artistic inclinations and the ability to work alone). If these fit your personality and you have these skills, you will be comfortable, and naturally effective in the assignment. If they do not, you may be very uncomfortable, and not effective even if you try. Imagine an uncoordinated business consultant attempting to do brain surgery. This would cause you to feel like and perhaps be a failure, which would reduce both your self esteem and the positive recognition coming from others. This then would have a negative effect on the personal benefits to you from attempting the task, and would decrease your motivation to do so.

10. Myself - that I can do it. If I'm going to be motivated to do anything, and especially to perform to a very high level of performance, then I must be convinced that I have the capability of achieving the performance that is asked of me. I must be convinced that I understand what is asked of me; that I have been provided the proper knowledge and skills through education and training to do the job properly. When I attempt the job, I must be convinced that it I will not be embarrassed or be thought of as a failure because I did not live up to the standards which have been established. Many children have failed in school because they didn't try to do the work. Then they had an excuse, because if they didn't try they couldn't be thought of as being stupid. They just were thought of as being lazy, and that wasn't as bad as being stupid.

"BELIEFS THAT" WHICH INSPIRE AND MOTIVATE

As leaders who motivate others to perform effectively, it is our job to help our people to hold all ten of the above "Beliefs In." But that is not enough. Now, we will discuss ten "Beliefs That" which also are very important for people to be motivated. Abraham Maslow in his "hierarchy of needs" lists five levels of motivation where a person can be at any particular time. The lower a person is on that hierarchy the more important these "beliefs that" are. Most people need to believe that most of the following "beliefs that" are true for them to be properly motivated.

"BELIEFS THAT"
WHICH INSPIRE AND MOTIVATE

1. Accomplishment will be measured and recognized
2. The benefit is more than the pain
3. The benefit is to me or mine
4. The task is doable
5. I can succeed
6. I will not get hurt or look foolish
7. The task is worthwhile
8. The task must be done, and now

9. The task is consistent with my needs
10. I have no other choice

1. Accomplishment will be measured and recognized.　Our people need to believe that their accomplishments will be measured and recognized, if we expect them to be motivated to think and act as we would desire.

"You never hear from anybody around here until you make a mistake!" Have you ever heard that statement?　In too many organizations the managers, or so-called leaders, only talk to people when they have something to criticize or correct.　They pay far too little attention to recognizing accomplishments.　Another failure, which is almost as prevalent, is to not measure accomplishment.　Too frequently we give someone a task to do and then do not check to see if it is performed properly, assuming it was done "okay" unless we hear something negative.

It was decided by Mary Jane, the director of customer service, in conjunction with the vice president of marketing, that she would train her people on effective listening and telephone techniques.　Also, she was asked to institute a policy in her department so that whenever a customer called in with a problem a short report would be prepared on the call, with a copy being forwarded both to the line department involved and to the director of marketing. A month later she was contacted about her progress, and gave a positive report. At the end of the training the vice president met with her and the members of her department to discuss what they had learned in the training and how they were now performing more effectively. Three months after that the marketing vice president arranged for an analysis to be performed on the number of complaints and how well the complaints were being handled. This included calling and questioning a number of customers. The customers were quite pleased with the results of the program, and the number of serious complaints had reduced steadily during this period, as compared to before the training.

As a result, a reception was held for the department, and the vice president and the president attended to thank the members of the department for their contribution and good work.　Notice of this reception and the improved performance of the department was reported in the company newspaper.

Now, the question is this, the next time Mary or her department, or any other manager is asked to perform a task, will they be more motivated or less motivated to do so because of the way that this particular situation was handled?　Suppose the vice president had given the assignment to Mary Jane and then had forgotten about it, had not followed up, and had not determined that they had done a good job, but had just assumed that the job had been accomplished, and had said nothing. As a result of that lack of action, what effect would have been had on the motivation or demotivation of Mary Jane, the department, and others in the company?

2. The benefit is more than the pain. In this context the "benefit" means the total benefit to the company, to the customer and to the individual. The "pain" could consist of the unpleasantness of working overtime, of working harder, or the personal stress from performing a new or unfamiliar activity. If our people feel that the effort and inconvenience involved in doing whatever is asked of them is "worth it," then they are going to be more motivated to take action.

3. The benefit is to me or mine. This relates to WIIFM discussed in 9 under "beliefs in." We are all selfish in our own way. Even the philanthropist gives his large gifts because of the resulting good feeling or some other benefit, either to himself or to someone who is important to him. The benefit can be recognition, either in this world or in the hereafter. The benefit can be financial. The benefit can be a good feeling received from doing something for someone else. It behooves us as leaders to determine what it is that our people are concerned with, and then package what we want them to do in such a way that it will benefit them or someone who is important to them.

4. The task is doable. No one likes to waste their time. If our people are asked to do something that they feel can't be done, or is without significant value, then they are not going to be motivated to do it. In motivating others it is important that we communicate to them that the task is important, and that it can be accomplished with a reasonable amount of effort. We might have to show them how to perform the task, or give them some evidence that it can be accomplished, or that it has been accomplished by others in the past.

5. I can succeed. We must convince or persuade our people that they are smart enough and capable enough to be successful in the tasks we ask of them. To do this we must first convince ourselves that the task is doable, and that the person that we are dealing with can do it. Then we can use the facts and evidence we use to convince ourselves to convince the other person.

6. I will not get hurt or look foolish. It is difficult to motivate someone to do something which they feel is not in their best interest. If an employee is afraid to appear before a group or to speak in public, it will be difficult to convince him to take a speaking assignment or lead an important meeting. We must deal with the fears of our people and overcome them through management, training, positive reinforcement, and the other tools available.

7. The task is worthwhile. If the task is worthwhile it is going to have substantial benefits to someone; to the customer, to the company, or to someone within the company. We must convince ourselves and then the other person that this task is worthwhile.

8. The task must be done, and now. This is not an absolute requirement, but can be very important. There are many tasks which are desirable but which do not have to be done. Certainly they do not have to be done immediately. Our people can be motivated to do these tasks because they want to do them, because they feel there are substantial benefits from doing them, or for any of a number of other reasons that we have been discussing. However, whether the person wants to perform a task or not, whether the person even believes in it or not, if that person believes that this task absolutely must be performed and it must be performed immediately, he probably will perform the task, and attempt to do it properly.

The following is an example. Suppose the company's top customer has been offended and he demands that the offending employee both make an apology and redo a piece of work. You know that neither your employee nor your company is totally at fault. However, you and your employee both know that to fail to comply will mean the loss of your most important customer. In this case, you both would be motivated to dismiss your pride and provide the apology and the additional work.

9. The task is consistent with my needs. We mentioned earlier Maslow's hierarchy of needs. Without taking the time to discuss Maslow in any detail let us just say that different people have different needs, and one person has different needs at different times. At a certain time an employee might need to feel secure in his job. At another he might need to feel liked by the other employees, to be one of the gang. Or at this time he might feel the need to be recognized and feel important. If the requested assignment is consistent with his needs, he is going to be more motivated to comply. If it completely fulfills those needs, then this belief in itself may be sufficient to cause motivation to action.

10. I have no other choice. This item is similar to number 8. In number 8 the task had to be performed, and now. Therefore, the employee was motivated to do it. Number 10 means the task must be performed by a specific person. They have no other choice but to do it; otherwise, the negative consequences would be unacceptable to that person.

PERSUASION TO BELIEVE

As we have been discussing, for our people to be motivated to take a specific action, they must "believe in" certain things and "believe that" certain things are true. One effective way for us to exert leadership is to determine in what areas our people are not yet highly motivated, and then to determine what they fail to "believe" that is blocking that motivation. We then can set out to persuade them that they should hold those beliefs.

For instance, if they don't believe that taking a certain action, such as cross-selling to present customers, will benefit them personally, then they probably will not be motivated to make an extra effort to cross-sell. They could hold the other nine "beliefs in," but failure to hold this one belief could stand in the way of motivation and resulting action. We then must persuade them that it will benefit them to cross-sell if we expect them to be motivated to do so.

Likewise, if they do not believe in our company, or in the management, or that the products will benefit the customer, or that they can be successful in cross-selling even if they try, or that their cross-selling efforts will be measured and recognized, then we must persuade them to hold these beliefs. How we do this is the subject of this section.

To persuade our people to "believe in" or to "believe that" anything, there are eight steps we need to take as follows:

PERSUASION STEPS

1. Develop Self Belief
2. Develop a Positive Relationship
3. Interview the Person
4. Analyze Self Belief
5. Display a Positive Attitude
6. Present Facts and Evidence
7. Obtain Agreement
8. Observe and Follow-Up

We will discuss each of these steps in turn. For the sake of illustration, we will assume that we are attempting to persuade our employees to "believe in" the personal benefits of cross-selling effectively and aggressively, and thus to be motivated to do so.

1. Develop self belief. If we are going to persuade someone else to believe in something, we must first believe in it ourselves. Concerning a task or job assignment, this means we must believe that it is worthwhile and in the best interest of the customer, the company and the person. It also means that we know the task and the person well enough to know that it "makes sense" for him or her, and that it does not require some personality characteristics and job skills that are incompatible with the nature of the person.

Concerning cross-selling, we would ask ourselves - and others as appropriate - just how it will benefit our people personally if they are effective in cross-selling. To answer this question we must know our people well enough, individually and as a group, to know what they want and why they want it. We must know what is important to them. Is it approval? Recognition? Friendship? Job security? Encouragement? A job title? More money? Trophies? Time off? A feeling of self importance? A feeling of having helped other? Or a number of the above?

We then ask and answer how their being effective in cross-selling will give them what they want and need. Perhaps to give them what they need it will be necessary for us to modify the company's measurement, reward and recognition program to match their wants and needs. Perhaps we will have to modify our own behavior or management style. In any case, we establish that we clearly understand that being effective in cross-selling will benefit our people personally, in ways they desire to be benefitted.

2. Develop a positive relationship. From the first time we encountered our people we should have been building a positive relationship with them so that they will respect and trust us, and hopefully like us. We do this by being competent in our own jobs, by being interested in and communicating with our people, by giving them firm direction, and by using the HULRAH human relations formula explained in chapter 8. When we have developed a positive relationship with our people, they are more likely to listen to what we have to say and to act on it.

3. Interview the person. The purpose of interviewing our people at this point is to confirm or modify our hypotheses as what they want and need, and why, as regarding this particular situation; in this case cross-selling to present customers. The interview can be structured, but is more likely to be effective if it is casual and as a part of general conversations and job interactions. If the other person feels we are asking questions to gather information so we can later motivate (or worse manipulate) him, he will be less open in his answers, and more on guard when we start presenting facts and evidence in step 6.

4. Analyze self belief. We convince ourselves to believe in step 1, and confirmed what our people want and need in step 3. In step 4 we then analyze why we believe as we do, how the facts fit with the wants and needs of our people, and what evidence is available to support our conclusions. We do this to clearly understand the facts and supporting evidence so we can present them to our people.

We make a list of what is important to our people and how being effective in cross-selling will give them that. We then list the evidence which supports that our thinking is sound. We can do this in our head or on paper, depending upon the complexity of the situation.

5. Display a positive attitude. It is not sufficient that we believe that cross-selling will benefit our people. It is important that we also show them that we clearly and enthusiastically believe that way. We demonstrate this with what we say and how we say it, to our people and to others with whom our people come into contact. We demonstrate it with our facial expression, tone of voice, body language and energy level when we are discussing the subject. Our people will subtly pick up from us whether or not we really believe what we are saying.

6. Present facts and evidence. We can attempt to persuade our people to believe by direct or indirect behavior. In either case, we need to communicate to them (to believe) that their wants and needs will be met by taking the action of assertively cross-selling. Usually, we also will need to supply some evidence that this is true. This evidence can take many forms, such as a demonstration, an exhibit such as a magazine article, an example or incident, an analogy to a similar situation, statistics, or testimony from an expert or someone our people will believe.

In a direct presentation we might sit down with them, explain what we want them to do and how it will benefit them, and what is our evidence that it will benefit them. Or we might openly explain that we believe they are having difficulty in a certain area of belief (one of the 10 "beliefs in" or "beliefs that"), why we believe they should believe this, and what is our evidence.

In an indirect presentation we might subtly and continually make comments and drop hints that build in our people the belief that the thing is true. In this illustration it would be the belief that it would benefit them substantially to cross-sell. This might be accomplished without ever explaining why it is being done. This is similar to the concept of leadership by "nudging," in which we continually make comments and give small recognitions and appreciations in an effort to nudge our people into a desired set of behaviors and actions.

7. Obtain agreement. Whether we present the facts directly or indirectly we attempt to get our people to vocalize that they now believe, that it will benefit them substantially to aggressively cross-sell. This is for two purposes. First, it gives us corroboration that our mission has been successful. Second, when someone speaks out that they believe something, it tends to drive that belief into their subconscious mind and make it even stronger.

8. Observe and follow-up. Continually, and as long as necessary, we will observe the attitude, behavior and actions of our people to see if the belief (in cross-selling) is bearing fruit; if they have been motivated and are taking action on that belief. If the attitudes, behaviors and actions stop demonstrating that they believe, then we need to determine the source of the problem. If they really believe, they will take action unless a countering belief is stronger. In that case we need to determine what is the countering belief and act on that.

MOTIVATIONAL INFLUENCES

There are a number of specific factors which influence the attitudes and the thinking of our people, and encourage them to be motivated (or demotivated) to work effectively and productively. Most of these influences affect the twenty beliefs discussed in the first section.

In this section, thirty seven separate influences are discussed and are listed under four sources: (a) influences primarily from the leadership itself, (b) influences by peers, (c) influences by the people on themselves, and (d) influences by the job, task or mission. Each of these influences can be affected by us as leaders.

A. THE LEADERSHIP

The following are motivational influences on our people which are provided directly by their leadership.

1. Sets the example. The leadership sets the example for effective performance. You remember the expression, "What you do speaks so loud I cannot hear what you say." If management and supervision comes in late, leaves early, and takes long lunch periods, then it will be difficult, if not impossible, to motivate the work force to come in early, stay late, and work hard all day. Alternately, if the managers work longer and harder hours than anyone else, set goals, and manage themselves and others to meet those goals, then their people will be influenced to do likewise.

If management is customer driven, treats the people in the company as intelligent and important, and demands excellence in performance from itself, then the people will tend to behave the same way.

2. Has enthusiasm. When a leader is enthusiastic about the projects and tasks of the group, then this enthusiasm will be contagious and the others will pick it up. This enthusiasm demonstrates that the leader believes in the assignment or objective and that it can be successfully completed. It also shows he feels that benefits will come to the participants from the successful completion of the work. If on the other hand, the leader shows little enthusiasm for the project, then others will be influenced to believe the project is of little worth, and they will not be motivated to put in their best efforts.

3. Deserves trust. Surveys indicate that the leadership quality workers desire from management more than any other is honesty and trustworthyness. If people trust the judgement and motives of their leaders, they will be motivated to support them and follow their direction. We can deserve the trust of our people by being honest with them, by keeping them informed of what is going on, by not springing surprises on them, and by showing them how their jobs fit into the overall corporate and department mission.

4. Deserves respect. People are inclined to be motivated by and follow someone who knows what he is doing and who performs effectively himself. We can deserve the respect of our people by knowing both our jobs and their jobs, by knowing what and when to delegate, by concentrating on essentials so we are being productive ourselves, by managing our time effectively, by paying proper attention to details, and by making effective decisions. Effective decisions generally are those which solve underlying problems rather than those which fight symptomatic fires.

5. Generates desire. The motivational leader generates a desire in his people to accomplish the proposed mission. He does this by presenting to them the benefits of completing the mission or assignment; the benefits to the customer, to the company and to themselves.

6. Demonstrates trust. It is motivational when people feel that their leaders trust them, their judgements and their intentions. Leaders can accomplish this by giving their people total responsibility for accomplishing certain projects that are within their capability. An effective leader delegates but does not abdicate responsibility. He observes performance without interfering in the performance.

7. Believes in the people. If our people feel we believe in them and their abilities to perform, their self confidence is increased and they are more willing to step out and perform. They also feel more loyalty to the organization, and more desire to help and please their leadership.

One way of showing that we believe in them is to ask them how to best solve difficult problems, such as how to increase productivity. Both the answers we get back and the resulting increase in employee motivation may surprise us .

8. Keeps them informed. Keeping people informed makes them feel more important, which satisfies their ego. It also makes them more effective and more comfortable in making decisions because they know what management wants, and how their assignments fit into the overall picture.

9. Treats them fairly. Everyone wants to feel they will be rewarded in proportion to their performance, and that others are not receiving preferential treatment. Leaders should not play favorites. This is a special problem when a friend is one of the subordinates.

10. Provides help and support. Enough help and support should be provided to allow the subordinate to perform effectively, but not so much as to interfere with his assignment or his ego.

11. Is interested and makes them feel important. Leaders should show a personal interest in their people and their accomplishments. They should find a way to spend some exclusive time with each. They make their people feel important by giving them important responsibilities, and by giving encouragement and positive reinforcement. Recognition and "feeling important" are major motivators.

12. Establishes a mission and goals. Effective leaders work with their people to establish a mission with accompanying goals for accomplishing that mission. As a result, their people will know what direction to take and what to do to get there. This gives them security and comfort. The mission usually is established by the leader or at a higher level. However, people should participate in establishing their own goals. This give them a sense of commitment to them. In addition, more realistic goals usually result.

13. Develops a workable plan. The worker and the leader should work together to plan for accomplishing the stated goals. The worker should be given as much responsibility as possible for developing the plan. Again, this encourages his commitment to the plan. An effective plan which the employee believes in is a major motivational tool. It increases his confidence in his ability to accomplish the assignment.

14. Measures results. Why is is that we should "inspect what we expect?" Everyone knows that people check up on those things which are really important to them. We are motivated to work on tasks which are important to those above us. In addition, we work to avoid the pain of having a result measured, and being found to fall short in the results produced.

15. Gives positive reinforcement. We all have a tendency to live up to the level of performance that is expected of us. Have you noticed that when you play sports you tend to perform better or worse, depending on the level of the competition? It is important to expect high performance from your people, let them know you expect high performance, look for small successes, and provide appreciation and recognition when you observe those successes. This will build confidence in your people and cause them to expect more of themselves.

A number of years ago an experiment was performed in a high school shop classroom. All the students in the class were given an aptitude test for mechanical and shop skills. The teacher was informed that one half of the class had a high aptitude for shop, and the other half did not. At the end of the school year the students which were tested out to have a high aptitude had done well and had received high grades. The opposite was true for the other group. Actually, the students had been assigned randomly to the two groups. The teacher had treated them according to his expectations, based on the test results, and the students had responded accordingly. Repeated tests have given similar results. Motivation and performance increases with increased confidence and expectation from the superiors. How many times have you heard the statement, "You never hear from anyone around here until you mess up." This demotivational management behavior is too prevalent and is unfortunate.

16. Encourages peer comparisons. There is considerable evidence that comparing performance between peers has positive motivational effects. The book, **In Search of Excellence**, gives a number of examples to support this. A particular example was told about Dana Corporation in which a "Hell Week" was held once each year, in which all of the operations managers were brought together to report their annual performance to each other. Managers had to justify their performance to their peers, in addition to upper management. The point was made that a manager frequently can "snow" upper management but cannot fool his own peers. Peer comparisons can be either constructive or destructive, depending on how they are handled. They need to be established in such a way that everyone can win, not so that there are always winners and losers.

Peer comparisons can be subtle rather than direct. For instance, if you are having problems with tardiness or absenteeism, one procedure that has worked effectively is simply to post a bulletin board with everyone's name, listing when people are tardy or on time, and when they are present or absent. Then everyone can see who is performing well and who is not. Without saying a word, through peer embarrassment, increases in performance occur.

17. Shares fundamental beliefs. When an organization stands for something important, then the people in that organization are proud to work for that organization and to represent those values. Once they buy in to the organization's beliefs and values, they are more motivated to work productively, and to follow those values as well. The effective leadership uses many avenues of communication to share its fundamental beliefs with its people.

B. PEER MOTIVATION

Peers can motivate one another in a number of ways. The leader can encourage this peer motivation through effective observation, planning and communication.

18. Peer pressure. If an organization is able to establish an attitude of positivism and moving forward, whereby most of the people are working for the organization rather than against it, then peer pressure develops against anyone who would thwart the objectives of the organization. Also, peer pressure supports those who are working for the benefit of the organization. Peer pressure can be a powerful motivation to perform or to not perform.

19. Peer challenges. Referring to the "Hell Week" meetings of Dana Corporation mentioned in number 16, one plant manager might challenge another plant manager to improve performance by a certain percent. The second plant manager then could take up the challenge, and go back to his people to notify them that they have been challenged by another organization. If handled properly, the organization because of its espirit-de-corps will respond to the challenge, thus motivating everyone to perform more effectively. In like manner, one salesperson could challenge another, or one production department another.

There is a story about Andrew Carnegie which illustrates how leadership can influence peer challenges. Andrew Carnegie was touring a factory and asked one of the shifts how many heats of production they had produced during that shift. They said, "Seven." When the next shift came to work there was a big "seven" chalked on the floor. The workers asked, "Where did the seven come from?" The answer was, "The big boss was in and wrote the seven on the floor, that is the number of heats the prior shift produced." When the next shift came on they saw a big "nine" on the floor. "So they think they are a better shift than we are," thought the first shift. When the second shift returned there was a "ten" chalked on the floor. The "eleven" heats produced by the second shift that evening became the new production standard.

20. Being on a winning team. If all of the peers working together believe they are a "winning team," this in itself is motivational. No matter what the present level is of our own capability or productivity, if we feel that our contribution can make the difference between the team winning and the team losing we will be motivated to perform.

As an example, suppose you were in a recreational softball league, and you were not a particularly good softball player. Let's say you play right field and have a rather poor batting average. If your team is doing very poorly, and you are in last place toward the end of the season, probably you and your teammates are going to just go out and have some fun and not particularly strain yourselves. If on the other hand, your team has a chance of winning the championship, then probably you will work very hard to do your very best to help your team win. You will be motivated, despite the fact that you are a rather poor softball player. You will be motivated, regardless of your skill level, because the team has a chance of winning.

This is a very important concept in business. It is very important for a person to feel that he is on, or has a chance to be on, a winning team. We as leaders must foster this attitude.

There are four ways to cause our people to believe that they are on a winning team, and we need to accomplish them all: (1) make them feel that the total organization or company is a winner, (2) make them feel that their leader is a winner, (3) treat them like winners, and (4) cause them to be winners by assisting them in setting goals, in making plans, and in effectively carrying out those plans.

21. Helping win. Individual workers can be motivated by their peers assisting them to be winners. Everyone has areas where they are strong and areas where they are weaker. If a worker feels he is part of a team, and that his peers are helping him to be more effective, then he is motivated by his team members.

22. Feeling responsible. As a corollary to the above; when someone feels responsible for helping his peers to operate more effectively then this will motivate him to perform. Leaders can encourage this motivation by pointing out to the workers where they have special abilities, and where they can be of special help to the organization and to their peers. This can encourage in them a feeling of responsibility to assist the other members of the team.

C. SELF MOTIVATION

There are certain attributes of the people themselves, that affect their motivations. When leaders influence these positively, they help to increase the motivation of their people.

23. Feeling a winner. When people feel that they are winners and that they are competent in their jobs, or when they are optimistic about their abilities to become winners, they tend to be motivated to perform. This is one reason positive reinforcement is so important. When we comment on the small achievements of our people and indicate that we have confidence in them, this helps them to feel like winners. We can help someone who is floundering a bit in his job by assigning him a series of easier tasks, thereby allowing him to achieve a series of small victories. We then can cause him to be successful by applying the practices presented in the next chapter.

24. Standing out. Everyone desires to stand out in some way, and is motivated to do those things which will help him to be special. We can help to fulfill this desire by designing the organization and making assignments to give people the opportunity to stand out. When they do, we can point this out in some special way.

25. Controlling their destiny. Everyone desires some control over his work assignments and his total career. Whatever we can do to share that control with our employees will help to motivate them. An organization with small work groups gives people more choices of what to do, a better idea of the overall picture, and usually more decision making power. A management by objectives system, when employed, should give the employee ample say in what his objectives should be. Employees feel they have more control over their careers when they clearly understand the bases of bonuses, salary raises and promotions in the company. When people believe there is a direct relationship between their performance and rewards, they are more motivated to produce.

26. Accomplishing results. When people know they have performed well and have accomplished meaningful results, this motivates them to repeat that performance. We can assist them by adequately measuring results, recognizing good performance, and causing their effective performance as described in the next chapter.

27. Having a positive reputation. If our people have a reputation as productive performers, and they know that those about them expect winning performance, they will be motivated to perform. We can encourage a positive reputation by giving appreciation and recognition, and by publicizing the positive results of our people. We also can encourage them by saying and demonstrating that we have confidence in them.

28. Feeling needed. If our people feel that the group or team needs their performance, if they feel they make a difference in the performance of the group, then they will be motivated to perform. Everyone likes to feel needed.

29. Desiring to achieve. If they have within them an innate desire to achieve then they automatically will be motivated, especially if the parameters of achievement are clearly spelled out. This is another indication of why it is important to clearly establish the mission, the goals, a plan of action for achievement, and the resulting benefits from successful results.

30. Responding to competition. Some of our people are much more competitive than others. If our people are challenged by competition, and if by nature they respond well to that competition, then they will be motivated. This points out the importance of our knowing our people and knowing what each responds to. The person who responds to competition should be encouraged to compete. The person who is not as responsive to competition should be encouraged based on his individual motives and belief system, and less based on competition.

31. Remembering past successes. Successful performance builds confidence and motivates people to do more of the same. If we have been asked to perform a certain task, no matter how difficult, we will be more motivated if we have had a series of similar past successes. The same is true of our people. As leaders, we can assist our people by making sure they have job successes, and by reminding them of their past successes.

D. TASK OR MISSION MOTIVATION

The task, job or mission, and how it is designed, can have a major effect on the motivation of our people.

32. Provides a challenge. Tasks, jobs or projects which provide challenges to our people will motivate them to work with vigor. Those which they consider to be impossible to accomplish, boring, uninteresting, or very easy to accomplish, will not be as motivating. We need to think through jobs and assignments to make sure they do provide an appropriate challenge to our people.

Suppose for example, there is an older sales manager who is not slated for upward movement within the corporation. Suppose we would like him to undertake a new assignment which includes administering the sales programs, developing a system for measuring sales performance, and being the source of competitive information for our sales force. This assignment could be designed and presented as rather boring and unimportant. On the other hand, it could be designed to be a very important assignment which gives the manager pride in performing it, and makes a major contribution to the organization. In addition to just gathering and disseminating the information, the manager might be asked to fly around the country and provide training programs to all the sales people on how to compete effectively against competitors, using the information that has been gathered. Adding this additional aspect to the assignment could make it much more important, more challenging, and more motivational.

33. Is interesting or fun. If our people like their jobs, if they look forward to coming to work, they are going to be much more motivated to perform effectively. The opinion has been expressed that some jobs are just dull and boring, and can not be made to be interesting or fun. This seldom is the case. One way to make a job interesting and fun is to make the person who is doing it know that the job is critically important to the organization. We should make sure that every job is important, and we should design each job to be as important and as interesting as possible. Then we need to clearly inform each person as to the purpose of their job, and how the job makes a contribution to the overall effort.

Many jobs have been redesigned to make them more interesting and more fun, with positive productivity results. Some substantial progress has been made in this area in the automotive industry, where teams were formed to produce certain sections of cars, rather than having each person to do his own monotonous piece of work.

Another way to influence the enjoyment of the job is through job assignment. Some people enjoy one type of work and others enjoy another type of work. Whenever we can, we should take personal skills and interests into account in designing jobs and in making job assignments.

34. Contributes to objectives. If each job or task is designed so that it contributes to the overall objectives of the corporation, and this is clearly explained to our people, then they are going to be more motivated. Likewise, if the tasks contribute to their personal objectives, then they will be more motivated to perform.

Suppose a regional sales manager is asked to design a computerized system for the sales force. The manager could consider this to be a dull, boring assignment, which does not contribute to his objectives of becoming a marketing vice president. If on the other hand, it is explained that some knowledge of computers, plus the additional knowledge of administration he will gain through designing the system, will be very valuable in higher level marketing management positions, then he would be more motivated to approach this task with vigor.

35. Is consistent with goals and abilities. When the task is consistent both with the goals of the department and of the individual, then the person will be more motivated to accomplish it. This makes sense, because our people should not be performing work which is outside the mission of their organization, and they know that. When it fits their personality, and their abilities and skills, they they will be better at it and more motivated to do it.

36. Is inspiring. Each of our people are different and are inspired by different things. When the job or task can be matched to a person's interest and needs, then it can become inspiring in itself, and the person is motivated to accomplish it. Once we understand the personal motivations of our people, it is helpful to explain any new job or task in line with how it matches and fulfills their personal motivations and ambitions.

37. Is worthwhile. No one wants to waste his time on a job, task or project that is considered to be unimportant. It is important to explain how each project fits into the overall mission of the department or the company, and why that project is important to the accomplishment of that mission. It also is helpful to clarify what the benefits of successful accomplishment are to the organization, to the customer, and to the person being motivated.

7

GROUP PERFORMANCE

MAKING PEOPLE PRODUCTIVE
A. Job Specifications and Design
B. Job Cybernetics
C. Treating People As Partners
D. Making People Winners
E. Roles of the Team Leader
CAUSING EFFECTIVE GROUP PERFORMANCE
A. Causing Performance Through Deserving
B. Causing Performance Through Motivating
C. Causing Performance Through Managing

An elderly gentleman, in Europe many years ago, was strolling along a country road. He stopped to watch a group of stone cutters who were in the early stages of a construction project. Approaching one of the men he inquired, "What are you doing?" "I'm building a wall," muttered the man, and said nothing more. The old gentleman wandered about the site a bit and asked the same question of another worker. This one was willing to talk. He stood up straight and said, with a touch of pride, "Why I'm doing a good job of stone masonry." The old fellow later inquired about the activity of a third worker who seemed to be working very hard. When asked, the man stopped, straightened up, and as he stretched the kinks out of his back, he tilted back his head and looked up thoughtfully as if he were studying something which the visitor could not see. He said quietly, "I'm helping to build a great cathedral."

Which one of these three workers represents the attitude which will best help your organization be a business leader? How can we manage and lead our people to be happy, productive workers like the third man? That is the subject of this chapter.

Building on the principles of motivational leadership discussed in chapter 6, we now deal with some concepts and practices which encourage and even cause our people to be motivated and productive. The first groups are discussed under the heading: **Making People Productive.** The second are thirty two practices for **Causing Effective Group Performance.**

MAKING PEOPLE PRODUCTIVE

This section presents five sets of principles which when employed will make our people more productive: (a) designing and staffing the jobs in the organization, (b) job cybernetics, or managing those jobs, (c) treating the people in those jobs as you would your partners, and (d) working with them to help them be winners. Section (e) presents the roles the manager fills when he operates not just as an administrator, but as a leader.

A. JOB SPECIFICATIONS AND DESIGN

It is important to find the right people and to place them in the right jobs. The following discusses how to do this.

1. Job design. Make every effort to design every job so it will make an obvious and productive contribution to the organization. The person who enjoys coming to work and receives self-fulfillment from the job is going to be more productive, and more willing to be concerned about the needs of his personal and commercial customers. All jobs, especially at the lower levels, should be designed so that the tasks are interesting, varied, and involve some challenge, learning and responsibility. Most jobs at upper levels already do.

The IBM company has been very successful in designing lower level jobs to generate high productivity. It follows three rules: 1. engineer the individual operations to be as simple as possible, 2. train each worker to perform as many operations as possible, and 3. design each job so as to require some skill or judgement, so as to make that job interesting. IBM also has been successful in involving their individual employees in redesigning their own jobs for increased productivity. IBM's no-lay-off policy helps to encourage their people to want to do this.

2. Job description. Prepare a written job description for each job, including the key purpose for the job, the specific key responsibilities, and the results desired.

3. People specifications. Determine the personal qualifications and characteristics of the people you want to work for the company generally, and those that are needed for any job specifically. These include personal characteristics, such as a positive attitude, agreeableness, and work-orientation. They also include personal characteristics, job skills and experience, which are specific to the jobs. As just a few examples, some jobs require enthusiasm and persistence; some considerable attention to detail; some listening and interviewing skills; some a facility with numbers; some a competitive spirit; some the ability to deal with ambiguity, etc. One way of developing people specifications for a job is to interview people who have been successful in the job, and determine what contributed to their success.

4. Hiring. Effective hiring is perhaps the most important practice in achieving an effective operation. It usually is easier to find the right person for the job than it is to motivate and train the wrong person.

5. Job placement. Place people in jobs in which they are interested, and where they have the strengths to be productive. Match people, both in-house and new hires, with the people specifications in 3 above.

6. Job orientation. An effective job orientation is important, not only to help the new employee to be effective, but to affect his attitude positively. Most companies we have observed do not have effective job orientations either when people first join the company or when they enter a new position.

7. Performance standards. Establish specific standards of performance for each job. Two people in the same type of job would have the same job description, but would have different performance standards for two reasons. First, the conditions of the job will be different. For instance, a sales manager in a large eastern city would operate differently from one in a western rural area. Second, people have different skills and experience. We can expect more from some people than from others in the same type of job.

8. Training. While general training and education is valuable, the specific needs of each person on each job should be defined, and training should be specified based on those needs. In IBM, for example, each employee has his own individual developmental plan which is updated on a regular basis.

9. Management vision. Share the vision of management with the employees, in such a way that they will "buy in" and get excited about their job performance and its contribution to the corporate vision.

10. Resource allocation. Communicate to the employees that the organization's resources are being allocated fairly and intelligently. Show each employee that his work is being supported; and that he is being fairly rewarded. Many employees do not understand the economics of business, and feel they and their departments are being slighted, when in fact this is not the case.

11. Communications. Keep the employees informed, and tend toward over-communications rather than under-communications.

12. Change. People resist change, especially when they see it as a threat to their job security. Some invest many years to become comfortable in their jobs as they presently exist. Consequently, all changes should be communicated clearly, with every possible benefit both to the company and to the employee being clearly explained. All employees need to understand how the change will affect them, and how to successfully adjust to those changes.

13. Productive Workers. Management usually seeks to improve the productivity of the less productive worker and leave the more productive alone. In many cases, substantially more benefit and increase in overall productivity can be achieved by reversing this, and concentrating on increasing even further the effectiveness and performance of the more productive employees. There are three reasons for this. First, the overall performance of an organization tends to adjust itself to the level of performance of the most productive workers. Second, the same percentage increase in performance of highly productive workers generates a larger increment of performance improvement. Third, it is the more effective performers who are more likely to discover the breakthrough, which can mean a large performance improvement for everyone.

B. JOB CYBERNETICS

A cybernetic system is one which achieves performance through providing controls and feedback. Managers and leaders should encourage systems to help all of the employees perform their jobs more effectively. The following cybernetic system will help to accomplish this objective.

1. Set objectives. Based on the job description and the job performance standards, each employee tentatively sets his own objectives for a period of time. He then reviews those objectives with his superior for input, adjustment, and approval.

2. Plans. The employee develops plans for accomplishing his objectives, and reviews them with his superior.

3. Results. The employee takes actions to carry out the plans on a timely basis.

4. Performance measurement. Performance is measured through a control system which feeds back measurements of the results both to the employee and to the superior.

5. Performance evaluation. Both the employee and the superior evaluate the results against objectives and then discuss the results and the differences.

6. Feedback from the superior. As results are accomplished the superior provides recognition and rewards. If the results are not being accomplished, the superior provides encouragement and guidance. Perhaps the plan is revised; perhaps training or closer supervision is provided.

7. Publicity. If results are positive, the results are made known to others, to provide recognition to the employee and to show the type of performance that is desired of others.

8. Revisions. As appropriate, new or revised objectives are established and new plans are developed.

The cybernetic system provides a system of self management for each employee which is monitored by the superior. In effect, each employee is his own quality controller. This system has worked well in Japan and in many successful American companies. Results are measured because, "What get's measured gets done." Reasonable pressure is applied for performance. Rewards are provided for results, not for efforts. Unsuccessful effort is rewarded with the right to try again in a positive and supportive environment.

C. TREATING PEOPLE AS PARTNERS

Both upper management, and immediate superiors have a significant influence on people and how they feel about themselves. There is considerable evidence that people respond to and tend to become like that which is expected of them. If we treat our people as partners, and expect them to behave as if they were a partner in the business, they will have a tendency to become that way - an effective, productive manager or worker. We are all familiar with the story of Pigmaleon, which was introduced on Broadway as the play, *My Fair Lady*. The unschooled char girl was treated like a lady and eventually acted as, and in effect "became," a lady.

How would we treat a partner? We certainly would expect a high level of performance. We would assist him in any way we could to help him achieve success. We also would treat him with respect and friendliness. The following are some specific ways we can effectively treat our employees as partners:

1. Positive attitude. Be genuinely interested in them and helpful in a friendly way.

2. Positive expectations. Expect a high level of performance, and work with them through a cybernetic system to generate performance and the resulting, deserved recognition.

3. Individually important. Treat each person as an individual, personally important to the company. Treat each as an individual, not as a cog in a machine. Take into account his or her individual interests, abilities, goals and concerns. Look for problems, and solutions to problems, which are specific to employees and classes of employees. Examples would include pre-menstral stress for selected women, and customer contact stress for those employees who are in continual customer contact.

4. Support. Give each person enough information, support, and authority to get the job done.

5. Training. Make available whatever training is necessary to improve specific skills and to accomplish the tasks at hand. In addition, consider instituting a policy of continuous learning. In such a system every employee is continuously educated and trained in a number of areas so they continue to grow and become more knowledgeable, mature and effective. Education and training is provided, based on an individual developmental plan. It includes overall company policies and objectives, personal performance and time management, technical skills needed to perform present jobs more effectively, and general education to prepare them for promotions and increased responsibility. This policy of continuous learning is employed successfully at IBM and is a policy of many successful Japanese companies.

6. Idea sources. See each person as a potential source of ideas. Have an open door policy, and be willing to talk to workers about anything that is important. IBM has effectively employed this policy. A factory worker once visited the president, Mr. Tom Watson, Jr., in his office. As a result, the entire corporate policy concerning the reward system for employees was modified. This particular employee was producing more than any other employee at his plant but was not being justly rewarded because he was a non-conformist. The old policy was changed. The new one resulted in increased corporate productivity.

7. Delegation. Delegate to each person those duties and responsibilities which will help him grow and which he is capable of accomplishing. This will help the superior as well, thereby releaving the superior of certain time-consuming duties, and allowing him to use his time on even more important matters.

8. Paperwork. Keep paperwork to a minimum, especially detailed task-oriented reports.

9. Job security. Do whatever you can to remove job insecurity. IBM in the late 1930's established a no-lay-off policy. This gave employees extreme job security and allowed them the freedom to make considerable productivity increases without the risk of losing their jobs. The matter of job security is very important when considering programs for increasing productivity. In a recent analysis, one division of the McDonnell Douglas Corporation concluded that to achieve anything close to maximum productivity a no-lay-off policy is required.

10. Creative work policies. Consider new types of work policies which can help the employee and the company. Some of these might include permanent part time employment, flexible work hours, work at home, partial retirement, productivity teams, and innovative benefit packages.

D. MAKING PEOPLE WINNERS

Everyone wants to be on a winning team. Everyone will work harder if they realizes that their team can win, and that they have the ability to influence the success of their team. Most of the practices discussed so far will make a contribution to helping the employee become a winning team member. Some more specific practices are discussed in this and later sections.

The most successful organizations have a knack for inspiring and requiring extraordinary effort and performance from ordinary people. Marva Collins is a school teacher who runs a private school in a low income area of Chicago. She has developed a teaching system which inspires extraordinary effort and accomplishment from low income students, who in normal circumstances would be totally disinterested and very unsuccessful academically. How do she and her teachers do it? The following paragraph gives a few hints. (Rewritten from the book, **Marva Collins' Way**.)

"A new and unkempt child enters the classroom for the first time; the teacher smiles, looks her in the eye, and says, "I'll bet you are going to be our smartest student." She cleans her up and treats her like someone important. The teacher enthusiastically presents the teaching material and shows to the students she is excited about this material. She explains to her students the benefits of learning; that by learning they can get better jobs and live a better life. She places a heavy work load on them and expects them to perform it. She gets excited and cheers whenever they are successful, which is often. She works with them on an individual basis when they are having trouble, and makes sure they are successful. As a result, almost all the students are excited about studying and learning, and are reaching high levels of academic achievement."

Like Marva Collins, we can lead our people to high levels of performance. The following are some ways to help our people be winners:

1. Provide a winning organization. Be proud of your organization (the company, the bank, the institution) and let your people know this. Present your organization in a positive manner, and help your people be proud of it too.

2. Be a winning leader. People are inspired when they work under a leader who is knowledgeable, is performing effectively, and is held in high esteem by his superiors and peers. Perform your own work successfully, and carry yourself as a winner.

3. New systems. Only start new employee-related programs and systems you plan to support and make work. Continually starting, not supporting, and then dropping programs, causes employees to lose morale and confidence.

4. Be an enabler. The job of each supervisor and each manager of people at any level is to enable his people to perform their jobs effectively. Therefore, be an enabler - an assistant, a resource, a teacher, a coach.

5. Be a people developer. A good manager and leader is not so much a producer of results as he is a producer of people who produce results.

6. Encourage action. The only person who does not make mistakes is the person who does nothing. Be tolerant of mistakes, but develop systems to prevent big mistakes which are business-shattering.

7. Encourage effectiveness. Encourage your people to do the right things more than to do things right, as important as that is. Said differently, what we do is even more important than how we do it.

8. Give rewards. Reward what you expect your employees to do. Make the rewards meaningful in type, amount and the way they are given. People respond to the way they are rewarded.

9. Have a service orientation. Guide and direct your people to be service oriented and provide effective service to both personal and commercial customers. This is the ultimate way to make everyone a winner.

10. Anticipate challenges. Be an anticipatory leader, and coach your people to be anticipatory performers. On a regular basis ask yourself, "What possibly could go wrong, and how might we prevent it?" Examples of "things that could go wrong," are: quality dropping below an acceptable level, employees forgetting to seek out customer needs and problems, an important customer feeling ignored or insulted, losing a major customer to a competitor, a top-performing employee quitting, or a series of sales opportunities being missed. You might meet regularly with your people and/or with a group of peers to answer the question, "What could go wrong and how might we prevent it?"

11. Cause effective performance. Use the principles and practices in the next major section to cause your people to be winners.

E. ROLES OF THE TEAM LEADER

Figure 7-1 on the following page presents a checklist of many of the roles you have as an effective leader. These roles are divided into six areas of responsibility.

This list can be valuable both in checking your own performance, and in checking that of your people, to identify any areas where you or they may be deficient in making people productive.

CAUSING EFFECTIVE GROUP PERFORMANCE

We wrap up this chapter on group performance by discussing in this section thirty two special practices of effective leadership, divided into three categories: (a) causing performance through deserving, (b) causing performance through motivating, and (c) causing performance through managing.

It is my opinion, as a business leader, as a business consultant, and as a student of the most successful corporations in the world, that through effectively employing these practices you essentially can guarantee that you will achieve effective performance from your people. You will cause them to be effective.

A. CAUSING PERFORMANCE THROUGH DESERVING

As you reflect on the practices discussed in this section you will see that many of them will be truly effective only if your people trust and respect you. This trust and respect must be earned. It must be deserved. The following six items discuss how you go about deserving the right to leadership and causing your people to perform effectively.

1. Earn extreme respect. Handle yourself in such a way that your subordinates, in addition to your peers and superiors, respect you so much that they will be ashamed to not perform well for you.

If you were once a young person on a sports team your team probably had a coach. If your coach "really knew his business," was interested in you as a person, really cared for you and your performance as well as the team performance, gave you effective training, hurt when you hurt and was happy when you were happy, then you probably worked very hard to please him, and were ashamed to do less than your best for him. On the other hand, if you had a coach who was a slave driver and who you did not

Figure 7-1

ROLES OF THE TEAM LEADER

AND EFFECTIVE TEAM MEMBER
IN ENCOURAGING GROUP PERFORMANCE

L — LISTENER & COMMUNICATOR
- ACTIVE LISTENER
- EFFECTIVE COMMUNICATOR
- COOPERATOR
- EMPATHIZER
- FEEDBACK EXCHANGER
- INFORMATION SHARER
- QUESTIONER
- RESPONDER

E — EFFECTIVE MANAGER & DEVELOPER
- COACH
- COORDINATOR
- COUNSELOR
- DELEGATOR
- DEMONSTRATOR
- EVALUATOR
- FOLLOW-UPPER
- GROWER
- HELPER
- INTERVIEWER
- SERVER
- SHOWER
- STRENGTH BUILDER
- TEACHER
- TIME-RESPECTER
- TIME-SUPPLIER

A — ADVANCE PLANNER & ORGANIZER
- GOAL SETTER
- HOMEWORKER
- MISSION DEVELOPER
- ORGANIZER
- PLANNER
- PREPARER
- PROGRAM IMPLEMENTOR
- RECORDER
- RECORD KEEPER

D — DYNAMIC PERSONALITY
- BELIEVER
- COMPETENT ONE
- COOPERATOR
- ENTHUSIASM FINDER
- EXAMPLE SETTER
- FUN ENCOURAGER
- INNOVATOR
- FAIR PERSON
- SMILER

E — ENTHUSIASTIC MOTIVATOR
- APPRECIATION GIVER
- ATTENTION GIVER
- BELIEVER IN
- BUILDER
- BENEFIT PROVIDER
- BRAGGER ON
- CELEBRATOR
- CHEERLEADER
- CONFIDENCE BUILDER
- CREDIT SHARER
- ENERGY SUPPLIER
- ENCOURAGER
- EGO BUILDER
- ENTHUSIASM GENERATOR
- FRIEND
- INSPIRER
- INTEREST SHOWER
- IMPORTANCE BUILDER
- MORALE BUILDER
- MOTIVATOR
- NAME USER
- NEED SUPPLIER
- OPINION RESPECTER
- PRIDE BUILDER
- SPIRIT LIFTER
- SUPPORTER
- SYMPATHIZER
- RESPECTER
- TOLERATOR
- TRUST DESERVER
- UNDERSTANDER

R — RESULTS & EFFECTIVENESS GENERATOR
- ACHIEVER
- CONCENTRATOR
- DECISION MAKER
- FOCUSER
- IDEA SEEKER
- IMPLEMENTOR
- MEETING LEADER
- NON-ABDICATOR
- PRIORITY SETTER
- PROBLEM SOLVER
- PUSHER/PRODDER
- SELF DISCIPLINER
- SELF MANAGER
- TIME MANAGER

like as a person, you may have worked hard to prevent being penalized, but not out of love or even respect. In addition, if you lacked respect for him because you felt he did not know his job; or because he did not train you well; then you felt less badly when your performance was less than excellent. You had a tendency, correctly or incorrectly, to blame him in part. Perform like the first coach to earn extreme respect from your people.

We all admire and want to follow someone who has the ability and willingness to make decisions. Be a decision maker and gain the confidence of your people.

2. Be trustworthy, competent, concerned. Your people respect someone they can trust, who is honest and "tells it like it is." They respect someone who is competent, who has earned the right to lead by performing effectively themselves. They also respect someone who is concerned about them and their welfare. They not only like him but respect him. People are concerned about producing for someone who is concerned about them.

3. Set the example through your performance. "Who you are and what you do speaks so loud, I cannot hear what you say." This statement is a reminder to, "practice what we preach." If we practice effective behavior, it is easier to persuade others to use that behavior. Also, subordinates tend to model our behavior. For instance, if we use good human relations practices and good consultant-coaching techniques while working with them, they will tend to use these with customers and with fellow employees.

4. Set the example through your attitude. The leader's attitude has a profound influence upon the attitudes of his people as well as their respect for him. The leader will generate trust, respect and a positive attitude toward himself, the company and its programs by demonstrating his support and enthusiasm for the company and its programs. He does this through his body language, his words and his actions.

5. Set the example by continuing to grow yourself. By continuing to study new materials, and keeping up with modern trends and methods, the leader inspires his people to do likewise. He also earns their respect by demonstrating that he is keeping up with the latest technology.

6. Generate confidence by making take-charge decisions. We all admire and want to follow someone who has the ability and willingness to make decisions. Be a decision maker and gain the confidence of your people.

B. CAUSING PERFORMANCE THROUGH MOTIVATING

Having deserved the trust and respect of your people you then can motivate them to effective performance through the following twelve leadership practices, keeping in mind the "beliefs in" and the "beliefs that" discussed in chapter 6.

7. Treat them like adults. The book, **In Search of Excellence,** presents a poem which made the rounds of a major automobile company. The point of the poem was, "You treat us like children, so why do you expect us to perform like adults?" This is a very important question. We need to ask and answer two questions. Have we not performed more effectively when we were treated like adults? And, how do we treat people as adults?

We show adults trust and respect. We treat them like we would partners in the company. We keep them well informed as what is going on; the objectives of the company, how their jobs fit into those objectives, and specifically what is expected of them in performance. We give them enough information and authority to get their jobs done, and without heavy supervision (unless required - as for new, inexperienced people). We explain company policies, and the reasoning behind the policies. We encourage them to take action and make decisions on their own in areas where they are qualified. We tolerate a reasonable amount of failure, and celebrate victory when it occurs. We provide training and coaching because we have given them responsibilities important enough to be of real concern. We avoid nonsense and time-consuming and unnecessary paperwork. This is how we treat our people as adults.

8. Treat individuals as personally important. Treat each of your people as individuals who are personally important. Include them in meetings concerning their areas of responsibility. Find time to meet with them specifically and exclusively. Discuss with them their jobs, their careers, and their home and family. Find ample time for face-to-face contact with those who report directly to you. Find some time to talk directly to those two levels below you. The top officers in many of the most successful companies spend a large amount of time each year in direct meetings with front line employees, sharing information first hand both ways. Most also spend some time walking through the work areas, talking to first and second level people informally, listening and observing.

9. Plan for winners. Plan for your people to be winners through properly designed systems; by celebrating winning with plenty of excitement; and by giving plenty of positive reinforcement. Ask yourself whether you are providing sufficient support in all areas to assure the successful performance of all competent subordinates.

10. Make positive reinforcement specific, immediate, based on achievable objectives, sometimes from top management, and unpredictable and intermittent. Make positive reinforcement specific so the employee knows exactly what was done well and what type performance will be rewarded in the future. Make it immediate, or as close to the time of performance as possible, so it is clear what was performed well. There is the story of the corporation president who when confronted with a task well done, had no reward to offer the employee. He pulled an uneaten banana from his desk and presented it to the employee so the reward would be immediate. The story became legend in the company, and later the "golden banana" award for performance was established. Positive reinforcement should be given only when deserved, or it will lose its meaning. Positive reinforcement should be available from top management for special efforts and results. This is especially motivating. Why should positive reinforcement be unpredictable and intermittent? If it is predictable and regular it becomes expected, and the failure to receive it regularly becomes demotivational. When it is intermittent, then it comes as a pleasant, motivating surprise.

11. Give meaning with company values. "One of the impressive accomplishments of the winning organizations is their ability to sustain a sense of mission and shared values over time." This quote from, **The Winning Performance - How America's High Growth Midsize Companies Succeed**, shows the importance of having meaning and company values, and sharing them with employees. Most successful large businesses have a "way of doing business," which is known by all employees and guides business performance. These values are shared by written creeds, by visits from top officers, and by employing these values as a basis for written objectives. "IBM means service," is clear and inspiring, as one example. Another IBM value would be, "At IBM people are important." Most companies say this, but many do not mean it and live by it. Only when you do, consistently and continually, does it become a "value."

12. Provide peer evaluation. In chapter 6 we discussed the value of peer evaluation and the generation of peer comparisons. A client of ours, a bank holding company, was attempting to encourage creative and innovative thinking, and a more results-oriented management style by each of its branch bank presidents. Following our analysis, it was decided to include in the regular presidents' meetings peer reviews of the performance of the branches. The report of each bank president was subjected to peer questioning, discussion and suggestions. The results appeared to be positive. The first presentation session did not result in as intensive questioning and discussion as we would have liked. But, new approaches already are being tried. The meeting appeared to generate more thorough analyses of banking results, sharing of ideas between banks, and more motivation within the banks in an effort to do well as compared to other banks.

13. Know strengths and limitations. Each of your people are different. They have different areas of specialization, different backgrounds, different abilities and different interests. Job assignments, job objectives, and performance standards should take these differences into account. This will increase the chances of each person being successful and making the greatest contribution. Those with great strengths in certain areas often need considerable support in other areas. For example, many high-powered sales representatives are very poor in administration. Many of these people should never be promoted to sales manager, but should be rewarded and recognized as senior sales specialists. Others, who are promoted, should be backed up with effective sales administration support.

14. Enthusiastically remind of personal objectives. Each of your people has his own personal objectives, which are distinct from his department or business objectives. For one person the objective may be a specific promotion or new job assignment. For another it may be to win a specific bonus so she can take a vacation. For a third it may be to become president of a civic club. If you can show each of your people how, by effective performance on the job, they will come closer to their personal objectives, they will be even more motivated to perform.

15. Provide a positive environment. This is one more way of saying; treat your people as if they are competent and important; treat your and their jobs as they they can be accomplished; and treat your daily tasks as if you enjoy working on them and for this wonderful company. This will set a good example for your people.

16. Tell motivational stories. Share with your people morale-building stories about the earlier days of the company, some of its superior performers, and others who were in similar positions to theirs and who have been successful within the industry. Stories about the founder or some of the key heroes of the company give rise to pride and ownership of the company. Likewise, stories of people in similar positions, who have been successful in this company or in another, give people hope and encouragement that by working hard and smart they can accomplish similar levels of achievement and reward.

17. Give them a positive reputation. When you were a child, if your father had bragged on you to his friends, as to what a good boy or girl you were or how well you played ball, what effect would that have had on your behavior? If you were in normal circumstances you would have broken your neck to show everyone that your father was right. The same psychology can be effective in business. In fact, it is just good common sense. If you will give your people a positive reputation to live up to; if you will look for what they do good; if you will tell them, their peers and other superiors what your people do good and that you believe in them; they will believe in themselves and respond accordingly. If you are sincere, your people will be highly motivated to prove you right.

18. Remind them they don't have to be super-human. Even

though you are requesting your people to produce at a very high level of performance, you need to make clear to them that you are not expecting something that is impossible, and that you don't expect them to be super human. If they fail along the way after an honest effort you might remind them that you too have failed, and that failure sometimes is the result of trying. You need to pick them up, dust them off, provide whatever resources and help that are needed, and give them solid encouragement to move ahead and succeed.

C. CAUSING PERFORMANCE THROUGH MANAGING

The following are management practices which you as a leader should employ to help - to enable - to assist - to make - to cause your people to be effective, productive and successful. By combining these fourteen practices with the previous eighteen, and operating with the Cross-Marketing™ leadership style described throughout this book, you essentially can guarantee successful performance by your people.

19. Know the skill level of your people. It is important that you know the capabilities and skill levels of your people, so you can properly utilize them and their talents. You should not promote them over their heads, or give them more responsibility than they are capable of handling. This would cause them to fail and would reduce their self confidence and their future performance. On the other hand, if you hold them back and do not utilize their talents fully, then they will tend to become bored and disenchanted. They will feel that they are being under-utilized, and that they could go to another department or another company and achieve more in the areas of status, position and remuneration.

When I was president of another corporation, I needed a high level manager to relieve me of some responsibilities. In my anxiousness to find someone for this position I promoted someone above his present experience and skill level. This was destructive both to him and to the company. He was not able to perform at the level required, and later had to be demoted. Had I been more aware of his skill level I would have made another decision. As a result of my error, the company lost a good man and quite a bit of money as well. Alternately, when I was a manager in two large corporations, I observed a number of outstanding personnel being under-utilized, in spite of the fact that the companies needed people with their capabilities. In every case that I can remember, the person that was under-utilized became demotivated and less effective, or left the company.

20. Become friend and counselor. As a manager and leader you cannot afford to become so friendly, so close to your employees, that it really impairs your judgement and prevents you from making hard-nosed business decisions. On the other hand, if you become very good business friends with your people, and gain their confidence, they will feel free to come to you as a business counselor when they have a problem. You then can engender their loyalty, and assist them to be more effective.

Most leaders are not as effective as they could be in the role of coach and counselor. One reason is that they do not have confidence in their own counseling skills. Another is that frequently they feel that the other person knows the job even better than they do. Both of these reasons cause them to lack self confidence. The optimum leadership situation exists when the leader knows both the person and the job very well, understands what is required to perform the job, and what the subordinate needs in training and guidance to perform the job effectively. He then can provide that light touch of guidance; showing how when needed, answering questions when they need to be answered, and keeping his mouth shut when they don't need to be answered.

21. Treat fairly and without favoritism. Favoritism is one of the most destructive practices of poor management. It is absolutely imperative that you manage everyone in your group in an objective, fair and evenhanded manner. You cannot afford to give favored treatment to anyone, no matter how well you know or like that person. This does not mean you must administer exactly the same discipline for the same infraction. One person may have a very fine record and may have slipped up just once, and another person may have a poor record with frequent infractions. However, if you are using the practices in this section you seldom should allow any situation to deteriorate to the point where one of your people has "a poor record with frequent infractions."

22. Do not mollycoddle; set standards and help them as needed. You should work with each of your people to establish performance standards based on the job situation and requirements, and the capabilities of the people involved. You should work with your people in establishing these standards of performance; and the standards should be set fairly, but so they stretch your people somewhat. You then should expect your people to meet the performance standards, with you providing help, training and guidance as needed.

A sales manager for a client company was meeting his sales budget, but was letting significant pieces of business slip away from the company. This was because the sales staff was not adequately covering the field. Also, while some of the sales force was outstanding in skills and performance, others were significantly lacking in certain very important sales skills. The sales manager was not totally at fault. He had come up through the ranks, and had never been trained to write job descriptions and establish performance standards. Once job descriptions were written, and standards of performance were established for him and his people in the areas of industry penetration and employee training, he managed these areas very well.

23. Set major objectives and follow-up. One of the most important practices of leadership in causing effective performance is working with people to establish effective goals and objectives, with timetables. There should only be a few objectives, and these should be in major areas of contribution. They should meet the criteria discussed in chapter 4. You do not want to nitpick your people, and be on their backs constantly asking about job progress. What you do want to do is to establish periodic checkpoints, at which you will meet with them, discuss their progress against goals, and if necessary, revise the action plans to effectively meet those goals.

When I was a plant manager, I required each of my department managers to evaluate their own situations and to recommend no more than three major goals to be accomplished at any one time. They also had to provide justifications for each of the goals. I then would review the proposed goals and ask questions. Generally they would be approved. What this accomplished was to cause each of my managers to think through their jobs, and what they needed to accomplish to make the most contribution with the limited resources they had available. When one of these department heads was promoted to plant manager he told me that this procedure was one of the most valuable that he had ever encountered. He instituted it in his own plant.

24. Cultivate the flowers and weed out the weeds. Flowers, if cultivated and fertilized, can become beautiful and make a major contribution to the landscape. If we don't cultivate and fertilize them, we won't get good results. However, no matter what we do with the flowers if we let the weeds run rampant they will strangle the flowers and cause havoc with the landscape or the crop. The same is true with people in a company.

You need to identify your best people and train and guide them to a high level of performance. You likewise need to identify those people who are trouble makers, and those who will never produce for you, and remove them from the organization as quickly as possible. As hard-hearted as this may sound, it is best for the organization and probably is best for the person.

Most of us are familiar with at least one extremely capable, but complaining and disruptive employee. Such a person performs his job rather well, but usually far more than compensates for that through the reduction in performance and dissatisfaction he causes in the people around him.

25. Keep your cool. One time early in my career, as a plant superintendent I once purposely became angry with an employee and flew off the handle with good results. However, I can site numerous other times that supervisors lost their cool with poor results. I learned over a period of time to keep my cool especially in business situations. A hot head, no matter how intelligent, loses respect from those around him. The calm, cool personality maintains respect. In addition, he maintains a level head to make wise decisions.

26. Listen and respond. Effective listening is one of the most powerful skills of any leader, and in fact of any person. When we listen to someone else we show them respect. Another advantage of listening is that we frequently learn something. It is important that you show your people the respect of listening to them thoroughly and responding to them with meaningful answers. This includes making sure that they have their questions answered, and that you understand their problems and their ideas.

One very important listening tool is to ask clarifying questions. For instance, suppose a bank employee says, "I just can't sell the new CD program." Instead of talking, or giving opinions, you might ask questions such as, "What about the program seems to be giving you difficulty?" Or you might ask, "Do you believe in the program? Would you purchase it if it were offered to you?" Their answers to these questions clarify their thoughts and give you the information to help them.

27. Communicate and get feedback. Communications in most organizations is not what it should be. If you communicate effectively to your people it will both motivate them and give them the information to perform their jobs effectively. The effective leader makes sure that his communications, what he says and writes to others, is clearly stated and clearly understood. He follows the rules of effective communications, which of course are too comprehensive to cover here. He conveys to his people everything they need to know, and in a language they understand.

One specific way to improve communications effectiveness is to ask for feedback. Not only can you ask your people if you have made yourself clear, but you can ask them to repeat in their own words their understanding of what they heard you say.

28. Criticize constructively. When your people are performing ineffectively or improperly it is your responsibility to observe this and to take action, once you determine that the situation is not self-correcting. Criticism can be offered directly or through asking questions to allow the other person to discover the mistake and the solution. In either case, your manner should be open and friendly, but businesslike. The other person should know you are serious and not kidding around.

It is wise to refrain from criticism until you have gathered enough information to be able to recommend potential solutions. Refrain from offering criticism just to get something off your chest. Constructive criticism is effective feedback to your people, showing where they are off course and what might be done to get back on course. Destructive criticism lowers both morale and long term performance.

29. Don't nit-pick; concentrate on the important. None of us cares to be a rooster-pecked wife or a hen-pecked husband. Likewise, we do not enjoy having our boss breathing down our necks checking every action we take. We want some room to make decisions and to act. As an effective leader you will want to concentrate on the essentials and encourage your people to do the same. When you give them an assignment to perform, you will make sure that they have agreed with you on how it should be accomplished and what the time frame should be for checking the progress. Then you will leave them alone to perform the assignment, perhaps observing their performance from a distance. You will provide for them training and help as needed. Hopefully, the need for any training and help can be established early in the task assignment.

30. Take the time to teach, train and coach. Employees can be divided into three categories: exceptional performers, competent performers, and new and not-so-competent performers. For the exceptional performers you generally can make assignments, and then get out of the way and let them perform. You should establish regular performance review meetings, but these probably would be at infrequent intervals. With competent performers, you should assign a task, and develop with them the goals and plans for accomplishing that task, including any training and guidance which would be needed. You then should establish reasonable timetables for performance reviews and task completion. Then you should stay out of their way except when they need help, to allow them time and space to successfully complete the task. Any training and coaching which would be needed would result from the regular review meetings.

You will want to watch the newer and not-so-competent performers more closely. You probably will be much more deeply involved with them, both in establishing their goals and the plans to accomplish those goals. They probably will require some training, and more frequent review meetings, along with some assistance from you in accomplishing their assignments. Still, you should attempt to give them as much breathing room as possible, and find areas where they are competent and where you can stay out of their way and let them perform.

Having said all of this, most managers and leaders are quite deficient in their abilities and dedication to teaching, training and coaching. As a part of the regular review meetings with their people, leaders need to determine the areas where they need training, and the areas where they need to improve their performance, and then work with them to provide needed training and guidance. When they do perform effectively, employees should be amply recognized and rewarded.

31. Provide specific training. We should work with each of our people to determine what specific areas of training and education would be most beneficial to them in increasing their immediate and long term performance. The key word here is specific. General education and training can be valuable and developmental. But specific education and training, addressed to the specific needs of a particular person with a particular assignment, can yield substantial specific results, both short term and long term.

For example, suppose one of the important responsibilities of your people is to serve as consultants and advisors to both customers and business associates. Suppose they do not yet have the education and knowledge to adequately perform as consultants. As a result, both their self confidence and their performance would be below the level desired. Let's assume that through an analysis of potential customer contacts the most frequent and most important questions and problems, which will confront them, have been determined. Then, specific education and training can be provided to them, along with backup support tools, to prepare them to effectively handle the most important and most frequently occurring questions and problems. For the time being, when other questions and problems arise, which they are not yet prepared to handle, they can check with an assigned "expert," and get back to the person who asked the questions, with the answers obtained.

32. Show them how. In many areas of leadership, especially at lower levels, it is important to show people how to perform effectively rather than just telling them how. This is especially true for tasks which require specific skill application. We can learn from observing a baseball pitching coach. The effective coach observes the performance of a pitcher, notices in what area the pitching style could be improved, and then demonstrates how this can effectively be accomplished. The pitcher who is being coached can then see exactly how to hold and release the ball. This same procedure of demonstrating skill application should be followed in many business situations.

For example, in training someone to make effective telephone appointments, you could first explain the fundamentals of making telephone contacts. You then could get on the telephone and demonstrate to him how to obtain appointments. Then the person being coached could make some phone calls, first alone for practice, and then with you in observation. You could then make suggestions, have him try your suggestions, and then again demonstrate to him the proper procedure.

There are three reasons managers and supervisors fail to "show how" rather than "tell how." First, it can be hard work. Second, they have to know how to show how. Third, they may not have the confidence in their own skills or their ability to coach. The manager who overcomes these blocks and coaches his people will be making a significant contribution to causing their effective performance.

8

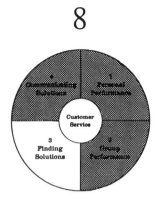

FINDING SOLUTIONS TO CUSTOMER PROBLEMS

CUSTOMER PROBLEMS AND NEEDS REQUIRING SOLUTIONS AND BENEFITS
RESOURCES AND STRENGTHS FOR PROVIDING SOLUTIONS AND BENEFITS
FINDING SOLUTIONS TO CUSTOMER PROBLEMS AND NEEDS
PERSONAL SERVICES ALL CUSTOMERS DESIRE
A. Make Customers Feel Heard
B. Make Customers Feel Understood
C. Make Customers Feel Liked
D. Make Customers Feel Respected
E. Make Customers Feel Appreciated and Remembered
F. Make Customers Feel Helped

In chapters 2 and 3 we discussed the importance of everyone in the organization identifying and effectively serving their customers.

Who are your customers? You know who the customers are of your company. They are the corporations, organizations and people who receive products and services from your company and who write checks to your company to pay for those services. They are *commercial customers*, and they are extremely important to you and to your company. They should receive the highest consideration and service .

But who are your customers, those who directly consume the results of your work? Many of us never meet the commercial customer face to face.

144

We all deliver valuable products and services from our jobs (at least we should if we plan to stay employed); but for many of us these are never directly used by the commercial customer. Who then are our *personal customers?* As we discussed in chapter 2, our personal customers are those persons and departments within or outside our organization, who make use of the products and services we provide as an output from our jobs. These people and organizations deserve the same consideration and the same service that an outside commercial customer deserves. This is a new concept to many of us. If we will grasp and utilize it, we will be performing a major service in assisting our organization to become the outstanding (Cross-Marketing) organization it can become.

For those of us who are in jobs as corporation presidents, market managers, salespeople, front desk people, bank tellers, or the like, our single most important customer category very likely is the "commercial customer." It is he who purchases, utilizes and pays us for the products and services we provide. However, even in these positions, there are personal customers within the company whom we serve.

In this chapter we discuss the three steps to *finding solutions* to customer problems (the problems of both commercial customers and personal customers). Once we identify the problems and find their solutions, we then must communicate those solutions to the customer in a convincing, and sometimes persuasive, manner. That is the subject of chapters 9 and 10.

CUSTOMER PROBLEMS AND NEEDS
REQUIRING SOLUTIONS AND BENEFITS
(STEP 1 OF 3)

The first step in solving customer problems is to identify what are the problems, needs and opportunities facing the customer. Figure 8-1 illustrates one way to categorize our personal and commercial customers, and then start looking for the problems and needs of each. We will discuss that table, after some intervening comments. (Note: items 1 and 2 of chapter 4 also list some questions to ask in identifying customer problems and needs.)

Since we are in business, we (as individuals, and also as companies) already must be serving certain customer needs and solving certain customer problems. Otherwise, we soon would be out of business or out of jobs. However, there are always new problems coming up and existing problems which have not yet been solved. Needs change over time and they seldom are totally fulfilled.

In the case of our personal customers within our company, if we do not properly identify their needs for our services and solve those problems of theirs which relate to us, then they may not have the resources to perform and serve their customers as they should. As a result, both our company and the commercial customer may suffer.

It is very important that we understand our customers' businesses (or jobs). This gives us a background for determining their problems and needs. Because we are customer driven (see chapter 2), we should understand parts of their business (or job) as well as or better than they do. As a result, in some instances we will identify customer problems and devise solutions, even before they know the problems exist. Otherwise, some competitor may, and we may lose some very important business as a result. Allen Mebane, The CEO of Unifi - the rapidly growing producer of textured polyester yarn - said, "I have to know my customer's business and problems as well as I know my own. If I can't show him how much I can help him, I won't keep his business for long."*

*The Winning Performance - How America's High Growth Midsize Companies Succeed, by Clifford and Cavanagh.

As a start in identifying customer problems and needs, we could make a list of all of the customer categories (and/or markets or departments) which we serve; then list all of the important customers which fall under each category. Following this, we might list the customers in order of priority. We also could group them by sub-category, such as by market or by type of need. Then for each category, and perhaps for each individual customer, we could think deeply about what are the problems and unfulfilled needs they now are facing, and which they may be facing in the future.

Whether we are performing an overall analysis, or dealing with an immediate situation facing us, we identify customer problems, needs and opportunities by asking questions. (Note: "problems" mean "problems, needs or opportunities.") We first ask (of ourselves, the customer, and those others who might know) what appears obvious, as far as what problems exist. Then we ask what might be any underlying or hidden problems. We then list everything we know about the customer and his business or job, and whether or not there resides a problem in each factor listed.

(For instance, the customer may be moving his location. We ask what problem might this cause for him, or what opportunity might it give him for improving his situation. Later, during steps 2 and 3 of the problem solving process, we will ask how we can help him solve the problem or need, or take advantage of the opportunity.)

After identifying each problem above, we take one further step and ask whether what we have identified is really the problem, or whether it is the symptom of a deeper, more fundamental, underlying problem. (For instance, the customer's manufacturing productivity may be too low. The problem may appear to be that the equipment is poorly designed. Upon analysis, it might be determined that the problem is not the equipment, but the policy for hiring and training of employees.) We satisfy ourselves that we have identified the real problem, not just a symptom of the problem, and that if we solve the problem the situation will not recur.

(If we have never performed a comprehensive problem analysis before, it probably would be worth taking time [a day or two?] to perform such an analysis on the customers or customer categories we serve. Following this initial analysis, we might update the analysis on a regular basis. We already are in possession of much of the information we need to perform such an analysis; however, we can fill in the informational gaps through market research, through visiting customers and discussing their problems and needs, through literature searches, and through discussions with other knowledgeable people in our company. Most organizations and people are anxious to share this information if they feel that we can and will help them. Editors of technical and business magazines can be especially knowledgeable and helpful.)

Let's now look at Figure 8-1 and discuss how it might be used.

As an example, suppose you are one of a number of market managers reporting to the director of sales and marketing; and you want to follow Figure 8-1 in analyzing your customer problems and needs. (Note: we might have chosen any position or job for this example.) You then will list all your present customers (commercial and personal) under the four headings: (1) associates and peers, (2) other departments, (3) the community, and (4) commercial customers. Depending on the number of your customers, and the depth of the analysis, you might list individual names, and/or you might list categories of customers.

1. Associates and peers. For illustration, let us assume that reporting to you as market manager are a product manager and a secretary. They are your personal customers, as are the other market managers in your department. As for *problems and needs*, under the right column, you might list their need for more effective systems of market research, and for gathering and storing market information. Thus, if in a magazine article, or if in your private study, you identify a helpful idea in one of these areas, you are reminded to share it with them, thereby benefitting them and the company.

2. Other departments. Under other departments you would list the regional sales managers. They need to be kept updated on changes in the market for which you are responsible, and on how to sell more effectively into this market. They need competitive information, information concerning their customers' customers, and how they can help their customers in new ways.

Figure 8-1

CUSTOMER PROBLEMS AND NEEDS

REQUIRING SOLUTIONS AND BENEFITS

CUSTOMERS & CATEGORIES   **PROBLEMS & NEEDS**

ASSOCIATES & PEERS

1. _____   1. _____
2. _____   2. _____
3. _____   3. _____

OTHER DEPARTMENTS

1. _____   1. _____
2. _____   2. _____
3. _____   3. _____

THE COMMUNITY

1. _____   1. _____
2. _____   2. _____
3. _____   3. _____

COMMERCIAL CUSTOMERS

1. _____   1. _____
2. _____   2. _____
3. _____   3. _____
4. _____   4. _____
5. _____   5. _____
6. _____   6. _____

3. The community. The corporation president or division vice president may be the official corporate personality responsible for being visible within the community. However, each of us can make our own contribution within the community. This is important for local organizations, such as banks and hospitals, and for major branches and manufacturing plants of national organizations. We could be active in local and civic organizations thereby making the public aware of us and our company. Using our marketing expertise, we could provide free market consulting to a local charity, and make sure our organization receives proper favorable publicity. We could speak to youth groups on the free enterprise system or some other appropriate topic.

4. Commercial customers. The market manager, just like the research manager and the production manager, usually works through the field sales force to serve the commercial customer. However, you may have identified a few key customers in your market to work with, and may visit them regularly with the blessing of field sales. You may be working on solving specific problems for these customers. In addition, members of the sales force may invite you to make joint sales calls on important customers. Some of these could become target customers or information-sharing contacts.

The first step to *finding solutions to customer problems and needs* is to identify, for customer categories and for individual customers, what they need and what problems need solving. This is what we have been discussing. The second step is to analyze what resources and strengths we have at our disposal for solving those problems and needs.

RESOURCES AND STRENGTHS FOR PROVIDING SOLUTIONS AND BENEFITS
(STEP 2 OF 3)

So, as a result of step 1, we have a pretty good idea of where our personal and commercial customers are hurting; where they have problems and where they have needs. So what? What can we do about it? How can we help? Where can we fit in? Some answers will come to us automatically, either because we have faced similar problems before, or just because of our reservoir of experience. Other problems will be more difficult to solve. By taking a structured approach, such as discussed here, we might generate newer and better solutions. We also might solve some problems we thought were unsolvable. To be able to solve customer problems most effectively, we need to understand what resources and strengths we have to work with.

Step 2, then, is to analyze the resources and strengths available to us for solving the problems and needs identified in step 1. Figure 8-2, for illustrative purposes, lists these under four categories: personal, department, the company and top management, and services/products of the company. When you perform this analysis for your job or department you may choose different categories. Some alternate categories could include management, manufacturing, marketing, research, finance, technical, and analytical.

We make an inventory of all of our strengths and all the resources available to us. A good first step is to sit alone for a few hours, or meet with our immediate associates. Then we may interview other associates and departments to add to the list.

The following discussion illustrates this procedure in brief form as displayed in Figure 8-2.

1. Personal. Under *personal* we have listed as illustrative examples; enthusiasm, hard-working, expertise in thermo-mechanics, and being a successful team manager. These could be some of our personal strengths which we believe can be employed to solve customer problems. Starting with these personal strengths, and adding others, we develop a picture of what we have available personally to help our customers. For example, a couple of our peer market managers might be assisted by our team management skills. Our expertise in thermomechanics could be helpful in assisting some of our sales force in working with customers in this area.

2. Department. The *department's* file of competitive information could be helpful to the field sales force, to product managers, and perhaps to upper management. Other department resources could include market and product analyses, and knowledgeable personnel in specific areas.

3. The company & top management. The *company's* domination in enzyme research could be used to develop a new product line for the market in which we are specializing. Also, any time we run into an enzyme-related problem or challenge we can attack it aggressively, since we are backed up by outstanding experts in this field. The company's reputation for quality could be the basis for some advertisements and market promotions.

4. Services/products of the company. A number of the major customers in the markets we serve might be able to increase their productivity by utilizing our newly-designed Zandu machine with the time-saving widget clamper. The high quality plant training programs might be offered to commercial customers as a free service or inducement, or as a new product offering. They also could be offered to non-profit organizations within the community as a good-will measure.

At this point, it might benefit you, the reader, to stop reading for a few minutes and to add to the table by inserting some of the resources and

Figure 8-2

RESOURCES AND STRENGTHS

FOR PROVIDING SOLUTIONS AND BENEFITS

PERSONAL

EXAMPLES	MY PERSONAL STRENGTHS
1. ENTHUSIASM	1.
2. HARD-WORKING	2.
3. EXPERTISE IN THERMO-MECHANICS	3.
4. SUCCESSFUL TEAM-MANAGER	4.

DEPARTMENT

EXAMPLES	MY DEPARTMENT'S STRENGTHS
1. FILE OF COMPETITOR INFORMATION	1.
2. EXPERTISE IN PRODUCT USES	2.
3. WATTS LINE FOR CUSTOMER CONTACT	3.
4. RESEARCH TECHNOLOGY FOR ANHYDRIDES	4.

THE COMPANY & TOP MANAGEMENT

EXAMPLES	MY COMPANY'S STRENGTHS
1. SOLID FINANCIAL BASE	1.
2. REPUTATION FOR QUALITY	2.
3. ADVERTISEMENTS IN BUSINESS WEEK	3.
4. DOMINATION IN ENZYME RESEARCH	4.

SERVICES/PRODUCTS OF THE COMPANY

KEY SERVICES/PRODUCTS	KEY FEATURES/ADVANTAGES/BENEFITS
1. ZANDU MACHINE	1. NEW TECHNOLOGY WIDGET CLAMPER
2. PLANT TRAINING PROGRAMS	2. TRAINS ASSOCIATES ON PRODUCTIVITY METHODS
3. SPRAY-DRIED CAULIFLOWER	3. LASTS LONGER WITHOUT SPOILING
4. AUTOMATIC TELLER MACHINE	4. 24 HOUR AVAILABILITY
5.	5.
6.	6.
7.	7.
8.	8.
9.	9.

strengths you personally have available to serve your own customers. At a later time, you probably should perform a comprehensive analysis of your resources and strengths, using the table as a guide. You may choose to use these four categories, or you may select a different set of categories.

FINDING SOLUTIONS TO CUSTOMER PROBLEMS AND NEEDS
(STEP 3 OF 3)

How do we go about *finding solutions* to customer problems and needs? In theory the answer is simple. We (step1) determine the problems and needs of our commercial and personal customers, (step 2) determine what are our resources and strengths, and (step 3) match our resources and strengths to the problems and needs, thereby generating solutions and benefits.

In practice, the problem solving process can be quite a challenge. Identifying the underlying problem, or discovering a need the customer is willing to admit, can require effort and insight. We may find that our strengths and resources are not sufficient for solving the problem or serving the identified need. In this case, we may attempt to seek out improved strengths or new resources. Once the problem is clearly identified, and the strengths and resources are clearly understood, the process of matching them up is fairly simple. However, explaining the solution clearly and convincingly to the customer can require skills in the areas of thought, organization and written and verbal communications.

The following examples illustrate all three steps of the problem solving process.

A bank teller noticed that a customer couple was going on a vacation out of the country. The customers may not have known they had a problem or a need, but they did. One problem they had was that they faced the chance they might lose their money (purse, wallet, money clip) and not have the funds to continue the vacation or to return. They needed both a way to obtain funds if money was lost, plus insurance against the possibility of losing their money or having it stolen. One of the resources the teller had available was the ability to issue travelers checks to solve such a problem. She *solved the customer's problem* (step 3) by matching their problem (potential loss of funds) with the bank's resources (ability to issue travelers checks). She then communicated the solution to the customer by effectively explaining the solution and the advantages and benefits of that solution. How to do this is the subject of the next two chapters.

A hospital patient was being visited by her family. The children of the family where being somewhat disruptive, including running up and down the hallway. The nurse could have been very strict and talked pointedly both to the children and to the parents, although this probably would not have been wise. The *problem* appeared to be that there were misbehaving children on the floor. The deeper *problem* was that the parents were not aware of the harm the children were causing. A less obvious *problem* (or opportunity) was the fact that this family potentially needed additional hospital services, and they had friends who also needed hospital services. They would be looking for the best hospital, as well as one which was not offensive to them. This staff nurse had both the strength of knowing that his hospital provides superior care, and the inner resources to be able to keep his temper and handle the situation using good human relations.* He *solved both problems* (step 3) by nicely stopping the children and by politely explaining to the parents and family that this hospital goes out of its way to provide the best in care, and when children are disruptive and make noise it is upsetting to the other patients. He offered to the parents a couple of alternative solutions to the problem, and promised them that this hospital would continue to provide the best in care to their loveone, who they were presently visiting.

    *   Note: the nurse in this example uses some of the HULRAH human relations skills discussed in the section below entitled, Personal Services All Customers Desire.

Because of some internal financial problems, a corporation was forced by its banks to hire an outside executive as chief financial officer. Consequently, the new financial officer was in a position to dictate financial policy to top management. The cost accounting system was determined to be inadequate in one major division. That system had been established by the present division vice president, who was highly respected by the president. That was *the problem*. The new financial officer identified two *resources and strengths* he had for solving the problem. First, his team had the expertise to design and implement an efficient, up-to-date system. Second, he had the human relations skills to present both the problem and the proposed solution to the division vice president in such a way as to not hurt egos. He *solved the problem* by utilizing them both.

The secretary to a division vice president received an irate phone call from a person of importance in a major corporate client. This person was unhappy because the salesperson had obtained a major buying decision without clearing it through him, and he felt the decision was wrong (*the problem*). The secretary recognized she had available the following *resources and strengths* for solving the problem: she knew her company's organization and who had what responsibility; she had some knowledge of the company's products; and she had reasonable human relations skills. She determined that the *solution to the problem* was first, to apologize sincerely and emphatically. Second, she asked to be given a few hours to contact some people internally, after which she would arrange for an appropriate high level official to get back in touch that day to discuss the matter. The communications skills she needed to effectively communicate with the caller are discussed in the following chapters.

As a concluding thought, suppose you were the sales manager of a medium-sized company such as a bank, or alternately you were a regional sales manager of a large corporation. Suppose you had six area sales managers reporting to you, each of whom had five to ten salespeople reporting to them, but no staff other than a secretary. In such a position you would be making sales calls with your salespeople on some of the larger accounts; these would be your commercial customers. *You would assist each salesperson in determining customer problems, and at arriving at solutions by matching the problems with the salesperson's and the company's resources and strengths.* You also would have a number of personal customers. Some of these might include: the area sales managers reporting to you, your secretary, the marketing department, the production department, the research department, and the marketing committee of the board of directors. *For each of these you would determine their problems as they related to you and your department (in other words what they need from you), and how to best solve their problems and serve their needs, based on the resources and strengths available to you.* You would do this consciously or unconsciously by the three step process described in this section.

PERSONAL SERVICES ALL CUSTOMERS DESIRE

During the problem solving process, and later during the customer communications process, we must be aware of and continually provide certain *personal services* all customers desire, relating to good human relations. The use of these were illustrated in three of the examples above. These human relations services have been assimilated into six categories, and nicknamed HULRAH. What might HULRAH represent? Before turning the page test yourself by attempting to fill in the blanks in the table below.

CUSTOMERS DESIRE TO BE -

H E A R D
U N D E R S T _ _ _
L I _ _ _
R _ _ _ _ _ _ _ _
A _ _ _ _ _ _ _ _ _ _ & R _ _ _ _ _ _ _ _ _
H _ _ _ _ D

Let's now discuss in turn each of the six HULRAH personal services that all customers desire.

A. MAKE CUSTOMERS FEEL HEARD

Customers, both commercial and personal, desire to be heard. It is important that we hear them. It is even more important from a human relations standpiont that they *feel* heard (that they believe that they are heard). Listed below are ten ways we can behave and perform to make our customers feel we are listening to them and are really *hearing* what they are saying.

1. Be agreeable and interested. Show a positive interest in the customer and in his business. Ask pertinent questions. Avoid negative or critical comments.

2. Listen actively. Listen to customers actively; ask non-interrupting questions showing that you are paying attention and that you desire more information.

3. Use eye contact. Look them directly in the eye. This gives them a feeling that you are honest, interested, and have self confidence. But, don't stare them down; glance away occasionally.

4. Acknowledge and give feed-back. Acknowledge their comments and ideas and give feedback on what you hear. Use comments like, "What I understand you to have said is ---?" "You feel ---, isn't that so?" "I agree with your position that ---."

5. Ask appropriate questions. Ask questions to obtain information and clarification. Avoid challenging questions.

6. Avoid distractions, and give complete attention. It is disrespectful to the speaker to be distracted by other people or activities. If you appear more interested in the appearance of someone nearby than in what the speaker is saying, the speaker will feel you are not completely hearing what is being said.

7. Hear them out first. Avoid the tendency to offer opinions or positions before clearly hearing and understanding the position of the speaker, and why he holds that position.

8. Avoid interrupting and interruptions. Wait for clear pauses or breaks in the conversation before making comments. Attempt to meet at a location where uninvited interruptions from others will not occur.

9. Display positive body signals. Use positive signals which indicate you are interested and are listening; such as leaning forward, smiling and nodding your head up and down.

10. Plan ahead. Plan the meeting with an eye to avoiding distractions and interruptions. If appropriate, suggest that phones and visitors be curtailed.

B. MAKE CUSTOMERS FEEL UNDERSTOOD

1. Talk in terms of their language or lingo. Learn the language of the customer's industry or technology, and phrase comments and questions in terms they understand. Avoid using technical terms with which the customer may be unfamiliar.

2. Be sympathetic to the customer's ideas. Attempt to be sympathetic and understanding while listening. Even if you disagree with what the customer is saying attempt to be agreeable and to avoid outright disagreement.

3. Be empathetic. Look at the subject from the standpoint of the customer. Attempt to see it as you would if you were in his position and with his background and experience.

4. Restate and confirm. Restate what you believe you heard, and ask confirming questions. Ask questions like, "What you are saying is ---, is that correct?"

5. Take responsibility for not understanding. When you do not understand what is being said, admit it and ask clarifying questions. Avoid negative statements like, "You are not making yourself clear." Replace them with statements in which you take responsibility such as, "With my background I am having some difficulty following you. Would you please re-explain ---."

6. Adjust your behavior style. Be perceptive to the emotions and the behavior of the customers and adjust your behavior accordingly. If they are quiet and talk in terms of a great amount of detail, then attempt to do likewise. If they are very forceful and move ahead aggressively to get at the bottom line, then avoid the small talk and proceed quickly to present the projected end results, followed by brief supporting statements. If they are fun-loving storytellers, then relax and join in the fun before getting down to business.

7. Avoid negative words and expressions. Replace negative or threatening expressions like, "I do not agree with you!" with expressions like, "My background causes me to see this a bit differently."

8. Control opposing prejudices or preconceptions. Like everyone, we have prejudices and preconceptions based on our past experiences. Avoid letting any of these get in the way of positive customer communications.

9. Project positive signals. Make an effort to convey verbal and physical signals which indicate that you understand and are *with* the speaker. Examples would be raising the eyebrows, nodding the head up and down, and replying, "Uh-Huh," and "Yes."

10. Pre-study the customer and the environment. Obtain information before the contact which will assist you in understanding the customer and his viewpoint.

C. MAKE CUSTOMERS FEEL LIKED

1. Smile. The smile is the universal indication of happiness and friendliness. Looking the person in the eye while smiling makes the person feel liked by you. Smiling into a mirror while speaking on the phone puts a *smile* into your voice.

2. Be friendly and warm. Take actions normally associated with friendly and warm personalities. Examples could be giving a warm friendly greeting, introducing customers to a friend, waving to them across a room, seeking them out to speak to them when not necessary. A friendly touch on the arm indicates warmth and closeness, but can be offensive to those with cooler type personalities.

3. Give genuine compliments. Look for positive comments to make to other people. Be sincere in your compliments. Offer evidence as to why a positive comment you say is true, such as, "I admire your good taste in furniture; the wall hangings are beautiful and match your chairs." Compliments are particularly effective in areas where people are unsure, and in areas which are particularly meaningful to them. Specific compliments are more effective and well-received that those which are general in nature.

4. Remember and use names. "A person's name is to that person the sweetest and most important sound in any language."* The first step to remembering names is to pay attention when the name is mentioned. Form a clear impression of the person and the name when you first hear it. Associate the name with the person in some way, perhaps with the physical appearance. The name also can be associated with a similar name, his business, a rhyme, or a mind picture. Repetition is helpful in remembering in general and in remembering names in particular. Few people object to your writing down their name; in fact they consider it a compliment.

* **How to Win Friends and Influence People,** Dale Carnegie

5. Talk in terms of the customer's interest. We all enjoy talking about that which interests us, whether it be about business or personal matters. We like and feel liked by those people who are interested in us and our problems and challenges. Effective business communicators, including salespeople, use this knowledge when they open a business conversation with a bit of informal chit chat in an area of personal interest to the other person.

6. Emphasize common traits and interests. Most of us feel more comfortable if the other person is like us in some way; the more like us, the more comfortable we are. Consequently, we should stress those areas where we agree with and are similar to the customer. Talk about mutual outdoor experiences when with an avid fisherman, not classical music, even though you may enjoy classical music more.

7. Avoid criticism, and a complaining attitude. It is difficult to be critical of, or to complain to or about, another person, and at the same time make that person feel that you genuinely like them. We should be positive when possible. We should be very careful when offering criticism, even constructive criticism.

8. Avoid embarrising the customer or making him feel uncomfortable. Protect the customer's ego. If the customer makes a mistake or does anything which might bring embarrisment to him, deal with the situation delicately. Someone will avoid you, and look for excuses to reject you, if they feel embarrised around you.

9. Avoid talking down to customers or showing them up. Be careful about implying that you are smarter than the customer. This endears us to no one. This principle must be dealt with carefully when we are identifying and solving customer problems, especially when involving an area where the customer might have found the solution himself, and perhaps should have.

10. Show genuine interest in them and their ideas. We like people who are interested in us and feel we are intelligent. We enjoy our ideas and interests, and we like being around those who show an interest in them.

D. MAKE CUSTOMERS FEEL RESPECTED

1. Take all of their concerns seriously. The customer is serious about his concerns even if they appear inconsequential to others. We will be, and appear to be, respectful if we will take those concerns seriously.

2. Be courteous and tactful. Proper manners, courtesy and tact demonstrate respect to the other person. We should be courteous even if the other person isn't. Referring to 6 immediately above, we purposely can be *rough around the edges* to make a less refined person feel comfortable with us, and at the same time be clean and courteous.

3. Keep customers appropriately informed. Keep the customer appropriately informed, but do not waste his time by over-communicating with him or continually providing details in which he has little interest. However, we more frequently err by telling customers too little and too late, than by too much and too soon.

4. Ask for the customer's opinion and input. We all feel we have something important to contribute, and appreciate someone who is interested in and respects our views.

5. Give them time and attention. Carefully evaluate the time and attention paid to the customer. If we give too little he will feel slighted. If we give too much, we may not be receiving an appropriate return to the company for the time spent. It is better to err in the direction of giving the customer too much time and attention, rather than too little.

6. Respect their time. Do not be late for appointments or overstay our welcome. Avoid asking the customer to spend time doing what we could accomplish a better way. As a result, the customer will be inclined to respect our time and give us time when we require it.

7. Do not ignore the customer. Maintain regular contact with the customer so he will never feel forgotten. Never fail to acknowledge his physical presence, even when you are busy and others of more importance are present.

8. Avoid telling a customer he is wrong. If the customer is incorrect, find a way of allowing him to save face. Avoid blatently disagreeing with him.

9. Introduce customers to important people. We show respect to customers when we go out of our way to introduce them to friends and important people. It is a nice gesture to introduce a visiting customer to a top company officer.

10. Have a respectful manner. Remain aware of the desires and comfort of the customer. For instance, do not crowd his "personal space." Different people have different personal space requirements. Be sensitive to his desire to be addressed formally as Mr. or Ms.

E. MAKE CUSTOMERS FEEL APPRECIATED AND REMEMBERED

1. Greet customers in a friendly way. Smile, and look happy to see them. Offer your hand for a handshake if appropriate.

2. Remember customer names. Concentrate on remembering names. Use their names often in conversation.

3. Treat them as if they are important. Ask yourself what you would do for a dignitary; do this for customers when appropriate. Do a little extra for them.

4. Do little things. Do something for the customer which is unexpected to show you care; such as providing extra copies of special instructions, or sending them a card during your vacation.

5. Provide extra service. Go a bit overboard. Do something extra. Make sure the service you provide is the best around.

6. Send thank-yous. Send thank you cards. Determine dates which are special to them such as anniversaries and birthdays, and remember them by card or phone.

7. Tell others. Mention to others what you appreciate about the customer and why. This probably will get back to the customer and will be even more appreciated than if told to them in person.

8. Clip and mail. Keep customers in mind when possible, especially when reading periodicles. Take notes on ideas and data of interest to them. Clip articles to send to them, perhaps with a personalized note. This shows them your interest and provides them helpful information.

9. Show special attention. Stay in contact. Phone when you could have written. Follow up a phone call with a thank you or clarification note. Contact them when unexpected with something worthwhile to share.

10. Thank them. Make sure they know you appreciate the time, cooperation and business given to you and your company. Say thank you in a number of ways. Do this even if you feel they are receiving more from you than they are giving to you.

F. MAKE CUSTOMERS FEEL HELPED

One of our principal responsibilities, no matter what position we hold, is to help and to provide service to commercial and personal customers. However, there are times when customers fail to recognize or *feel* that help, even when it is being received in great measure. The following are ideas for providing extra help and making the customer *feel* that help.

1. Seek out and solve problems. Spend some time thinking about each individual customer, what he is trying to accomplish, and how we might be of help. Aggressively use the principles discussed in this chapter to assist all customers, and especially the more important ones.

2. Make their jobs easier. Most of us feel we are overworked. Our customers will feel well-served by us if we can assist them in saving time and being more efficient, especially if we subtly let them know we have done so.

3. Provide benefits and evidence. Make it easier for the customer to use our services and understand their value by clearly explaining the benefits of those services to the customer. When necessary, supply convincing evidence that those benefits will, in fact, be received.

4. Treat customers fairly. The majority of our time and effort should be spent with the more important customers, assisting them and solving their problems. This is both smart and fair. However, we should allocate a fair amount of time and effort to less important customers; and in various ways let them know we are spending time on their problems and opportunities.

5.   Be responsive and cooperative.   Act promptly on customer requests. Carry out our promises. Keep them clearly informed when our responses will be delayed. Have an attitude of being service oriented and cooperative.

6.   Follow-up.   Make reminders for ourselves, so we remember to do what we planned and promised. Follow-up with others in our company who have the responsibility to carry out the services we have promised our customer. Even in a customer-oriented and team-oriented company, there are those who are ineffective and inefficient.

7.   Call in reinforcements when needed.   Be sensitive to times when specialists and back-up personnel can be helpful in working with us to solve the customer's problems or serve his needs even more effectively.

8.   Be consistent.   Attempt to deliver consistent service. Avoid surprises, especially unpleasant surprises. Customers appreciate dependable and consistent service. Communicate with the customer as soon as you know there is a problem on our end which will negatively affect our service consistency.

9.   Make customers aware of developments.   Make them aware of new ideas and events you observe which relate to their jobs or businesses. Send them clippings and notes as applicable.

10.   Make the customer look good.   When dealing with customers keep in mind their desire to look efficient and effective to their peers and superiors. Give them credit for solutions. Give them worthwhile ideas. Talk about them positively to others.

9

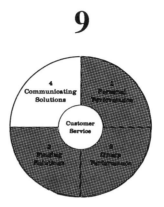

COMMUNICATING SOLUTIONS TO CUSTOMER PROBLEMS AND NEEDS

KEYS TO CROSS-MARKETING COMMUNICATIONS
I. BELIEVE
II. INNOVATE
III. CONCENTRATE
IV. TOUCH
V. COMMUNICATE
VI. SERVE
APPLICATION OF CROSS-MARKETING COMMUNICATIONS

The four stages to Cross-Marketing effectiveness presented in chapter 3 were (1) personal performance, (2) group performance, (3) finding solutions, and (4) communicating solutions to customer problems. Chapter 8 addressed stage 3, finding solutions to customer problems. Chapter 9 is the first of two chapters dealing with stage 4, providing effective customer service through communicating those solutions effectively to customers.

The communications principles and practices presented in chapters 9 and 10 will appply almost universally both to commercial customers - those outside our organization who purchase our goods and services, and to personal customers - those mainly within our organization to whom we provide information and other support. These principles and practices apply to the corporation president who is communicating a new and controversial policy to the board, or communicating our customer service theme to the front line employees; to the department manager who is negotiating support from other department heads; to the bank calling officer who is establishing a business relationship with a Fortune 1000 corporate customer; and to the office receptionist and telephone operator who is regularly contacted by customers and others outside the company. In other words, they apply to everyone in the organization.

If you or your people happen to hold a direct customer service position, or are a front line employee for an organization which directly serves the public (bank, airline, hospital, etc.) then you will need to modify or restate some of the practices in this chapter to make them meaningful to your job. For instance, practice no. 1 listed under *III. Communicate* states, "classify customers by importance." You may need to restate this as something like, "classify customer situations by their importance to the customer," and then make appropriate modifications to the discussion to fit your situation. The information in *VI. Serve* should be very valuable in building your personal marketing expertise, but much of it may not be directly applicable to your immediate job responsibilities. However, chapter 11 was written specifically for you.

KEYS TO CROSS-MARKETING COMMUNICATIONS

This chapter discusses six keys to effective customer communications, along with a number of practices you can use to implement those keys. Some of these practices help you to prepare for effective service and effective communications. Others are employed during the process of face-to-face communications, to deal effectively with the customer and to present your ideas and your solutions.

SIX KEYS TO IMPROVED COMMUNICATIONS

    I. **BELIEVE**
   II. **INNOVATE**
 III. **CONCENTRATE**
 IV. **TOUCH**
  V. **COMMUNICATE**
 VI. **SERVE**

First you must *believe*. Without belief you have nothing to communicate about. With belief you have confidence in your knowledge, and the enthusiasm to share ideas and solutions with the customer. Most people are not nearly as effective as they can be at most things. One way to become more effective at communicating is to *innovate*, to think of and to apply new and different ways, both to serve the customer and to communicate that service. If you *concentrate* both on the more important ideas and on the more important customers, you will communicate ideas which are of value and interest to the customer, and you will achieve higher results. By *touching* customers emotionally, through using good human relations, they will be more receptive to you and to what you have to say. By developing and using specific *communication skills,* you will be more effective in your face-to-face communications. And finally, if you are *service* oriented and take specific actions to increase your customer service, the customer will know he is benefitting and will continue to be receptive both to further communications and to increased business relationships.

So, let's look at the first and fundamental key to effective customer and Cross-Marketing communications, belief.

I. BELIEVE

If you really believe in your company and what you have to offer it will be easy for you to develop the enthusiasm to communicate that to the commercial customer or to the business associate.

In chapter 6 we discussed in detail that which you and your people need to believe, to take any significant action. In that chapter, in the section titled, *Motivational Beliefs Which Inspire People to High Performance* we discussed ten *beliefs in* and ten *beliefs that* which inspire and motivate. We then discussed how to persuade your own people to increase those positive beliefs. Those same principles and practices apply to increasing our self-motivation for effectively communicating problem solutions to customers. It is recommended that those sections of chapter 6 be reviewed before continuing.

In review, the following are the ten *beliefs in* discussed in chapter 6.

BELIEFS IN, WHICH INSPIRE AND MOTIVATE

1. The Industry	6. Product Quality & Purpose
2. The Company	7. Customer Benefits
3. The Management	8. Company Benefits
4. The Job or Profession	9. Personal Benefits
5. The Program and Purpose	10. I Can Do It

The importance of *belief* to effective communications cannot be overstated. On the one hand it is a simple concept which we would all tend to accept. There is a danger in this. It seems so simple and acceptable that most of us do not really understand its full importance. Consequently, we do not address it with the time and attention it deserves.

Do you really believe in your *company?* Why? What makes your company so good? Then why were you complaining about it last week? You mean you can believe in your company and still complain about parts of it? Give some evidence to support what you say! If you do not really believe in your company; if that belief is not deep down in your subconscious; then you probably will not have the conviction, confidence and persistence to look the customer dead in the eye, and believe, and explain to him what the facts are. You need to believe so you can explain to him that he will benefit substantially by using or continuing with our products and services, and that he will suffer in the long run if he does not.

The same is true for the *product,* and the other areas of belief. What about the product, service or course of action you are recommending to the customer? What is so good about it? How is it better than something else? Why does the customer need it ? How will it benefit him? What evidence do you have to support that? Do you believe that evidence yourself? Would you pay money out of your pocket for that product or service? Will the customer really be sorry down the line if he fails to utilize your product or service? Why? It is important that we convince ourselves that each of these ten areas of belief are true. Answering questions like the above is one way of convincing ourselves.

Some of us are naturally enthusiastic, and tend to believe in whatever we are involved with; we look for the positive points. But most of us require more convincing. For the rest of us, the majority, it would be beneficial to have a group think session to help build our belief in those areas of greatest importance. In the think session you should list as many advantages and benefits as you can, along with supporting evidence, to explain why you should hold each of the ten *beliefs in* and most of the ten *beliefs that.* For the sake of the non-believers, you might also list as many negatives about each of these twenty beliefs that you can think of, and then have the group answer each negative as successfully as possible. Following this think session, on balance, you should hold very positive beliefs, and even be enthusiastic about your products, services and problem solutions. You then should remove all negative thoughts from your mind and concentrate exclusively on the positive beliefs and their supporting points.

Once you believe in what you are doing and what you are offering, you are in a position to address the remaining five keys to effective communications.

II. INNOVATE

Innovation consists of thinking of and implementing new and better ways to serve the customer and to communicate with the customer. Innovative thinking not only generates real benefits to the customer, it also gives us ideas for presenting our services and solutions in new, more interesting ways. For instance, British Airways generated several thousand ideas for improving customer service in a recent three year period (1982-1984) by concentrating on innovation with those at the front line.

The following are specific ways to apply innovation to Cross-Marketing communications at the organizational and at the personal level.

1. Develop a data base. Keep a file or other information repository for important commercial and personal customers, and the industries and subject matters which pertain to them. Depending on your business or position, this could be done for categories of customers, or individual customers. As information and ideas pertaining to each category, customer and subject are uncovered, clip or make note of them and deposit them into the appropriate file. Plan to set aside time on a regular basis to think about the problems and needs of each customer, with or without others thinking with you as appropriate. File all ideas developed for future reference. Some of the ideas, such as how to communicate more effectively and persuasively, and how to learn more about customer needs, will be applicable to all customers across-the-board.

This procedure will yield two positive results. First, each customer or category will remain in your subconscious if not your conscious mind, and ideas and events related to them will occur to you from time to time, more frequently than most people would believe. Second, when the time comes to communicate an important idea or problem solution to a customer, a significant amount of background and specific data will be in hand.

2. Encourage constructive discontent. Encourage an attitude of *if it ain't broke it probably soon will be,* instead of the more normal attitude of *if it ain't broke don't fix it.* Encourage your people to be unsatisfied with the status quo and to be looking for new and better ways. Make it uncomfortable for people to be conservative.

3. Look for new ways. Think *new.* Be alert to new and different ways for serving the customer. Ask how present tasks and actions could be accomplished in new and different ways.

4. Look for better ways. Have a *better way* attitude. Always be looking for better ways to serve the customer, better ways for your customer to serve his customer, better ways for the customer to do his job or produce his product or service, better ways for the customer to deserve and receive positive recognition.

5. Look for new capabilities. Look for new skills and abilities which you might acquire to serve the customer more effectively. Do your competitors have different or better expertise than you do? Would it benefit you to learn or improve technical skills to help the customer perform more effectively? Do you need to listen better; gather information more effectively; become more skilled at analysis; improve your human relations skills?

6. Look at your own special capabilities. Evaluate any special or unusual capabilities you or your people have, and ask how they might be applied to customer situations. If your customer is a stamp collector, do you know someone who collects stamps, and what can you learn from them which would be helpful in building relationships or communications? One of your people studied drama in college and presently leads church seminars; another held a job as a draftsman; and another used to sell copy machines. Maybe part of your experience includes financial analysis and justifications. Can knowledge or skills related to these be useful in dealing with any of your present customers?

7. Encourage non-conformity. Often the most creative people are non-conformists by nature. Encourage these people, and encourage unusual and different ways of thinking in yourself and in your people. Encourage discussions of new and different ideas and approaches. If your people are operating in an *accepting* environment in which new and even *silly* ideas are not frowned on, they are much more likely to be innovative in their thinking. Note: you do not implement silly ideas; you modify them and develop them into useable ideas.

8. Hold brainstorming sessions. Creative brainstorming sessions can yield numerous ideas for both serving customers and communicating with them more effectively and persuasively. Brainstorming sessions can yield hundreds and even thousands of ideas. If only a few of these have real merit the results can be substantial. Brainstorming sessions are run in a totally positive environment in which there is a free flow of ideas and suggestions. All ideas are accepted regardless of merit. Frequently a useless idea from one person can trigger a useful idea in the mind of another person.

9. Provide training on creativity and innovative thinking. Properly designed training should result in three positive effects. The first effect would be a more positive attitude of your people toward creativity and innovation. Second, all of you would be more alert to and would more readily recognize new and innovative ideas and approaches. Third, specific skills for developing and implementing new ideas would be acquired by your people.

10. Borrow from other industries. Study related, and even unrelated, industries and businesses for ideas which might be applied to your industry and to your customers. How do the best insurance people obtain appointments? How do the best advertisers make their case? What can a study of McDonalds, or IBM, or Citibank, or British Airways, or savings associations in Chicago tell us about how to operate your savings association (or your type of business) more effectively?

11. Allow mistakes. When people are dealing with the tried and true the possibility for mistakes is much less than when they are dealing with the new and unknown. An organization which penalizes all mistakes inhibits creativity and innovation. Encourage an attitude of *if you haven't make any mistakes you probably haven't done anything.* But, establish guidelines, and checks and balances, to head off mistakes which could be very damaging.

12. Reward innovative ideas. People tend to do what they are rewarded for. Rewards could be formal. Or they could be informal, such as bragging on those who generate new ideas.

III. CONCENTRATE

One expression of Pareto's Rule is that in most situations 80% of beneficial results come from addressing only 20% of the problems facing us. Consequently, in Cross-Marketing communications, we want to concentrate and focus our efforts whenever appropriate. The following are some ways to concentrate effectively.

1. Classify customers by importance. Analyze the list of present customers by meaningful categories such as customer size, sales level, profitability, customer industry, and type of potential need. Then list customers in order of their importance. For commercial customers this could be by sales level, but probably should be in order of projected long term profitability. For personal customers this relates to the relative importance of their outputs to the company, to our commercial customers, and to our department's mission. Our allocation of time and effort will be strongly affected by these listings.

The best opportunities for improved effectiveness and new business most often come from your present customers. Organizations too often fail to fully serve and obtain business from existing customers, especially the larger ones. You should give emphasis to analyzing the problems of, and communicating with, your largest and highest potential present customers. You should develop relationships with a number of important people in the larger and the more progressive organizations. There usually are people at many levels and in many functions who influence a company's needs for your products and its system of satisfying those needs. Likewise, some of these will know about and be involved in developing technologies which will influence future business and product purchases.

2. Allocate resources based on projected results.   Allocate the time and effort you spend on specific customers and customer categories based on the projected match between their problems and needs and your resources and strengths.   In other words, allocate your resources based on your projected ability to effectively serve and generate substantial results.

3. Establish a reputation as an authority.   By specializing in industries and technologies, by developing specific expertise, and by promoting yourself wisely, establish yourself as an expert.   As a result, customers will welcome your contact, will gladly invite you to their facilities, and will openly provide needed information to assist you in understanding their problems and needs.

4. Concentrate on major problems and opportunities.   Identify the most important problems and opportunities facing the customer.   There are three definitions of *most important,* and all three deserve consideration. Primary importance should be placed on those areas where solutions will benefit the customer the most.   Solutions in this area should earn additional business for us and will earn us the customer's respect and appreciation.   A second most important area involves those solutions which will yield our organization the largest dividend in sales and long term profitability.   The third most important area concerns problems which if solved, the solutions can be extended to other companies and other industries.

5. Concentrate on your organization's major problems and opportunities.   Your company or department may be facing certain obstacles or opportunities; their solution may generate substantial benefit to the customer.   You may be lacking technical knowledge in a new or important area related to a major customer industry.   To overcome this lack you could hire knowledgeable people, you could assign people to study the area, or you could study the area yourself.   Alternately, you recently may have solved a major problem for a customer, and you now can see opportunities to apply those solutions to a number of related industries. These types of problems and opportunities deserve your attention.

6. Concentrate on personal major problems and opportunities.   To accomplish your job more effectively, and thus serve your organization and your customers more effectively, you might need to change your job responsibilities or obtain training in specific technical or communication skills.   This is illustrated by the following brief examples. You might potentially become your company's highest producing salesperson, in addition to your responsibilities as a corporate officer.   You might delegate substantial time-consuming responsibilities, releasing that time for more important tasks.   With the proper personal marketing, you might establish yourself as a recognized industry authority, with substantial benefits to your organization.   Improved leadership on your part might cause your people to substantially increase their productivity; perhaps you should allocate more time to effective people management and less to your own personal output.

7. Concentrate on past customer receptivity.   Identify the types of solutions customers have been receptive to in the past and aim toward those types of solutions.   Small changes usually are accepted more readily that large technical jumps, especially over a short time period.   As an example, it was easier to gain acceptance from secretarial personnel for word processors than for computers.   It has proved easier to persuade a company to change advertising strategy and retain their present advertising media, than to persuade them to change advertising media.

8. Establish specialist task forces.   Frequently very large projects and opportunities require more time and expertise than one person can supply.   Many effective companies have been successful in pulling together task forces to address major sales and internal productivity opportunities.   The task forces bring together all the needed technical disciplines and decision makers to accomplish an objective.   Some of the most successful have had limited staff support and operated only as long as the project lasts.   IBM has made many large sales using task forces, as have other major computer equipment companies.

Suppose the central marketing research department determines that the major growth opportunity for the company lies within the technology of one of the four divisions, and that corporate management agrees.   Then despite the fact that the other three division managers may not be overjoyed, the marketing research manager may allocate over half of the department's resources to studying the opportunities and markets for that one division.   The department may participate in one or more task forces to research markets, and to analyze the opportunities in each market.

9. Delegate.   Make a policy of delegating as many as possible of those responsibilities and tasks which do not require your full attention.   This will free up your time for concentrating on those areas where you can make the most   impact   and   contribution.   You   still   should   review   final accomplishment in the areas delegated.   Depending on the tasks and the ability of the delegatee, you also may check on accomplishment at various checkpoints along the way.   You should design the delegated tasks so they will be interesting and challenging to those to whom they are delegated.

10. Remove distractions.   By making a concentrated effort to remove less important distractions from yourself and from your people, you both free up time and remove unnecessary interruptions which reduce concentration and effectiveness.   The following could be examples of distractions to be addressed: unwanted visitors, time-wasting associates, urgent phone calls concerning matters of low importance, and unnecessary assignments from superiors or related departments. Some of these will have to be handled in a creative manner, so as to not offend the people involved.

11. Delete or reduce less important tasks. The most effective way to save time and resources is to totally eliminate unnecessary tasks and projects. We are all familiar with the myriad of government programs which frequently get reduced in scope, but seldom are totally eliminated. As a result, large budgets continue, to carry the overhead staffs. Correspondingly, you might operate your department or job on a zero-based budgeting approach, eliminating all activities you would not start now, if they were not already in progress. In addition, if you will reduce time and resources allocated to all other tasks which absolutely cannot be eliminated, you then can allocate your remaining available resources to those which will make the most contribution to the corporate and department mission, and to the areas of major opportunity.

12. Allocate resources to those customers, problems and opportunities which will yield the largest long term results. As you are successful in doing this, you will have the best opportunity of achieving the largest long term results. For instance, you might focus on a single industry, a single technology, or even a single customer. As an example, Boeing Company has appointed sales and marketing people to specialize in serving single major airlines, and with great success.

IV. TOUCH

Communications involves transferring words and impressions to the mind of another. It also involves a transfer of emotions. If during the communication process you *touch* other people in a positive emotional way, if they like you and feel comfortable with you, they will be much more receptive to your message. This section lists twelve ways to emotionally touch another person positively. The material is closely related to, and is supported by, the discussion in chapter 8 entitled *Personal Services All Customers Desire.*

1. Greet customers in a friendly and warm way. This will establish an immediate positive attitude and an inclination toward receptivity.

2. Smile and be happy to see them. The smile is the universal sign of happiness and friendship. Most of us like to be around people who are genuinely happy and who are friendly. If a person is happy to see me then I feel he likes me. If he likes me he must be a pretty swell fellow, and probably has my interests at heart.

3. Make them feel important. We all have a desire to be important and to have that importance recognized. You want to make people feel important without using insincere flattery, or appearing to manipulate them. To make them feel important, mention or ask them about their ideas, interests and accomplishments; listen intently, and ask meaningful questions in conversation.

4. Show them sincere appreciation. Thank them in various ways for their cooperation, their business, and whatever is appropriate. Most people in most situations feel relatively unappreciated and respond to those who appreciate them. Do you feel you receive enough appreciation from your superiors or your spouse for the effort and results you have contributed? If you are like most of us the answer is, no!

5. Remember and use their names. It gives a warm, positive feeling to hear our name used repeatedly in conversation, if it is handled properly. If you can recall someone who uses your name frequently in conversation, you probably will be thinking of someone you like and would be pleased to cooperate with.

6. Be sympathetic with their ideas and their situations. Our ideas hold special meaning to us. We appreciate those who recognize their importance, and we are upset at those who scorn them. Likewise, most of us do not take full responsibility for any negative situations in which we find ourselves. We usually feel someone else is at fault in some way, and do not appreciate being told otherwise. We can expect this reaction from our customers.

7. Take all their concerns seriously. If a person has a concern it is important to him, no matter how trivial it may appear to us. Do not ignore or downgrade any concerns of customers.

8. Be empathetic. Empathy is the ability to understand what a person believes and why he believes that way. If you can think like the customer thinks, and see the situation from his standpoint, then you can tailor your communications to solve his problems and make him clearly understand that solution.

9. Talk in terms of common interests. We feel comfortable with people who are like us, and feel uncomfortable with people who act and think differently from us. This is the source of much of the world's prejudice. As quickly as possible you should learn as much as you can about the customer, and make him comfortable by talking about things that interest him. You also can share, subtly and as appropriate, the interests and backgrounds you have in common. If you enjoy both fishing and classical music, and you are talking with a New York banker, you may share fishing stories with him instead of discussing classical music, because you learned in early conversation that he is an avid fisherman and dislikes everything related to culture and the city. If you had not learned this early in the conversation, you might have assumed his interests were something different.

10. Show them respect. We all desire to be respected, and will respond to those who show us respect, especially in a way we desire it to be shown. Your challenge as a communicator is to know the other person well enough to determine how to show appropriate respect. For instance, one person desires to be called Mister, perhaps because of insecurities, while another considers that silly. The second person may be very sensitive about not finishing college, and may be threatened by any discussions about college graduates.

11. Ask for customer opinions and input. We all feel we have ideas to share, and appreciate being asked about them. In **How To Win Friends And Influence People,** Dale Carnegie shared how a large sale was made when the salesperson asked an important customer to evaluate and give opinions about a new piece of machinery.

12. Be genuinely interested in them and their ideas. We like and are interested in communicating with people who are interested in us and our ideas. If you show a genuine interest in others you generally will find them receptive to your communications.

V. COMMUNICATE

Discussed below are specific skills and practices which relate directly to the communications process, generally on a one-to-one basis. If you develop and use these practices all of your communications will be enhanced.

In my personal business and consulting experience I have observed that most organizations suffer from inadequate communications. More specifically, employees at all levels tend to lack an understanding of communications skills and how and when to use them. The following are some examples.

The bank accounting clerk learns that a customer is unhappy about his loan terms, but does not tell anyone. Important information, which would be helpful to working personnel is distributed to department managers, but is never dissiminated to their people. Decisions are made about people's jobs and workload without getting an input from them; then they are not informed about the resulting changes until the last minute. A corporate market researcher does not know what an operating vice president wants of him, and the vice president wonders what the market researcher is doing wandering around talking to his personnel. The corporation president visits one of the branches for a meeting, leaves without speaking to any of the branch personnel, and wonders why morale is down.

The supervisor gives a complicated instruction to one of her people, does not ask for feed back to make sure the instruction is understood, does not check to see if the assignment is performed properly, and wonders why her people never understand instructions. Skill training is given in listening and telephone skills without auditing changes in performance, and management wonders why customers feel the organization's people are unfriendly and uninterested. We get excited about a proposed solution to a customer's problem and ask him to accept it, without first listening to his ideas and opinions, and we wonder why he says no. These are just few examples of where we fail to communicate effectively on a daily basis. The following are some ideas for overcoming these failures.

1. Develop an atmosphere of trust and respect. Behave toward the customer as if you trust him, you are trustworthy yourself, and you expect to be trusted. Be totally honest, and stand behind your word. Follow up to make sure all promises are kept. If possible, refrain from actions which imply a lack of trust, such as requesting written guarantees. Use non-threatening language; instead of saying "you implied," say "I understood you to say." Carry yourself as if you are dealing with a trusted friend. Save hard-nosed or unpleasant subjects for later in the conversation after rapport has been established.

2. Listen carefully to others and their ideas. Pay close attention to them and to what they are saying. Look them in the eye and do not be distracted. Respond to them with positive body signals. Analyze what is being said and relate your questions to the subject they are presently discussing.

3. Ask meaningful questions. From prestudy and preplanning, and from listening to the customer's comments, develop hypotheses of what his problems are and what solutions you might offer. Then politely ask and obtain answers to the questions which will confirm or deny those hypotheses. To clarify what you are hearing, ask clarifying and confirming questions. But be careful to not interrupt the speaker's thought; wait for a clear pause before speaking. Avoid threatening questions or those which are off the subject.

4. Confirm understanding with feedback. Confirm your understanding of important points by repeating what you believe you have heard in your own words, and get confirmation from the speaker that you understand correctly.

5. Remove Barriers to Understanding. You should be aware of potential barriers to communications and prevent them from occurring. Barriers can be created from differing assumptions, attitudes or prejudices. The use of unfamiliar technical language can create a barrier between participants. You should adjust to the customer's situation and personality style when possible, saying nothing to offend him, and speaking in terms of his language and jargon.

6. Talk in terms of customer benefits. We all are interested in ideas which will benefit us and ours. The statement, "Your department needs better market information," is less interesting and persuasive than, "With improved information on your customer's capacities and needs, you would be better able to design effective selling proposals." The statement, "You need and will benefit from this training," conveys less information and is less persuasive than, "Through the increased human relations skills your people will gain from this training, your people will better understand the needs of both associates and customers, and they will increase their communications and their selling results."

7. Make communications specific. Focus on the information needed and the points to be made, and avoid extraneous conversation and unnecessary details. An executive who is planning to use a preprogrammed personal computer does not need to understand how to program a computer, or even how the computer works; he needs to understand how to operate the computer with its specific program, and how it will benefit him. If you are talking to a bottom line, results-oriented manager, she needs to know the cost justification and the major advantages and benefits, not who invented the item and why, and all the steps required to make it work properly.

8. Inform all appropriate people. Determine the names of everyone who needs to be informed about upcoming actions and decisions, and to what extent they need to be informed. Take actions to keep them properly informed. However, do not waste the time of those who have no desire or need to be informed. If we are involved in selling a product to a commercial customer, or in selling an idea within the company, we can have the sale blocked by someone who is resentful about being left out of the consideration and communication process.

9. Use and learn to read body signals. By understanding positive and negative body signals you can both influence others positively, and understand whether they are thinking positively or negatively about your proposition. Folding the arms and leaning backwards are recognized as negative signals. Smiling, leaning forward, and asking questions about the ideas being proposed are recognized as positive signals, indicating genuine interest. If you look apprehensive and unsure you will imply to the customer a lack of enthusiasm and confidence. On the other hand, if you are smiling, leaning forward, looking them dead in the eye, nodding your head up and down and talking with a bit of excitement in your voice, you are indicating confidence and enthusiasm in what you are saying. The customer will be positively influenced by these signals.

10. Make statements clear and unambiguous. Use simple, straight-forward language. Avoid fancy and unusual words, and technical language which might be unfamiliar to the customer.   Make statements in as few words as possible. Use visual aids such as graphs and pictures. Confirm important communications in writing.

11. Lead effective meetings.   Much time is wasted in many organizations by improperly run meetings.   Invite to the meeting all important participants, but no one else. Have an agenda and stick to it. Start the meeting on time and finish on time. At the end, summarize results and actions to be taken, when and by whom. Send a written summary to those who should know about the results, all participants, and those from whom action is expected.

12. Plan ahead. Before initiating important communications, gather all needed information, determine specifically what is the goal or purpose of the contact, and outline a general plan of action for accomplishing that purpose.

For example, suppose you are a production quality control manager. A specific, very important customer has been refusing to accept some of your shipments which you know have been within agreed-upon specifications. You need to meet with the customer to clarify the situation. You first gather and review records, and talk to appropriate people in both companies to prepare your case.   You establish a goal of convincing the receiving department to change its present criteria for accepting shipments, and to do it in good spirit. Your plan is (1) to ask them for the reasons they have been refusing shipments, (2) to clearly establish the agreed-upon criteria, (3a) to explain how they have misunderstood the agreement - and (3b) how it is understandable that they could have done so, (4) to get their agreement to change their criteria, and (5) to confirm the above in writing.

VI. SERVE

A principal purpose of your job or position is to serve the needs of your personal and commercial customers.   Once customers realize you are offering truly effective service, they will be receptive to all your communications efforts.

As indicated above, by being innovative you can develop new and better ways of communicating to and serving your customers. This can give you a substantial advantage over your competition. By concentrating and focusing your efforts you can can make your service more effective and rewarding. By believing in your products and services, by emotionally touching your customers, and by employing effective communications skills, you can cause your customers to be even more receptive to your service proposals. Listed below are a number of additional ways of offering and communicating superior and extra service to your customers.

The material in this section is very important to anyone who plans to deserve and hold an important position in any organization. For most managers and potential managers the material should be easy to grasp. Consequently, if you can't seem to grasp this section, or can't relate to it, then I suggest you find a mentor, someone who will explain the material in this section and discuss it with you. The same holds true for the entirety of chapter 9.

1. Study customer trends and needs. The more you know about the customer, and the industries and technologies which relate to him and his needs, the easier it will be for you to discover problems needing solving, and to solve those problems. Also, it will be easier to effectively and persuasively communicate your solutions to the customer, and to the responsible people who affect the customer's decisions.

If, for instance, your financial institution provides bank financial services to the construction industry, you can research the market to determine which industries will be doing the most building of plants and facilities, where, when, and of what type. We then can look at what financial requirements they will have, and which of those financial requirements they will pass back to the construction companies. You then can ask and answer questions about the types of construction financing and related services you can design to help all involved and to compete most effectively. While developing the above information you will be developing numerous personal relationships which will be helpful to you later in serving the industry.

Suppose as another example, your company or division produces molded plastic resins to go into shoe heels. Then the shoe industry (or at least the shoe heel industry) is one of your major customers. In studying the industry and companies in the industry you might determine that the fashion in women's high heels is moving toward longer and thinner shafts. If so, you might advise your product development department to develop a resin with more shear strength and which adheres more tightly to a metal shaft. On the other hand, if the trend is toward brightly colored heels, then you might recommend the development of resins which better hold bright and bold dyes. Having been involved in this business, you would have developed a close relationship with major heel manufacturing customers. If you determined that they were developing equipment to manufacture the heels more quickly and at higher temperatures, then your company probably should be developing resins which are compatible with the new equipment and manufacturing processes. These are examples of studying customer trends and needs, and taking action based on those studies.

2. Study the trends and needs of your customers' customers. There are two benefits of studying the customers and the industries served by your immediate customers, especially the major ones. First, you gain perspective as to which of your customers and industries will be growing and changing, based on the pull-through effects of the customers and the industries they serve. This input will help you in determining which customers and industries to emphasize, what challenges and problems they are facing and will be facing in the future, and what products and technologies you should be improving and/or developing. The second benefit is, it will give you an understanding, sometimes even better than that of many of your customers, of what your customers can do to market more effectively to their customers. If you can help them to market more effectively, you are serving them, gaining their appreciation and loyalty, and developing increased business for your company.

In the two situations in 1 above we implied examples of customer's customers. The direct customer of the bank could be either the construction company or the companies they build for, depending on who the construction loan is to. In some cases the construction companies will take out the loan and be your direct customers; then the companies for which they are building will be the customer's customers as defined in this section. The direct customers of the resin company are the shoe heel manufacturers. If they in turn sell heels to shoe manufacturers, then the shoe manufacturers are your customers' customers. If the shoe companies manufacture their own heels, then your customers would be the shoe manufacturers, and your customers' customers would be the general public, which buys the shoes from your customers, the shoe manufacturers.

In an internal situation, if you happen to be an operations manager, then one of your personal customers might be the corporation president; a customer's customer could then be the board of directors.

3. Develop customer-related expertise. Once we have committed ourselves to certain industries and certain customers, we then can commit resources to understanding both how their businesses work and to learning the technologies upon which those businesses are based. If for instance your company sells raw materials to the manufacturers of polymer resins, and if as a result your chemists and engineers study the technology of resin manufacture, then your company may develop improved raw materials and supplies for your customers. You also can assist the customers in increasing their manufacturing efficiency by sharing with them your developments in improved procedures and equipment.

Suppose some of your bank calling officers understand the intricacies of the construction business; including the details of prospecting, bidding, labor relations and sub-contracting. Then your bank can devise innovative financing plans, inform the contractors of better ways of prospecting, and develop cost-saving computerized bidding programs. Each would be a service designed for the construction industry, based on your customer-related expertise.

As a credit union president or controller, you could examine the types of problems and challenges your members are facing and hire or develop expertise to handle some of those needs. Some of these needs could include personal financial counseling, computerized financial planning, computerized tax preparation combined with expert consulting, identifying and reporting on better and less expensive home repair services, advising on types of investments available and their relative security and earnings potential, discounted insurance, and other discounted purchasing.

4. Provide a customer information service. Gather and analyze information about your customer-industries, and formally or informally provide valuable information to customers. This information could be disseminated by newsletter, personal letter, phone call update, phone-in service, or by (planned) casual conversations during normal business communications. This will increase your welcome when you make personal contacts, and will establish you as being committed and knowledgeable within the industry.

5. Be change oriented. Continually look for changes everywhere that may result in problems or opportunities for customers; these can provide you with new and different ways to serve customers. Increased transportation costs combined with new teleconferencing technology can give a motel chain the opportunity to establish teleconferencing and teletraining centers for associations and large corporations. Population shifts, life style changes, income redistribution, and housing trends will affect the branch locations and marketing methods of financial institutions.

Internal changes in your organization can affect department objectives. Suppose many more production executives are being promoted to general manager, with responsibility for the marketing function. Then as director of the marketing or marketing research department, you may decide to modify the approach of your department to internally communicating the importance of the marketing function. You may decide to schedule internal seminars and informational programs on up-to-date marketing and marketing research principles and practices, primarily for the benefit of these new and potential general managers.

6. Interview customers effectively. There are many ways to obtain information about industries and companies; and their trends, problems, opportunities, wants and needs. One of the best is the personal interview. You need to develop your interviewing skills for two purposes: (1) gathering information from initial contacts with industry experts, sales prospects, and customer employees you are encountering for the first time, and (2) continuing interviews with your regular industry and company contacts.

A hospital administrator might interview selected government officials, looking for first hand information on trends and decisions which will affect hospital strategy.   He may do this formally, or informally in *casual* conversation.   A motel executive housekeeper might informally interview a number of customers to determine what in housekeeping service is most important to them. A bank teller might casually interview customers at the window, while processing their checks and paperwork, to determine which of present and proposed bank products give the most positive reaction.

7. Be a problem finder. Look at every situation, both inside and outside the company, from the standpoint of what is wrong with this; how could it be better; what resources and knowledge do you have that could help this situation; how might a change in this area help the customer? Frequently, finding the problems can be much more difficult and more valuable, than finding the solutions after the problems have been properly identified.

The entire credit union industry; the universal credit card; the IRA; the word processor; the personal computer; the transistor radio; the specialized direct mail insurance company; the money market fund; all these were valuable solutions to existing problems. However, the solutions were fairly easy to comprehend; the clear identification of the problem which led to the solution was in each case the more difficult and more valuable contribution. By your concentrating on problem finding, you possibly could make the same level of impact on your company and on your customers as those who found the problems above did on the overall economy.

8. Talk in terms of benefits.   Every customer, commercial or personal, is *primarily* interested in how his organization and how he personally can benefit from any idea or any proposal. We are all interested in *what's in it for me* ?   This may be the singly most important truth of motivation, persuasion and sales; it is certainly *one* of the most important. Consequently, we should continually be thinking in terms of customer benefits.

Suppose you want a division manager's support for adding an employee to your staff department, or for giving another division more than its allocated share of services; how will it benefit him and his division to give you that support?   You want a congressman to influence others to support a certain piece of legislation; how will it benefit him or his constituents? You want a customer to transfer her savings account and her IRA to your institution; how will it benefit her or her family? You want the secretary to a department manager of one of your major customers to talk favorably about your company and its outstanding service; how will it benefit her or her boss or her company to do so?   When possible, every statement you make to a customer about your company and about one of your products or services should contain a customer benefit.

Referring to the above, let's look at some benefits. By your applying the extra effort to a different division there is an excellent chance of developing exceptionally profitable business for the company, which will later make available additional financial resources to all divisions. These benefits should be explained to the division manager. The congressman's constituents will be better served (benefitted) in some specific way if the legislation is passed; you should explain the specific way as a benefit. By transferring all her accounts to your financial institution the customer will have to deal with only one institution, and she will have more influence on that institution; tell her. The secretary's department has been receiving poor service and it would benefit her and her department to have that changed. Talk in terms of benefits and suggest this to her.

9. Provide justifications. Whenever you desire a commercial or personal customer to take a particular action, or refrain from an action, you should be prepared to justify why you recommend that decision. The justification consists of presenting the benefits, the value of those benefits (frequently in dollars), the costs involved (frequently in dollars) and the difference, or the benefits minus the costs.

Purchase of "equipment A" will reduce your customer's manufacturing time and lower his per unit labor costs, resulting in a savings of $100,000 per year. Since total costs, including installation and startup, are only $50,000, the purchase will pay for itself in only six months. Note: your controller can inform you of more sophistocated methods of calculating payout, such as the present value method.

By transferring her account to your bank your customer will lose 1/4 % on her interest rate, but she will have the assurance that no checks will be bounced, and you will offer her a $5000 open-ended line of credit; isn't that more than a fair trade? Ask her.

You might justify a special request to another department as follows: "Department C will not be pleased if you put my project in front of theirs; but you can see how critical my project is to reaching our department's and the company's time objectives. By giving my project priority you will be demonstrating to all in the company your ability to make wise decisions to benefit the company, based on hard-nosed value analysis."

10. Utilize experts. As you become involved in more important activities, you will find, more and more often, that you do not have all the expertise needed to adequately analyze or solve customer problems. You will need to bring together others, mainly from within your company, to work with and serve your customers.

A doctor calls in a physical therapist to work with a patient because of his special needs. A marketing or technical manager brings in a computer systems analyst to design an improved instrument package for a customer's operations. A product manager brings together representatives from research, manufacturing and marketing to analyze an important customer service problem. These are examples of calling in outside expertise to serve the customer's needs.

11. Serve other departments in your organization. The effective performance of not just yours, but a number of the company's departments is required for the company to give good customer service *across the board.* Consequently, when you treat each of the other departments in your company as an internal or *personal* customer, and provide outstanding service to that department, you are helping them to be effective and to serve the commercial customer effectively. Each of us have experienced cases where we as the customer have been are treated well by some departments of a company and poorly by others. If this happens too frequently, you find another company to deal with. The poor service by the *other* departments may have come from a poor attitude of those within the department. It also may have been caused by these *other* departments not being properly served by their back-up departments, and therefore not having the information to adequately serve us. This is one of the reasons the Cross-Marketing system emphasizes giving top quality service to both commercial and personal customers.

12. Do your own job well. When each of us performs our own assigned responsibilities and tasks effectively, whatever they may be, we are contributing to serving the customer. As stated in chapter 1, the purpose of any business is to effectively serve the customer. And as related in number 11, above, each person and each department is important in that effort.

When everyone in the organization is productive, the organization is operating as a smoothly running, well oiled machine, which is effectively serving the customer. Customer problems and needs are identified on a timely basis. Products and services are researched and developed to solve those problems and to serve those needs. They are presented to the customer in a professional and convincing manner, so the customer can easily make positive decisions which will benefit him. Staff departments efficiently serve the line departments. Engineering engineers high quality products. Production produces products of high quality at low or competitive costs, and on a timely basis. Distribution ships the products to correct addresses and without delay. Accounting sends properly prepared invoices on a timely basis. Moneys are received and efficiently handled so as to prevent waste of interest and expenses. As a result, customers are happy and well served, the company is profitable, higher wages and benefits can be paid to productive employees, and perhaps prices can be lowered a bit, which makes the company even more competitive and able to effectively serve all the customers.

When you believe in what you do, innovate and concentrate your efforts, improve your communication skills, and effectively touch and serve the customer; you have developed a fertile environment for further effective communications, and for communicating solutions to customer problems.

APPLICATION OF CROSS-MARKETING COMMUNICATIONS

Figure 9-1 on the following page is provided for you, and your people, to copy and use as an action plan for improving your Cross-Marketing communications. To use this table properly, and to obtain the greatest benefit from this exercise, follow these steps in order:

1. Choose one of the above six keys to Cross-Marketing communications. Choose the one in which you feel improvement would give the most job-related benefit. Complete the steps below for that key. Then repeat the procedure with that or a different key. Proceed through the six keys in this manner.

2. Review the twelve principles and practices listed under the chosen key. Add any other related principles which you believe applies to your job and your situation.

3. Choose the principle or practice listed (from one of the 12, plus any you added) from which you feel improved performance would yield the most benefit.

4. Choose a commercial or personal customer on which to concentrate when using the chosen principle or practice. Under 1 and 2 on the table, write the name of the customer chosen, and a brief description of the situation concerning that customer. Indicate under step 3 why that customer was chosen.

5. Write a short action plan in step 4 on how you will apply this principle or practice to the chosen customer.

6. Over a period of days continue to use the chosen principle or practice with the selected customer, and with other customers as appropriate. Make notes of the results.

7. Review your performance at the end of each day and note where the results were good, where the results were not as good, and what you plan to do in the near future to improve performance and results. Note: if the action plan is not working then revise the action plan.

8. When you are satisfied with your performance or progress on this principle or practice then return to step 1.

Figure 9-1

APPLICATION OF CROSS-MARKETING
COMMUNICATIONS

1. CUSTOMER NAME (OR CATEGORY): _____
   _____

2. CUSTOMER SITUATION: _____
   _____
   _____

3. AT THIS TIME THE CUSTOMER NEEDS MOST FOR ME TO BETTER (CIRCLE
   ONE OR MORE AND EXPLAIN) -

   - BELIEVE   EXPLANATION: _____
   - INNOVATE
   - CONCENTRATE   _____
   - TOUCH
   - COMMUNICATE   _____
   - SERVE
                      _____

4. ACTION PLANNED - THIS IS WHAT I WILL DO AND WHEN I WILL DO IT:
   _____
   _____
   _____
   _____
   _____
   _____
   _____
   _____
   _____
   _____

10

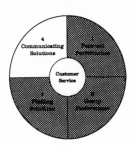

PERSUASIVE COMMUNICATIONS

POSITIVE PERSONAL ATTITUDES AND TRAITS
PERSONAL SKILLS
THE PROCESS OF PERSUASIVE COMMUNICATIONS

Leaders deal with their people daily. All employees deal daily with their personal and commercial customers. As a result, all continually face the need to sell their ideas, and to persuade others to make use of their services and their problem solutions.

The purpose of chapter 9 was to show how to communicate in a smart and effective way. Chapter 10 rests on the foundation of chapter 9, and takes the next step of showing how to communicate ideas and solutions in such a way that the other person (customer or otherwise) will accept them and act on them.

To achieve a high level of effectiveness in persuading - in influencing - in inducing - in convincing - in impelling - others to take a desired course of action, we must concern ourselves with three areas of performance: (1) our personal attitudes and traits, (2) our personal communications skills, and (3) the "process" of persuasive communications.

As we address these three areas in this chapter we will illustrate them by applying them as they relate to a **functional specialist**, one who has been asked to assist the sales department in selling to and providing effective services to a major customer. This specialist may be a product or service manager, an engineer, a technical department head, a computer programmer, a financial accounting expert; any type of functional specialist who might from time-to-time assist and make joint sales calls with the sales department.

The product being sold and supported in this case could be a physical product such as a commodity chemical, a new type of bicycle, or a piece of machinery; or it could be or a service, such as a banking service, hospital care, or a special motel package. In this chapter we will use the word *product* to represent any of these. We will use the word *service* to represent any service that the functional specialist is providing either to the sales department or to the commercial customer. These services could consist of general consulting, problem solving visits, gathering needed information, solving specific problems, preparing specialized literature, serving on a sales team, or even just being friendly and cooperative.

POSITIVE PERSONAL ATTITUDES AND TRAITS

The following are six personal attitudes and traits which are required for effective persuasive communications.

1. Belief. The foundation of effective communications, and the foundation of persuasion, is belief. If we really believe in the value of what we are presenting, it is relatively easy to develop the courage, the conviction and the inspiration to present it to others. Chapter 6 discussed a number of specific beliefs we should develop to be effective in persuasive communications; among them, belief in our company, in our product, in ourselves, and in the benefits of our product or idea to the customer. We can increase our positive belief in each of these areas through a three step process. First, for each belief, we can list the many reasons we should have that positive belief. Second, we can study and learn those positive reasons. Third, we can concentrate on the positive reasons and remove from our minds any negative, competing thoughts.

2. Enthusiasm. Enthusiasm is generated from belief, and gives the customers the honest impression that we really believe that what we are offering and supporting will benefit them and solve their problems. Many sales have been consummated because the customer observed, "If the company representative believes so strongly in what he is saying, then it must be true." If we are not on fire for the product or service we are representing, then the customer may feel uncomfortable in making a positive decision, and may be inclined to wait and continue evaluating other alternatives. We develop our enthusiasm through increasing our multi-faceted beliefs as discussed in chapters 5 and 9.

3. Persistence. If we really believe in what we are representing we are not going to be easily discouraged, or dissuaded, even when the customer hesitates and appears to reject us or our proposal. If we are sure that what we have to offer is the best solution for the customer's problem, then we will *hang in there*, and continue to ask questions, answer questions, remind him of the benefits, and attempt to persuade him that we and our recommendations are in his best interest.

Some people are conditioned to say no at first to any proposal. In such a case it is only when the proposer demonstrates his positive conviction by continuing to support his position, despite their continued objections, that they seriously consider his proposal. Some people have a habit of testing the strength of the proposer's beliefs by automatically refusing to make a decision early in any discussion. This can be true whether we are attempting to sell a product to a customer, a new program to our management, or cooperation on productivity improvement to a peer or to a subordinate.

There is a significant difference between being persistent and being obnoxious. In all matters dealing with other people we need to use good human relations skills, such as those discussed in chapters 8 and 9. If we disagree with the customer, instead of saying, "I disagree," or even, "Why do you say that?" we would be more persuasive to respond, "Could I ask how you arrived at that conclusion?" Notice the softness of the statement which started with the phrase, "may I ask," and its professionalism and delicateness. And yet the statement represents persistence in solidly *hanging in there* and generating additional information to carry the communication forward.

4. Self discipline. We must discipline ourselves to do what we know we should do. The particular assignment in question may be in addition to our normal work load. We must discipline ourselves to use our time wisely, so as to accomplish the important normal tasks, and at the same time allocate sufficient time to this project. We must discipline ourselves to practice and use the principles discussed in this chapter, and perhaps to review our performance each evening if we have not yet arrived at a high level of performance. We must discipline ourselves to prepare effectively and professionally for each meeting so as to give our team and our organization the best chance of success.

5. Friendliness. Not everyone prefers to deal with a person who is joking, laughing, loud, and telling lots of humorous stories. But, everyone prefers to deal with someone who demonstrates genuine friendliness; a warm smile and handshake, a look in the eye, interest in the other person and his welfare, willingness to listen and not interrupt, a helpful and cooperative attitude, understanding, appreciation and respect. To become an even more friendly person, we might ask some peers and friends to make one suggestion which we might employ to become even more friendly and to make those around us even more comfortable. Many of us prefer to do business with our friends. All of us prefer to do business with a friendly person.

6. Interest in the customer's welfare. We know intuitively when someone is attempting to genuinely help us, as compared to when they are trying to *sell* us something from which they will be the prime beneficiary. If we keep the customer's welfare primarily in mind, realizing that our organization must benefit as well, then the customer will be responsive to our communications. As long as we genuinely are trying to solve the customer's problems, and do not let our egos get in the way, the application of this principle should not be difficult.

PERSONAL SKILLS

Eight personal communication skills need to be employed during the communications process, in order for us to be persuasive. By being persuasive we motivate the customer to first evaluate, and then agree, with our problem solution.

1. Having empathy. "If I were you, and had had your experiences and background instead of my own, then I would look at the situation just as you do." This statement represents empathy, the ability to look at a situation through the psychological and mental eyes of the other person. It is important that we develop the skill to ask ourselves and understand, what the customer is looking for? What fears and concerns does he have? What does he consider the problem to be? What type of solution would be most acceptable to him and to his company? How does he like to dealt with - in an open and friendly way; by analyzing lots of data; with a simple presentation of the facts and backup evidence; or with numerous testimonials from satisfied customers? What type of presentation and what type of proposal would be most helpful to and most meaningful to this customer?

2. Maintaining eye contact. By providing the customer with firm, and consistent eye contact, we are demonstrating that we are confident, honest, and interested. We want to avoid the wide-eyed gaze, or the cold, hard stare. But, at the same time, we want to avoid looking shifty-eyed, or not consistently looking the customer in the eye. There are two advantages of proper eye contact. First, we gain considerable information from the facial expressions and body signals of the customer during the meeting.

Second, we develop an attitude of trust and respect toward us within the customer. In our society good eye contact is considered to demonstrate honesty and self confidence.

3. Asking questions. We will want to ask questions both of our sales department and of the customers themselves. (Note: now, we are thinking in the context of the functional specialist.) We want to find out from the sales department what are their objectives; what do they know and what don't they know about the customer and his problems and needs; what do and don't they know about the solutions to those problems and needs; what input do they need from us; how do they plan to proceed with the customer; and what part are they looking for us to play? From the customer we need to determine how does he perceive his problems and needs; what has he considered already; how does that compare to what we have recommended to date; what might further develop if this project is successful; who are the knowledgeable people and the decision makers; and how are they best contacted? We need to know what will happen if the problem is not solved, and how the solution of this situation might benefit the customer personally.

The questions to be asked will differ for each situation. Some can be planned ahead of time. Others will develop as face-to-face discussions proceed. How we ask the questions can be as important as determining the questions to ask. We must develop the skill to do both. The book, **The Evaluation Interview,** by Dr. Richard Fear presents some valuable information on interviewing and effective question asking. Also, it is important to perceive when to ask questions and when to just be observant and listen.

4. Listening. We must be effective listeners if we are going to be good communicators and good persuaders. We need to be listening intently and at all times. The customer may say or imply something of great importance while we are on the phone making an appointment, when we first meet him, while he is explaining his situation, while answering our questions, while walking us through his facilities, during lunch, while responding to our suggestions, and even during follow-up conversations.

To increase listening effectiveness we need to be empathetic, avoid distractions and mind wandering, pay close attention to what is being said, avoid unnecessary interruptions, ask clarifying questions, avoid pre-judging, listen for underlying meanings, make notes of main points, and encourage in-depth discussions. Books and training programs are available on this valuable skill from our company and from others.

5. Developing product/service knowledge. It is important that we have, and know how to obtain, adequate knowledge about the products and services with which we are dealing. In providing information (features, advantages, benefits, and evidence) concerning any product or service, it gives us confidence to know considerably more about the product or service than we need to make the presentation. This knowledge also provides us with a solid foundation for asking and answering questions.   As a functional specialist we would normally have far more product knowledge (concerning our specialty) than would the average person.

Many times we find that inadequate possession of product/service knowledge is the reason that so many people fear to make persuasive or "selling" presentations, either inside or outside the organization. Often the person feels that management should be providing him information about products and services. He is correct, and that would be the case in a well-run company which is effectively applying the Cross-Marketing system. However, if we find ourselves in a company where we are not being provided with adequate product knowledge, it is relatively easy for us to dig out that knowledge for ourselves, and we should do so if we are truly competent. We can read a few, very important books in our subject area. We can subscribe to one or two of the more important magazines in the field. We can obtain product and technical literature produced by our organization and review it. We can arrange meetings with knowledgeable people in our company to discuss the subject area and the materials we have reviewed. We even can phone and meet with knowledgeable experts in other companies, at universities, in consulting organizations, and at the editorial staff of trade periodicles.

Generally there are only a few major products and services and a few applications of those that we really need to know about. We should concentrate our efforts on obtaining product knowledge on those few products and services. While we are doing this, we should be looking for ways those products and services are advantageous to the customer as compared to not using them, and as compared to competitive products and services. We also should be looking for customer benefits from our products and services, as well as evidence to back up claims of customer benefits.

6. Presenting benefits.   In evaluating any proposed product or service the customer is always interested in WIIFM (What's in it for me? - and - What's in it for my organization?).   Consequently, we need to develop the skill to analyze for and explain product and service benefits, what's in it for the customer.

When presenting or recommending a particular product or service we will describe the product or service, its features, and how they are used. However, the customer is even more interested in, "What are the advantages of these products or services, and in what ways will they benefit me? Will they save me time? Will they reduce my costs? Will they generate me more profit? Will they make it easier for me to do my job? Will they bring me prestige and make me a hero? Will they make someone else's job in my organization easier? How will they accomplish these, and what is your evidence that these benefits are true?" These are questions we need to answer.

We can spend a lot of time describing our wonderful product or service, but if we do not explain how it benefits the customer, the customer remains unsure as to why he should utilize or purchase it, as compared to taking some other course of action, or no action at all. Sometimes it appears to the customer we don't ourselves understand how the proposal will benefit him. In addition, all too frequently we believe we understand how our proposal benefits the customer, but we assume incorrectly that the customer can clearly see those benefits. It is important for us to explain the benefits of our proposal, and not give the customer the opportunity to misunderstand what those benefits are.

Good persuaders frequently ask customers questions to confirm that they understand the benefits. For instance, suppose we are proposing a new financial program which will save the customer twenty hours per year. After explaining the benefits, we might ask the confirming question, "Would it be important to you to save twenty hours per year?" If the customer answers, "Yes," it indicates he understands and appreciates the benefit. If the customer answers, "No," or "I'm not sure," then either he doesn't understand, or he does not regard the *benefit* as important. Either answer is important information. Likewise, if the customer responds by asking a question, then we have an opportunity to answer that question and keep the communication channel open.

7. Developing and presenting evidence. It is one thing to claim we have a wonderful product or service which will solve the customer's problem. It is one thing to claim that our product or service has numerous advantages and benefits, and even present those to the customer in a clear fashion. Frequently, it is something else again to convince the customer that what we are saying is true. The way we convince him that the features, advantages and benefits we are professing are true is by developing and presenting evidence to support our claims.

If what we are saying is true, then there must be some evidence to support what we are saying. There may be satisfied customers who have used the product or who have been served by us. They may be willing to write us a testimonial letter, or talk to us on tape, or be available to be interviewed by a prospective customer. We may possess written documents or scientific data to support our case. Or just the logic of the situation, or an analogy to a related situation, may provide evidence to support our claims. In any case, it is important to be skilled in determining what evidence is needed, and in presenting that evidence effectively.

8. Asking for action. If we believe in our proposal or solution, there is no reason we should hesitate to ask the customer to commit himself, at the earliest possible time, to make a positive decision. One of the reasons that so many of us fail to be persuasive communicators; and one of the reasons so many people are ineffective in selling; is that they do not have the courage, conviction and skill to ask for action.

As a functional specialist assisting the sales department, it would not normally be our responsibility to ask a commercial customer to take action; that is, to purchase our problem solution. That would be the responsibility of the sales department. However, there are a number of smaller decisions that must be made along the way, for which we might ask for action. We will ask the sales department to provide us with background material. We may ask the sales department to obtain certain information and data from the customer. We may ask the customer to allow us to visit a certain sensitive location, and make observations.

In summary, whenever we are involved in persuasive communications, as soon as we believe the customer has received sufficient information to make a positive decision we should suggest that a positive decision be made at this time. There are a number of ways to ask for action. One way is to say, "Well, why don't we go ahead and ---(take this action)," and then wait for a response.

THE PROCESS OF PERSUASIVE COMMUNICATIONS

Persuasive communications is a proactive process. We must take action, and do and say certain things, to cause the other person to believe what we say sufficiently to act on that belief.

There are ten steps to the process of persuasive communications. Sometimes we will consciously and methodically move through these ten steps. At other times, many of them will happen automatically, or the customer will take some of the steps without us having any input.

STEPS IN PERSUASIVE COMMUNICATIONS

1. Making contact
2. Getting acquainted
3. Explaining the purpose
4. Interviewing for problems and needs
5. Generating solutions
6. Presenting solutions
7. Explaining advantages, benefits and evidence
8. Answering questions
9. Obtaining action
10. Following up

As explained earlier, the steps of this process will be presented as seen through the eyes of a functional specialist who has been asked to assist on a sales team. He will take certain actions (move through some or all of the 10 steps) to persuade our salesperson (his personal customer), and then later the commercial customer, to take certain actions, once it is determined what those actions should be.

Let us assume that we, as the functional specialist, are informed by our superior that one of our important customers has a problem, which if we can solve will represent considerable business for our company. Unfortunately the salesperson feels she can handle the assignment alone and that she does not need our help; but upper management has decided otherwise. Consequently, we need to employ our persuasion skills first with our own salesperson, and then with the commercial customer.

1. Making contact. The first step in persuasion is to make contact with the person whom we desire to persuade. At this point we may or may not know what we want to persuade them to do. Also, during the 10 step process, what we want to persuade them to do may change as we gain more information.

In this particular case we make contact with our salesperson (our personal customer) by phone. We call, introduce ourselves, be as friendly as possible, tell her the purpose of our call, and ask for a personal appointment. If she resists or attempts to delay the appointment we are as persistent as we need to be to arrange the appointment at an appropriate time. (But, we are not obnoxious. We use the HULRAH human relations rules presented in chapter 8.) We may have to "sell" the appointment, by explaining why we need to see her and how the appointment will benefit her and others.

Note: the situation determines how persistent we should be. If we absolutely must see the customer within a week, we insist on that. However, if it would not substantially harm our mission to delay a few weeks or a few months, and the customer has a genuine reason to delay the appointment, we may have no choice but to graciously comply with the customer's wishes.

If our initial contact was face-to-face, we might move to step 2 immediately, or we might introduce ourselves and make an appointment to return at a later time.

As we will see, in this particular case, making contact (step 1) with the commercial customer is taken care of by the salesperson.

2. Getting acquainted. When we first meet any customer (at this point, our personal customer, the salesperson) face-to-face we probably will not immediately get down to business. It is important to relax the situation and develop some rapport with the customer. Therefore, we will take the opportunity to have some small talk, about some items of interest to the customer. We might mention that we have heard some very fine things about her, especially concerning her knowledge in a certain area of expertise. We might ask her how she got started in that area. She then can feel good as she brags a bit and explains this to us.

This "Getting Acquainted" process can take just a very few minutes and should not last an extended length of time. After all, we are with her to do business and to accomplish effective results.

In this case, as we enter the salesperson's office we notice on the wall some public speaking plaques. Instead of immediately getting down to business we comment on the plaques, and have a short discussion about her public speaking experiences and her experience with the Toastmasters organization. This discussion is about her and her accomplishments, and helps her to feel more relaxed and more friendly toward us. Then, in a non-threatening way, we bring up the subject of the sales team and ask if we could ask her some questions.

We move through steps 3-9 with our salesperson, finally arriving at an agreement as to how we will approach the commercial customer.

The salesperson makes an appointment with the commercial customer (step 1). The two of us meet with and get acquainted with the customer, much as described above (step 2).

3. Explanation of purpose. After a few minutes of "getting acquainted" conversation with the commercial customer we get down to business, and explain the purpose of the visit. One of our team makes a comment similar to the following: "We appreciate your taking the time to discuss with us your problems and plans concerning the Abalone unit. We have some preliminary ideas and possible solutions, but before discussing them we feel we need some additional information and insight."

4. Interviewing for problems and needs. This may be the most important step in the entire persuasive communications process. We already have some ideas on how we might help the customer, but we may not be fully knowledgeable concerning all of the intricacies of the problem. In fact, we may be entirely on the wrong track. Just as with a doctor, who prescribes treatment before understanding the entire condition of the patient, if we give our ideas and solutions before thoroughly understanding the situation and the problem, we may prescribe some very bad medicine.

We might describe the situation as we understand it and ask for the customer to give us clarifications and corrections. Probably, even before doing that, we will ask the customer to give us a run down on the situation. We will listen intently with very few interruptions, except for occasional clarifying questions. We will use the appropriate personal traits and personal skills discussed earlier in the chapter.

During this interviewing process we may offer some encouraging comments concerning our ability to help the customer solve the problem, but without getting into any details as to what our solutions are. This will start to condition him that we have answers and can help him, but without impeding the flow of information from him to us.

We will behave as a consultant who is gathering and analyzing information in order to help the customer. This raises our prestige in his eyes, and encourages him to provide us with more and in-depth information. Having developed this client-patient relationship, we may subtly ask him questions concerning what other solutions he has investigated, and what are the advantages, benefits and costs of those (competitive) solutions.

We will continue the information-gathering process, both in the customer's office and out in the field, until the solution becomes apparent, or until we believe we have sufficient information to analyze and arrive at a solution.

5. Generating solutions. As discussed in chapter 8, we compare the customer's problems and opportunities with our strengths and resources (both those in hand and those which can be obtained). We arrive at a solution which we believe will satisfy the customer and meets his decision criteria. We prepare a presentation which presents the solution, what it will do for the customer (the benefits), and our evidence that it will work.

6. Presenting solutions. Once we have arrived at our solution to the customer's problem, we then face the task of presenting it to him in a clear, understandable and persuasive way. We can present the solution now or later. We can present it verbally on a one-to-one basis, in a written letter or report, as a presentation to a group of customer representatives, or as a combination of these. In any case, our solution needs to be well-thought-out so it will be received positively by the customer, both mentally and emotionally.

We need to be thoroughly convinced ourselves that the solution will work, and be prepared to answer any questions which will arise. In fact, we should attempt to anticipate all the questions the customer might ask. We might hold a dry run of our presentation, having our own people attempt to pick our solution apart.

When we make the presentation, whether it is on-the-spot or after careful preparation, we should carry ourselves as consultants who have thoroughly analyzed the problem and have arrived at the best solution. It should be clear to everyone that we are convinced that our solution is in the customer's best interest, and that any benefits to us or our company are clearly secondary considerations. (However, everyone knows we also are in business to increase profitable sales, and we need not be ashamed of this.)

7. Explaining advantages, benefits and evidence. During the presentation of the solution in step 6 we will clearly explain the advantages and benefits of our proposal, along with our evidence which supports what we say. This is so important it is listed as a separate step.

The customer is interested in comparing this solution with others which might be available, or with doing nothing at all. He will compare the advantages and the benefits to be derived from each, along with the associated costs. He will weigh the evidence provided to determine which course of action seems to be best proven and best supported.

To assist him we may prepare a comparison of all the known opportunities or solutions, with the features, advantages, benefits and supporting evidence for each. We may decide to provide a cost-justification, indicating the payout on any costs or investments required.

Likewise, if in a different situation we are trying to persuade our superior to support one of our ideas, or our people to be motivated to take a certain action, or a different commercial customer to make a certain decision, we need to support our proposal with the advantages, benefits, and supporting evidence.

8. Answering questions. The customer is going to have a number of questions concerning our proposal or recommendation. As a matter of fact, if he does not, that generally will indicate a lack of interest on his part. We should answer his questions as directly and as clearly as possible. We even will want to ask, at appropriate times, whether he has questions or whether he understands or agrees with what we are saying. Sometimes his questions will be posed in a negative way, indicating a rejection of all or part of our idea or proposal. We should be careful not to resent this or to show resentment. If we do, this will build a negative attitude and concern in the mind of the customer.

When we receive negative questions or comments it is wise to cushion our response with a softening statement. For instance, if the customer were to say, "That kind of solution will not work in my business." We might respond, "Experienced managers frequently have believed that way, until they knew about......." Another way of responding to such a comment would be with a softened interrogative question such as the following: "Could you explain why you feel that way?"

It is important that we ferret out any questions that the customer has in his mind concerning our solution or proposal and answer them. Otherwise, it is unlikely that the customer will make a positive decision. One way to do this, especially later in the presentation, is to ask a comprehensive revealing question such as the following. "If you were going to make the decision to go ahead with this proposal, what further questions would you need to answer before you would be comfortable in making a positive decision?"

9. Obtaining action. Once we have presented our solution or proposal to the customer and have explained how it will benefit him; once we have answered all his pertinent questions, and believe that if we were in the customer's shoes we would be ready to make a favorable decision; it is time to ask for action. One way to do this is to make a positive statement such as, "Let's go ahead and get started; okay?" Another is to make a positive statement such as, "I believe the best action now is for you to go ahead and install this piece of equipment; do you agree?"

We might give him a choice of two different courses of action such as, "Do you want me to get started right away, or would it be better to wait until the first of the month?" If the customer is somewhat hesitant, we might help him weigh the advantages for going ahead with this proposal against the reasons for hesitating. We might say, "Why don't we treat this decision like any major business decision; why don't we take a sheet of paper and list on the left side the advantages and reasons for going ahead with this proposal and on the right side the ideas which might cause us to hesitate?" Following the comparison, assuming it indicates we should go ahead, we then suggest that we do so. However we ask for action, the important point is to "ask for action!"

There may be times during the presentation when we are not sure as to whether the customer is agreeing with us or not. We are not sure whether he is ready to take action, or has some severe reservations. At such a time we might ask a temperature-taking question. We might say something like, "If you were going to go ahead with this proposal, would you want to do it right away or wait until next month?" With this question, we have not assumed that he is going to take action. We have just asked what his timing would be, if he were to take action. If he responds very favorably to this question, we might go ahead and ask for action immediately. For instance, if he were to respond, "Oh, I'd like to get started right away," then we would immediately go ahead and ask for action with a statement like, "Would Monday be a convenient day to get started?" On the other hand, if he responds negatively to our temperature-taking question by saying, "I'm not at all sure that this proposal will fit my needs," then we might respond with a question such as, "What concerns you most about the proposal?" We are now generating further information to understand his thinking process.

In the illustration we have been using, it probably would be up to the sales representative to ask for action from the commercial customer. However, in other situations, such as making a proposal to our superior or to our people, it would be up to us to ask for action, not to wait and hope that they would volunteer to take action.

10. Following up. Having obtained a positive decision from our customer to agree to and act on our proposed solution; we should follow through to make sure that no one procrastinates or slips up in implementing the decision. We may confirm the positive decision in writing. We may inform those persons who need to take supporting actions of the decision, and even assist them in taking those actions. We may make information-gathering and reminder phone calls to make sure everyone is doing what they should do.

Just because we have been successful in persuading the other person to approve a certain action, that does not mean that person, and others involved, will remember to take all the implementing steps on a timely basis. If the decision is important enough, we can spend the time and effort to coordinate the implementation of the solution.

11

"The performance of the front line worker
makes or breaks the company."
                                        Baber

TO THE FRONT LINE WORKER
"THE IMPORTANT PERSON"

CROSS-MARKETING
THE PROCESS OF CROSS-MARKETING
TWENTY-FIVE CUSTOMER SERVICE MISTAKES
DOS AND DON'TS FOR HANDLING THE UNHAPPY CUSTOMER

The purpose of this chapter is to further put the book and the Cross-Marketing concept into perspective for you, the front line worker - the bank teller or customer service representative, the hospital nurse, receptionist or department secretary, the airline steward or counter representative, the hotel housekeeper or front desk clerk, the restaurant waitress or maitre d', the secretary, the mechanic, the production line worker, the office worker - the important person who directly does the company's work, with or without supervising others.

You and your associates do the work that causes your company to have products and services to offer to the customers. Many of you provide those services directly. Your superiors strategize, plan, organize, coordinate and sometimes direct and control. They sometimes even do part of the work. But, most of the work - the production of products, communications and services - is performed by you. If you and your associates do your work well (*if you are efficient and highly productive, if you pay attention to details and perform work of high quality, if you communicate well with and cooperate with customers, superiors and fellow employees, if you have a positive attitude that is "catching," if you are a positive influence on others)* then your company will prosper, and you and your associates will prosper because there are income and resources to share all around.

If you are fortunate enough to directly come in contact with the commercial customer you have an important job indeed. Frequently you become "the company" to the customer. How well you deal with each customer will have a major impact on whether that customer will (1) continue to do business with you and your company, (2) expand business with you and recommend you to others, (3) stop doing business with you, or (4) bad-mouth you and your company to your other customers and to potential customers. Most of your interactions with customers are performed outside the eyesight of supervision. Therefore, oftentimes you must act as your own supervisor and make those decisions and perform those actions which you would advise others to do, if you were supervising them.

You have an important responsibility. What you and your associates do or do not do will <u>make or break the company</u>. This chapter discusses what you can do to help "make" your company (bank, hotel, hospital, etc.) be successful.

CROSS-MARKETING

Cross-Marketing consists of "activities by which solutions and benefits are effectively communicated from numerous parts of a supplier (you and others in the company) to numerous receivers, and ultimately to the customer."

In other words, you and your company will be effective and prosperous only if you and your associate employees, at all levels, learn to be productive and to work together cooperatively as a team to serve one another and to serve the commercial customer. To accomplish the last part of this requires that you understand who your customer is and what he needs, and then supply that need effectively.

You can be effective in Cross-Marketing by following *"The Process of Cross-Marketing."*

THE PROCESS OF CROSS-MARKETING

Chapters 1-3 discuss corporate business leadership and the bases and theory of Cross-Marketing. This will be valuable for you to read for the following reasons: (1) you will get a clearer understanding of the challenges facing upper management and how they should be addressed, (2) this understanding will make you more valuable and more qualified to be promoted, (3) you will learn how to be a better personal leader at home and on the job, (4) you will better understand customer and fellow employee needs and how to do your job better, and (5) you will better understand the advantages and benefits to all from following the practices discussed in this chapter. You especially need to read and understand the section in chapter 3 entitled, "Customer Support."

Chapters 4-10 discuss the details of *"The Process of Cross-Marketing."* The following are some specific comments on each of the four stages in the process.

1. Personal performance. Chapter 4 discusses 40 ways for you to be more effective and more productive in your job. It discusses how to set goals, make plans, and manage your attitude and your time. Chapter 5 shows you how to be more highly regarded by your customers, peers and superiors. It also discusses the twelve keys to personal success.

Chapter 2 presents the section on "Personal Assessment." This is a list of questions you can answer to determine how effective you are being and how you can improve your performance and productivity.

You and your associates are on the "firing line." You are in a position to see what the company needs to do to improve performance; to increase productivity; to better serve customers; to improve the morale and motivation of employees. You should think these ideas out and then share them with your supervisor or manager; at least you should if you want to be of the most value to your company. Not all your ideas can or should be implemented. But, your supervisor should be eager to receive them and should show substantial appreciation to you, both for your effort and for any really good ideas received and used.

Your supervisor should be equally interested in hearing from you about problems and roadblocks you face in doing a good, productive job. It is his or her job to help you solve those problems and remove those roadblocks. However, be careful about one thing. Many supervisors are less than perfect, and many are insecure in their jobs. If what you say sounds like it is criticism of them or how they do their jobs, they are liable to be quite upset and resistive to your ideas. This is not as it should be, but as it often is in the real world. (If supervisors are chosen properly, and are properly trained, this should not be a problem in your company. However, "proper training" exists in only a very small percentage of companies today.)

2. Group performance. Chapters 6 and 7 discuss how to motivate yourself and others. You need to believe in what you are doing, and help those around you to believe. If you bad-mouth the company, the management, the company's products, or anything - even a little - you will hurt your own motivation and the motivation of those you are speaking to. By understanding the information in chapters 6 and 7 you will better understand the challenges and tasks facing your superiors, and how you can work with them to guide and motivate those about you.

In an effective organization your supervisors will work with you to set performance objectives. They won't let you do this alone, and they won't set your objectives for you without your input. Your performance objectives could include increasing the number of units produced, or reducing the number of customer complaints, or increasing the number of times you identify a customer problem or need with a corresponding solution, or increasing the number of times you suggest to customers that they purchase or utilize your product or problem solution. Your superiors then will work with you to establish plans to achieve those objectives; to provide you with needed training and assistance; to measure your performance against the objectives and feed the results back to you; and to reward performance or make suggestions for improvements in performance. The more you yourself know and are able to do, the less guidance and help you will need from your supervisor or manager to accomplish these tasks.

We don't come to work to have fun. We come to work to produce and market a product or service, and to do it efficiently and productively. However, we all work best when we enjoy and are fulfilled in our work. It is management's job to help you to be productive, and to help you enjoy being productive at the same time.

3. Finding Solutions. If in your job you come in direct contact with the customer, as does a hotel front desk clerk or a bank teller, then you need to find solutions to customer problems in two ways. First, you need to understand your customers generally and what needs and problems they have as a class that you can solve. For example, all customers visiting a hotel or motel have a need to be treated with friendliness and respect. They want to be efficiently processed and get to their rooms quickly, and they have a problem if their rooms are not clean and fresh when they get there.

Second, you need to be alert to problems and needs of the specific customer you are talking to at a certain time. A businessperson visiting a hotel may require the services of the concierge - for instance, he may need some letters typed or an overhead projector for a meeting. You may have to ask questions and make suggestions to uncover such needs. The lady who deposits a large sum of money to her bank account may have the problem of deciding where to best invest it. The industrial customer who phones to check on the availability of a duplicate piece of equipment may be interested in purchasing a recently introduced test kit or a piece of enhancement equipment, but only if he is told about it. By suggesting the additional products and services, when appropriate, you are solving customer problems. You frequently are increasing the sales and income of your company as well.

In addition, all of us come in direct contact with other departments and employees (our personal customers). We need to have a cooperative attitude and be seeking out ways we can help them to do their jobs and serve the needs of their customers better. Chapter 8 discusses how to find and solve customer problems. It also includes the HULRAH formula for good human relations with customers and fellow employees.

4. Communicating solutions. Chapter 9 discusses how to be a better and more effective communicator. It presents some concepts which may be if interest to you in a number of ways. These include, how to be more creative and innovative, how to make people like you, how to communicate more clearly, and how to be more service oriented. Chapter 10 presents how to be more persuasive, and how to convince others to do what you feel is best for them.

It is important that you pay close attention to the customer (and to your fellow worker as well), and listen carefully to what he says. As a result, he will believe that his concerns are important to you, and you will understand more clearly what he wants and needs.

Once you decide to tell him about some product or service which you believe he should use or purchase to solve his needs, you will want to do so with enthusiasm, using the personal attitudes and skills presented in chapter 10. You will use the steps to persuasive communications presented in chapter 10, but probably in a much simpler way than presented there. (Read chapter 10, and modify the presentation to fit your particular circumstances.)

If you and your associates really try to improve your performance through using the practices in *"The Process of Cross-Marketing,"* the benefits to you and your company will be far beyond what you can imagine. You will be more productive and will waste less time. Your associates will be happier and more cooperative, and cooperation increases performance and reduces costs. Many fewer customers will become upset because of poor service; in fact, some will be thrilled because of the unusually good service. Many more customers will do business with you and purchase more when they do. This is because you handled them well, found out what they needed, and suggested that they take action to satisfy that need.

TWENTY FIVE CUSTOMER SERVICE MISTAKES

In the late 1970's a study was performed for the White House Office of Consumer Affairs by a consulting company called Technical Assistance

Research Programs, Inc. (TARP). The TARP studies indicated that, on average;

- For every customer which complains there are 26 who are unhappy and do not complain,
- The average unhappy customer tells 9-10 other people about it, and as a result,
- For every complaint your company receives, there are about 250 people who know you performed poorly, and who may hesitate to do business with your company.

The study also indicated that every time you do something good, which catches the customer's attention, he will tell 3-5 other people about your good performance.

It pays to give good customer service, and to avoid customer service mistakes. This section discusses twenty five mistakes you should avoid, when dealing with both commercial customers and fellow employees, regardless of your position in the company.

1. Being unappreciative.   The customer expects you to show appreciation for his business. You can do this with a smile and a genuine, "Thank you." Sometimes a thank you note or letter is appropriate.

2. Not being interested.   It is important to show interest in the customer and his problems and concerns.   The HULRAH formula presented in chapter 8 is helpful in accomplishing this.

3. Not listening. If you do listen closely to the customer you may offend him. You also may miss hearing important information needed to provide him the service he wants and deserves.

4. Unfriendliness. We all prefer to deal with friendly people. Show your friendliness with a smile, genuine interest in the customer, and application of the HULRAH formula.

5. Lack of empathy. When one fails to understand how the customer thinks and feels about the situation, then it is difficult to understand how to satisfy the customer's needs. Ask yourself, "If I were this person and were in this situation what would I want; what would make me happy?"

6. Ignoring customer input. When we don't listen effectively or we ignore what the customer is saying and implying, we stand a good chance of misunderstanding what the customer wants. When we think we are smarter than the customer, and prescribe a solution before diagnosing the problem, we frequently miss the mark and make the customer unhappy.

7. Not asking questions. By asking the right questions you will determine what the customer wants and needs. Open-ended questions like, "Would you describe you feelings about that?" or "What do you want from this product?" generate large amounts of useful information.

8. Forgetting customer benefits. The customer is not as interested in what you are proposing as in how it will benefit him. If you only describe the features of your problem solution and not the benefits, the customer may not be able to figure out why he should accept your solution or buy your product or service.

9. Jumping the gun. Don't make the mistake of suggesting a problem solution before you clearly understand what the problem is and what the customer wants, needs and will find acceptable.

10. Lack of sympathy. The customer's sprained shoulder, bounced check, or lost reservation is more important to him than the airplane crash in South Africa which killed 100 persons. He will appreciate and like us if we are interested in and sympathetic to his problem.

11. Keeping customers waiting. Most people resent waiting a long time for service. Make every effort to process people quickly and efficiently. When someone must wait longer than a normal period, speak to him in a friendly way. Apologize for and explain the reason for the delay.

12. Being pushy. It is important that we be enthusiastic about our company and its products and services. We will even be persistent at times in encouraging customers to accept our products and our problem solutions. However, we want to avoid being and acting "pushy" and trying to get the customer to do something he really does not want to do, or does not feel comfortable doing now. This can occur when we do not clearly understand the customer's situation and problem. That lack of understanding comes from improper question asking and listening.

13. Being discourteous. There is no excuse for not being courteous and tactful to customers; to our fellow employees; to everyone.

14. Arguing with customers. You may win the argument but you will seldom win the war - the customer's long term business. When you believe the customer is wrong, and it is important to establish that, ask questions. Ask questions like, "May I ask why you believe that to be true?"

15. Not admitting you are wrong. "When you are wrong admit it quickly and emphatically," advised Dale Carnegie many years ago. This builds customer respect. If you or your organization has wronged the customer, admit it, apologize in a friendly and sincere way, and attempt to make amends.

16. Allowing distractions. When you are distracted from the business of the customer you are showing lack of respect for the customer. Usually you also are giving poorer service than you should.

17. Rushing the customer. There are times the customer is not in a hurry, such as when you are suggesting he make a decision. Rushing him can make him feel uncomfortable and pressured.

18. Being insensitive to behavior styles. The book, **Non-Manipulative Selling**, by Alessandra, Wexler and Dean discusses clearly and simply the fact that different people have different styles of behavior, and are comfortable doing business in different ways. Some customers want to get down to business immediately and look at the facts and the bottom line. Others prefer to deal on a more casual and friendly basis, and are concerned with who you have helped before. Some feel more comfortable examining details and all available data. Others want to make friends and do business with friends. We need to adjust our communications to the style of the person we are dealing with.

19. Being undependable. If the customer feels he can't depend on you he will not want to deal with you. Once a decision is reached it is important for you to act promptly, and to make sure the decision is properly implemented. If it is not, the customer will lose confidence in you and your company.

20. Being inconsistent. No one likes unpleasant surprises. People prefer for you to be consistent in your actions and your behavior. This gives them a feeling of assurance and security.

21. Allowing them to be embarrassed. If a customer does something, such as making a mistake, which causes him to be embarrassed in your presence, he will avoid you. Thus, he will avoid doing business with you.

22. Criticizing customers. None of us really like or appreciate criticism, even constructive criticism. Therefore, avoid being critical. Instead, ask questions such as, "Could I ask how you happened to decide that?" Then perhaps say, " Have you considered this alternative?" The alternatives you suggest should have solid reasons, or evidence, to back them up.

23. Becoming angry. Customers can be very difficult and even unfair. If you become angry with the customer you will establish communication barriers which will be difficult to remove.

24. Expecting customers to be fair. If you expect the customer to be fair, respectful of you and your time, and appreciative of your efforts on his behalf, you may be very disappointed. This can negatively affect your attitude and morale. Customers can be, and frequently are, fickle and unfair.

25. Wasting the customer's time. The customer will resent your wasting his time by not being prepared, not being knowledgeable of your products and services, and not being time sensitive.

DOS AND DON'TS FOR HANDLING THE UNHAPPY CUSTOMER

Suppose the customer is unhappy. Perhaps you have made one of the customer service mistakes listed above. Perhaps there has been a mistake in communication with one of the members of your organization. Or perhaps you have slipped up and failed to provide the exact product or service that was promised to the customer. In any case, whether he has a right to be or not, the customer is unhappy. Perhaps the customer confronts you personally or over the telephone, and with flushed face says, "What are you going to do about it?" The following are some suggested dos and don'ts for handling the unhappy customer.

DOS

These are ways that we should deal with the unhappy customer.

1. Be friendly and understanding. Do approach the customer in a friendly and understanding manner. Even if the customer has been wrong and ugly, you still want to maintain him as a customer, and you want to maintain his friends as your customers. Remain calm, collected and mature. Act to him just as you would to a good friend who has been wronged by someone else. Be understanding; ask questions to determine the facts; listen intently.

2. Take the situation seriously. This is not the time for humor. The customer obviously is very concerned and feels he has been wronged. An attempt at humor could easily backfire and indicate to the customer that you are being flippant and disrespectful. On the other hand, do not take yourself too seriously. Realize that this person would be acting toward anyone in your same position in the same way.

3. Hear him out. The customer will appreciate your paying full attention to the problem at hand, and your asking questions and listening intently. Get all of the information and make him feel that you are interested in getting all of the information concerning the situation.

4. Show concern. Show concern for the customer and the problem at hand. Help the customer feel that you genuinely are concerned about his welfare and about a rapid solution to the problem.

5. Be sympathetic. Be sympathetic to his concerns. Even if you know the customer is wrong do not tell him this at an early stage. Continue to listen, to ask clarifying questions, and to show your concern. Statements like, "I'm sure that made you feel terrible," can be helpful.

6. Be respectful. Treat the customer with the same respect that you would your most important customer. Take him to a private office if available.

7. Ask questions. At times you will want to ask permission to ask questions. There are certain questions which may appear threatening to the unhappy customer. You can soften these questions with a preliminary phrase such as "Could I ask-----?" For instance, instead of asking, "Why did you do that?" you might ask, "Could I ask why you did that?" Before asking any questions you might ask, "Could I ask you some questions concerning how this matter was handled?"

8. Find the source of the problem. Seek to quickly and correctly discover the source of the problem.

9. Solve the problem. Try honestly to solve the problem as quickly and as effectively as possible.

10. Admit being wrong. When you or your organization is wrong, admit it and apologize for it. Depending upon the seriousness of the matter you may have to get authorization from a higher source to make this admission.

11. Find grounds for agreement. Even when the customer is wrong you frequently can let him save face. Find some grounds for agreement. This will soften the problem between the parties, and will encourage agreement and future communications and good relationships.

12. Find a fair solution. If appropriate, consider asking the customer to offer a fair solution. Frequently, once the customer has been allowed to vent his emotions, and has been treated respectfully, he will bend over backwards to be fair when deciding on a way to correct the situation. Frequently, the customer will offer a solution that is more to the advantage of your organization than if you offered one yourself.

DON'TS

Avoid these actions when facing an unhappy or angry customer.

1. Don't smile too big or act too happy. The emphasis here is on the word **too**. If you act too happy you will appear to consider the problem to be unimportant, and that you do not care about the customer or his concerns. A pleasant, understanding expression is advisable.

2. Don't interrupt. Do not interrupt the customer while he is explaining the situation. The policy here is to listen and to listen and to listen some more. Let the customer vent his feelings and at the same time gather information concerning what has happened.

3. Don't blame. Do not overtly imply that the customer could be wrong, especially early in the conversation. To do so would appear to be defensive and attempting to place the blame on the customer. At this point the customer is angry and is looking for sympathy and not blame. Later in the conversation you can ask questions which may lead the customer to the conclusion that he is wrong.

4. Don't promise. Do not make promises you cannot keep. The customer may be demanding immediate decisions and actions. The best defense against answering with quick decisions is to continue to ask questions.

5. Don't make excuses. As a matter of fact, early in the conversation, until all of the information is gathered and analyzed do not even offer reasons for why a problem has developed. Those reasons can be interpreted as being defensive excuses.

6. Don't be smug. Do not appear to be or act as a "know-it-all." Even if you do know all of the answers, a humble attitude will have a softening effect on the customer. Of course, the customer will appreciate dealing with a knowledgeable professional who is understanding of the customer's problem. So don't act ignorant.

7. Don't take criticism personally. Realize that the customer is upset, and that he would act as he is behaving to anyone representing your organization who is in your situation. This realization can be especially important for keeping continuing relationships pleasant.

8. Don't expect rational behavior. Do not expect the customer to be rational or to act in an understanding way. The customer is upset and wants redress of his grievances.

As a final comment, don't fail to apply the human relations practices in the HULRAH formula presented in chapter 8.

12

"The great end of life is
not knowledge but action."
Thomas Huxley

IMPLEMENTATION

BUSINESS ASSESSMENT
TRAINING PROGRAMS
THE CROSS-MARKETING SYSTEM
Individual Action Plan
Leader/Coach Meeting Report
Action Plan Leadership
Cross-Marketing Teams
IN SUMMARY

Suppose you have read this book, or you have attended one of the nationwide seminars on **Integrated Business Leadership Through Cross-Marketing.** You believe that this philosophy and the resulting business system makes sense. You can see how the strategies and practices contained herein were the secrets to the success and leadership of IBM, and a host of leading larger and mid sized companies in many fields. You would like to implement this program, or part of it, within your organization. How would you go about doing it?

If you are the CEO of a large organization you would want to assign a competent, full time coordinator to arrange for a business assessment, supportive training programs and implementation of the system. These are discussed in the sections below.

If you are a department manager, or the CEO of a smaller organization, you might arrange for a part-time coordinator, or perform the arrangements yourself. You might even delete the business assessment step because of your intimate knowledge of the business. However, it has been our experience that in organizations of all sizes the business assessment has revealed important attitudes and needs which were not fully understood by top management.

In any case, successful implementation requires commitments and actions from three levels of the company. Deletion of any of the three will significantly reduce the success of the program.

1. First, top management must be committed to the program and must give it adequate financial and moral support. Top management must make this clear to middle management, to supervision and to front line workers, through both word and action. How to do this was discussed in chapter 1.

2. First and second levels of management and supervision must support the program, and must have the leadership skills to help, and not hinder, front line workers. In most cases first level supervision also must have the skills to demonstrate proper performance to front line employees, and to assist them on the line when needed.

3. Finally, front line people must have the skills, through experience and training, to carry out the program or system as assigned. For Cross-Marketing these skills include meeting and greeting people, being a business friend, seeking out and solving customer problems, self management, and effective and persuasive communications. The attitudes of front line people are heavily influenced by the attitudes and leadership skills of those supervising and managing them.

BUSINESS ASSESSMENT

The first formal step to program implementation, and the first step our company probably would recommend if we were to assist you, would be to analyze your organization, from top to bottom and from side to side. This would require an experienced, objective business analyst to interview you, your top people, the heads of major departments and divisions, and a sampling of managers and workers throughout the company. He or she would be looking for strengths, weaknesses, attitudes and unexploited opportunities. Based on these results, he might suggest sending written questionnaires to a broader sampling of employees and/or customers, and having them completed and returned to him on a confidential basis. Or he might suggest limited telephone surveys.

Using the analyses presented in chapter 2 as a starting point, he would evaluate, perhaps by division or department, where your company and your people are effective and where they need to improve. Then working with you, and perhaps with your division or department managers, he would establish with you a series of objectives for moving your company in the desired direction.

He would prepare and submit a written report outlining the findings, and presenting recommendations for (1) objectives, (2) training, and (3) revised business systems. This business assessment would take far less time and require far less expense than the uninitiated would expect. A lot can be learned by a competent business analyst in a short period of time.

TRAINING PROGRAMS

Based on the strengths and the needs determined from the business assessment, and the resulting objectives worked out with management, a series of training programs probably would be recommended. These could be designed by an in house training group, a training company, experts in the areas of training required, or a combination of the three.

Some training companies are like ours, and provide a train-the-trainer approach, in which for the more comprehensive programs line and staff employees of your company are trained to present the training programs, and the companion business systems, to the individual employees. The direct involvement in the training of your company's line managers and recognized authorities generally will make the program more effective, and better received by the workforce at all levels. This is true even when the needed specific skills are presented by an outside consultant.

One effective approach is to put every employee through the same training program. With this approach, the basics would be presented to every employee at every level; while some specifics could be modified for different divisions and levels of management. Both Scandinavian Airline System and British Airways put every one of their employees through a two day training program as a part of their successful efforts to redirect the attention, efforts and financial performance of their companies.

A second approach would be to design different training programs with different emphases for different levels, different divisions, and even different individuals, based on their strengths, needs and objectives. One group may need training in business leadership concepts, another in personal leadership and supervision, another in personal effectiveness, another in problem solving, and another in persuasive communications or sales. Some may need training in time management, others in personal motivation, others in customer service and customer relations, and still others in creativity, innovation and change.

A third approach, and a good one, is to present a short, theme-oriented motivational/informational seminar to all employees, and follow this with specific formal training as needed, by department or by individual. When your people complete the Individual Action Plans, presented in the next section, then their needs for any specific individual training should become apparent. All three approaches have been employed effectively.

Regardless of the training approach chosen, it should be designed to be supportive of the mission and objectives of the company, the departments and the people involved. In addition, the training should be followed by on-the-job application, and by an effective follow-up program. This is to inspire application of the information and skills learned, to measure performance and provide feedback, and to provide direction and coaching toward improved performance. One way to accomplish this is to implement a continuing operational system, such as the Cross-Marketing system explained in the next section.

THE CROSS-MARKETING SYSTEM

Even before undertaking the business assessment, your company probably will have established a mission, a set of corporate values, and a series of interrelated goals and objectives, for the corporation and for the various departments. These may be changed, or added to, based on the results of the assessment.

Assuming the company is going ahead to implement its tailored version of the system on **Integrated Business Leadership Through Cross-Marketing**, then related and specific long term and short term objectives will be established at all levels. Support training will be provided as discussed in the prior section. A mechanism will be established to tie in the efforts of each employee to the company and department objectives. One way to accomplish this is through Individual Action Plans.

INDIVIDUAL ACTION PLAN

An Individual Action Plan would be completed by each employee at every level. *This concept was considered to be so important by John Hanley, the CEO of Monsanto Company, that in the mid 1970s he assigned a top official of the company to coordinate it. This "top official" was Earl H. Harbison, Jr., who became president of Monsanto Company in 1986.*

Figure 12-1 presents one format for the action plan which has been successfully employed. This particular version assumes the department objectives are, "for all employees to be customer oriented and to 'sell' the products and services of their departments in such a way that the (personal and/or commercial) customers benefit substantially."

The action plan serves as a communication device between the employee and his superior, and is a means to establish and measure performance against meaningful objectives. It is recommended that this action plan first be completed in draft by the employee. It then would be shared with the superior in advance of a meeting, at which time the two would discuss it and negotiate a revised action plan. The action plan is for a period of time, perhaps one month. It is modified on a regular basis.

The discussion below explains the Individual Action Plan, Figure 12-1, section by section.

Section A. In this first section of the plan the employee puts on paper his attitudes toward our industry, our company and its products and services, the importance of Cross-Marketing, and a statement concerning his ability to do what is being asked. To complete all four parts the employee needs some solid communication with his superior concerning the program and what will be expected of him.

There are a number of advantages of having the employee put this information on paper. It assists the employee to think through just what his attitude is toward these items. It communicates this attitude to his superior so the superior can deal with it, in whatever way is appropriate. If the employee has a negative attitude toward any of the items, it provides the superior the ammunition and information to deal with that attitude; to ask questions concerning the reasons for the attitude, to answer questions, and to provide assurance that certain actions will be taken. The employee may write down that he has a positive attitude concerning all four items. If this is true, he is reinforcing in his own mind the fact that he can and should be successful with this program. If it is not true, if he is lying and writes down that he has a positive attitude when really he has a negative attitude, then he still is committing himself to positive performance. He is removing later excuses for negative performance.

Section B. This establishes and clarifies in the minds of both the employee and the superior, the benefits of the Cross-Marketing program. Again, if the stated benefits are substantial, the employee is reinforcing why he should work effectively on this program. If the stated benefits appear to be meager, then the superior has the opportunity either to explain why the benefits are more substantial than he thought, or to make arrangements and adjustments to increase the value of the benefits.

Section C. This clarifies the employee's strengths as related to this program or system. It can be used to modify the employee's assignment and objectives, or to define needed education and training.

Section D. This identifies potential needs for education and training, and will influence the assignments and objectives.

Section E. This communicates the products and services which will be emphasized, and whether their benefits are fully understood.

Section F. This further identifies the benefits of selected products

Figure 12-1

INDIVIDUAL ACTION PLAN

THIS ACTION PLAN IS FOR: _____

A. THIS DESCRIBES MY ATTITUDE TOWARD –
   1. OUR INDUSTRY:

   2. OUR COMPANY, AND ITS PRODUCTS AND SERVICES:

   3. THE IMPORTANCE OF CROSS-MARKETING:

   4. MY ABILITY TO DO WHAT I THINK IS ASKED OF ME:

B. IF I PERFORM EFFECTIVELY IN CROSS-MARKETING AT OUR COMPANY
   THIS IS HOW IT CAN BENEFIT ME AND THE COMPANY:

C. IN CROSS-MARKETING THIS IS WHAT I CAN DO WELL:

D. IN CROSS-MARKETING I NEED TO IMPROVE THE MOST IN THESE AREAS:

E. THESE ARE SERVICE AND PRODUCT BENEFITS I WILL CONCENTRATE ON
   CROSS-MARKETING AND COMMUNICATING TO OTHERS:

F. FOR EACH SERVICE OR PRODUCT LISTED IN E, THESE ARE THE REASONS
   I AM PLEASED TO ENCOURAGE CUSTOMERS, ASSOCIATES AND EVEN
   PERSONAL FRIENDS TO BENEFIT FROM THEM:

INDIVIDUAL ACTION PLAN - PAGE 2

G. My cross-marketing goal is:

H. This is my plan to achieve that goal:

I. I will know I have achieved my goal when the following has been accomplished:

J. I plan to have my goal achieved by this date: _____

K. When I have achieved the listed goal the following is planned at that time:

L. Other comments:

_____   _____
SIGNED - ASSOCIATE   APPROVED - COACH/SUPERVISOR

_____   _____
DATE   DATE

Action plan date record:

    Original action plan: _____
    Revision # 1:   _____
    Revision # 2:   _____
    Revision # 3:   _____
    Date of this plan:

and services, and increases the commitment of the employee to successfully implementing the program.

Section G. Listed here is the specific goal(s) or objective(s) which is agreed to. All goals should be clearly stated, specific, reasonable, results oriented, measurable, and compatible with other goals.

Section H. Described here are the steps in the plan to achieve the goal (or goals). More space may be needed than is provided here, depending upon the detail-orientation of the employee and the superior, and the need for that detail. Completion times should be included with each step in the plan when possible. As appropriate, each step should answer the questions of who, what, when, and where; and sometimes even how. "Why" is not needed, but could be discussed face to face.

Section I. This is a restatement of the goal(s) giving the indicators to be present when the goal(s) is completed.

Section J. This states the target date for goal completion.

Section K. Listed here can be tentative future goals, and/or rewards and recognition which would be expected by the employee following completion of this goal. Whether or not they are stated here, the quality and quantity of the recognition and rewards to be received from successfully completing the Cross-Marketing goals, as compared to the recognition and rewards received from other competing work, will directly influence the employee's opinion of the importance of this effort to the superior and to the company. It will affect the effort which will be applied to the program.

Section L. Other comments. This adds flexibility to the action plan.

Final Section. The action plan is signed or initialed by the employee and the superior. A listing of the dates of previous action plans are shown for reference.

LEADER/COACH MEETING REPORT

Following each regularly scheduled (monthly?) action plan meeting, the leader or superior needs to make personal notes. Figure 12-2 presents one format which has been found to be useful. This particular format is designed as a checklist to assist the leader in identifying potential stumbling blocks to completion of the action plan. These can be used as a basis for observation and coaching during the action plan period.

ACTION PLAN LEADERSHIP

To effectively implement the Cross-Marketing System each superior at

Figure 12-2

LEADER/COACH MEETING REPORT

ASSOCIATE: _____ COACH: _____

MEETING #: ____ DATE: _____

1. ATTITUDE OBSERVED:

2. COMMENTS HEARD:

3. HELP NEEDED:

4. HELP GIVEN:

5. PLANS FOR FUTURE HELP:

6. GOALS SET:

7. ACTIONS PLANNED BY ASSOCIATE AND COMPLETION DATE:

8. ACTIONS PLANNED BY COACH AND COMPLETION DATE:

9. APPRECIATION/SUPPORT GIVEN BY THE COACH:

10. SCHEDULED DATE OF NEXT SESSION:

each level will need to employ the principles of leadership discussed throughout the book. They will need to manage themselves effectively as follows:

1. Being genuinely interested in their people's situations, and helpful to them in a friendly way.
2. Being open to suggestions and feelings of employees; and being good listeners.
3. Being enthusiastic about Cross-Marketing, and concentrating on how to be successful, not whether to be successful. Setting the example.
4. Setting objectives in line with the individual capabilities and maturity of the people.
5. Rewarding success and progress.
6. Being encouraging and supportive of the company, the program, and their people.
7. Applying the principles of concentration, time management, and innovation.
8. Setting the example by effectively carrying out their own assignments, especially in Integrated Business Leadership and Cross-Marketing.

As superiors work with their people on completing and implementing the Individual Action Plans, the superiors will need to keep the following principles in mind. They need to -
9. Evaluate the strengths and performance of their people, in relationship to the program being implemented.
10. Determine from their people their present attitudes, knowledge and skill levels.
11. Discuss, listen to, and help them with their concerns.
12. Help them set fair performance goals. Get their ideas, and their agreement on fairness. Get their commitments.
13. Help them develop plans to achieve their goals.
14. Identify where they need help.
15. Conscientiously provide and arrange for help needed. This can include finding specific answers for them, demonstrating skills, arranging for training, coaching and role-playing, developing tools to increase their effectiveness (such as promotional materials), etc.
16. Follow-up. Check on results. Locate problems. Give program support. Give encouragement and appreciation. Reward results.

CROSS-MARKETING TEAMS

Implementation of the system has been assisted by the establishment of

Cross-Marketing teams. These are groups of 5-10 employees each with a leader. The leader can be one of the group, or the formal supervisor of the group. The team discusses ongoing problems and roadblocks to effective performance. They share ideas which have worked in particular situations. They receive ongoing training and assist each other with role-plays and other exercises.

Some teams meet weekly for one hour on company time. Others meet during off-hours. Sometimes this time is paid for and sometimes it is not, depending on the particular organization and its arrangement with employees. In all cases, the teams should be clearly supported by upper management, and meaningful rewards and recognition should be supplied to the teams which deserve them.

IN SUMMARY

This entire book is designed to be about **implementation; how to** operate a successful business and **how to** be an effective personal leader or front line worker, through integrating a number of effective strategies and practices; and then how to implement those strategies and practices.

Chapters 1, 2 and 3 present the current wisdom on business leadership, from the viewpoint of how to make strategies and practices work in our work-a-day world. They add some new concepts which should be helpful to corporations, institutions and individual leaders in applying that wisdom.

Some of the new concepts are: the purpose of a business, twelve steps to business effectiveness, being customer driven, personal customers, Cross-Marketing, the flow of solutions and benefits, the process of Cross-Marketing, customer support, and customer service management.

Chapters 4-11 discuss, present specific examples and illustrations, and show: how to increase personal performance, how to have a winning image, how to motivate others, how to achieve effective group performance and teamwork, how to find and solve customer problems, how to plan for and implement effective communications with customers and others, how to be persuasive in your communications, and how to perform as an effective front line employee.

The book discusses in some detail how to implement the keys to business leadership, how to assess yourself and your business as leaders, how to become customer driven, how to be customer-service oriented, how to implement plans, how to control your behavior, how to manage your time, how to plan for personal success, how to make a good first impression, how to motivate others to believe, how to make people productive, how to cause effective performance, how to identify customer problems and needs, how to analyze for your own resources and strengths, how to match resources and needs, how to be effective in human relations, how to believe, how to innovate, how to concentrate, how to communicate, how to persuade, how to serve, and how to implement.

All of this is supported with stories and illustrations, most from real life business situations. They are provided with an eye to sharing insights which will remind the experienced leader of important principles he may have forgotten. They also are provided to give the less experienced leader, and the front line worker, insight and wisdom concerning achieving high performance, and concerning the importance of being customer-oriented, teamwork-oriented, and company-oriented. This is insight they otherwise may never obtain.

Many books have been written, especially recently, about customer orientation and about business leadership. Where this one stands alone is in providing practical information and proven practices for applying and implementing the principle of leadership, to effectively serve both the needs of commercial customers and the needs of in-house employees. This generates, throughout the organization, effective personal performance, group performance, solving of customer problems, and effective communications with those customers everywhere.

REFERRED BOOKS AND SUGGESTED READINGS

Referred Books

1. A Business and Its Beliefs: The Ideas That Helped Build IBM, Thomas J. Watson, Jr., McGraw-Hill, 1963.

2. Build a Better You Starting Now! 12, Michael Baber, et. al., Showcase Publishing Co., 1983

3. Competitive Strategies, Michael Porter, The Free Press, 1980

4. Dress for Success, John Molloy, William Morrow & Co., Inc., 1981

5. How to Make Big Money Selling, Joe Gondolfo, Harper & Row, 1984

6. How to Win Friends and Influence People, Dale Carnegie, Simon & Schuster, 1964

7. In Search of Excellence, Peters and Waterman, Harper & Row, 1982

8. Innovation and Entrepreneurship; Practices and Principles, Peter F. Drucker, Harper & Row, 1985

9. Managing in Turbulent Times, Peter F. Drucker, Harper & Row, 1980

10. Managing for Results, Peter F. Drucker, Harper & Row, 1964

11. Marva Collins' Way, Marva Collins and Civia Tamarkin, J. P. Tarcher, Inc., 1982

12. Molloy's Live for Success, John Molloy, William Morrow & Co., 1981

13. Non-Manipulative Selling, Anthony J. Alessandra and Phillip S. Wexler with Jerry Dean, Reston, 1979

14. Quality is Free, Philip Crosby, New American Library, 1979

15. Quality Without Tears, Philip Crosby, Mc-Graw Hill, 1984

16. Service America, Karl Albrecht & Ron Zemke, Dow Jones-Irwin, 1985

17. The Effective Executive, Peter F. Drucker, Harper & Row, 1966

18. The Evaluation Interview, Richard A. Fear, McGraw-Hill, 1958

19. The Marketing Imagination, Theodore Levitt, The Free Press, 1983

20. The Practice of Management, Peter F. Drucker, Harper & Row, 1954

21. The Winning Performance - How America's High Growth Midsize
    Companies Succeed, Clifford & Cananagh, Bantom Books, 1985

Suggested Additional Readings

22. Bankers Who Sell: Improving Selling Effectiveness in Banking,
    Berry, Futrell & Bowers, Bank Marketing Association, 1985
    (Applicable to any industry; explains steps to a successful selling and
    marketing program)

23. Effective Psychology for Managers, Mortimer Feinberg, Prentice Hall,
    1965 (Filled with lists of practical, useable techniques)

24. Excellence in Leadership, Frank Goble, Caroline House Publishers,
    1972 (A practical explanation of principles and theories of management
    leadership)

25. Eyes on Tomorrow: The Evolution of Procter & Gamble, Oscar
    Schisgall, J. G. Ferguson, 1981 (A history of the success of Procter &
    Gamble)

26. Grinding It Out: The Making of McDonalds, Ray Kroc, Henry
    Regnery Co., 1977 (A history of the success of McDonalds)

27. High Output Management, Andrew Grove, Random House, 1983
    (Management practices followed by the president of Intel, a successful,
    rapidly-growing, entrepreneural corporation)

28. IBM Colossus in Transition, Robert Sobel, Bantom Books, 1983
    (Explains how IBM became successful through marketing more than
    through technical expertise)

29. Leadership Effectiveness Training, Thomas Gordon, Wyden Books,
    1977 (Effective person-to-person communication and leadership skills
    by the author of "Parent Effectiveness Training")

30. "Like No Other Store in the World": The Inside Story of
    Bloomingdale's, Mark Stevens, Crowell, 1979 (A history of the
    success of Bloomingdale's)

31. Management: Tasks, Responsibilities, Practices, Peter F. Drucker, Harper & Row, 1973 (A complete presentation on management prinicples by the "founding father of the science of management")

32. Service Management: Strategy and Leadership in Service Businesses, Richard Norman, John Wiley & Sons, 1984 (Service management theory; and experiences in Europe)

33. Successful Management by Objectives - An Action Manual, Karl Albrecht, Prentice Hall, 1978 (A clearly presented, human relations oriented manual)

34. The Art of Japanese Management, Pascale & Athos, Warner Books, 1981 (Explains the success of major Japanese corporations; reaches similar conclusions to those of "In Search of Excellence")

35. The Change Masters: Innovation and Entrepreneurship in the American Corporation, Rosabeth Moss Kanter, Simon & Schuster, 1983 (Explains that change must come from the top)

36. The Human Side of Enterprise, Douglas McGregor, McGraw-Hill, 1960 (Originates the X and Y theories of management)

37. The Managerial Grid, Blake & Mouton, Gulf Publishing Company, 1964 (Analyzes the effects of being results-oriented vs people-oriented in management and leadership)

38. The Situational Leader, Paul Hersey, Warner Books, 1984 (Explains a theory of varying leadership style by the maturity and motivation of the subordinate)